D1338058

HISTORY OF
GARHWAL
1358-1947

An Erstwhile Kingdom in the Himalayas

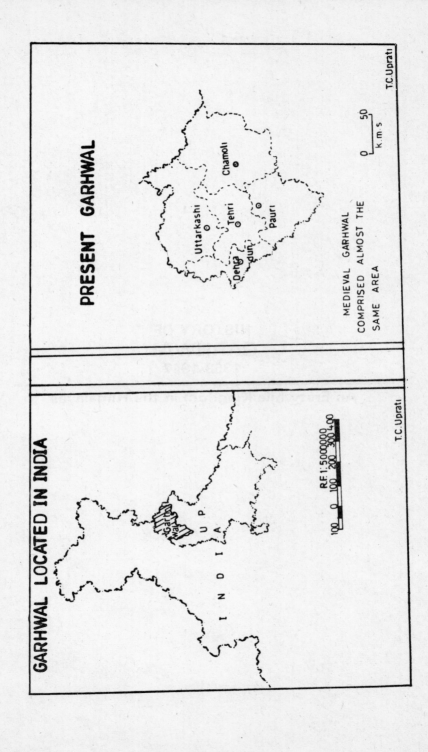

PRESENT GARHWAL

Uttarkashi

Tehri

Dehra
dun

Chamoli

Pauri

0   50
k.m.s

MEDIEVAL GARHWAL
COMPRISED ALMOST THE
SAME AREA

T.C.Uprati

GARHWAL LOCATED IN INDIA

U. P.

Garhwal

I N D I A

R.F. 1:5000000

100 0 100 200 300 400

T.C.Uprati

HISTORY OF
GARHWAL
1358-1947

An Erstwhile Kingdom in the Himalayas

AJAY S. RAWAT
Kumaon University, Nainital

INDUS PUBLISHING COMPANY
New Delhi

First published in 1989 by Indus Publishing Company
FS-5, Tagore Garden, New Delhi 110027, India

© 1989 Ajay S. Rawat

ISBN 81-85182-18-3

Published by M.L. Gidwani, Indus Publishing Company,
FS-5 Tagore Garden, New Delhi 110027, and printed at
Gidson Printing Works, FS-5, Tagore Garden,
New Delhi 110027

Dedicated to

Dr. M.D. Upadhyaya
Vice Chancellor
Kumaon University
Nainital

Preface

The present study is an innovative endeavour to reconstruct the political and administrative history of Garhwal during the period 1358 to 1947. Upto the middle half of the fourteenth century, Garhwal was divided into fifty-two principalities; Raja Ajay Pal of the Parmar dynasty consolidated these fifty-two principalities into one kingdom. After his conquest, Ajay Pal's domain was recognised as Garhwal owing to the exuberance of forts. He became famous as 'Garhwala' i.e. the owner of forts and his kingdom as Garhwal. Raja Ajay Pal and his scions ruled Garhwal from 1358 to 1804 A.D. In 1804 A.D., Garhwal was occupied by the Gurkhas who ruled this terrain upto 1815 A.D. when they were defeated and driven away by the British forces. After the British occupation of Garhwal, it was divided into two parts, 'British Garhwal' and 'Tehri Garhwal State'. British Garhwal became a part of Kumaon Commissionery and in Tehri Garhwal State, the erstwhile Parmar rulers were reinstalled.

Hitherto very less has been written about this area and these works throw a sporadic light on the political and administrative history of Garhwal. Most of the authors have relied absolutely on Atkinson's Gazetteer of the Himalayas. It may be pointed out that this gazetteer is beset with several shortcomings, e.g. spatial and temporal incoherence, unverified and unverifiable facts, based largely on hearsay and folk lore and lack of total historical perspective imbued with a pronounced bias of an alien administrator. Moreover, Atkinson has not compiled the history of Tehri Garhwal State since it was written in the nineteeth century. Further no attempt so far has been made to present a scientific account of this area based on primary sources like copper plate inscriptions, original manuscripts, rock edicts, numismatic evidences, archival sources, etc.

In the broad scope of the study, there is a two-layered examination from 1358 to 1804 A.D. On the one hand it throws light on the Parmar kings of Garhwal, the correct fixation of their dates and bridging the historical gaps between their rule on the basis of primary sources (like copper plate inscriptions, contemporary manuscripts, rock edicts, numismatic evidences) hitherto unused, and on the other, the study highlights administrative policies of the rulers.

From 1815, when the Parmar kings were reinstalled in Tehri Garhwal State, upto 1949, the objective of the study is an examination of the interaction between administrative policies and their political repercussions in the form of political dissent. However a comparative study has also been undertaken as regards the British administration in British Garhwal, and its counterpart, the indigenous rule in Tehri Garhwal State.

I must avail this opportunity to express my deep gratitude to late Dr. R.N. Nagar, and Mr. Rajendra Singh Bhandari for their invaluable suggestions and persistent encouragement. Thakur Shoor Beer Singh, Purana Durbar Tehri, a scion of the royal family of Garhwal was not only a mine of information on the history of Garhwal, but his paternal love and assistance will always remain a source of inspiration to me.

Acknowledgements are also due to Dr. (Mrs.) S. Dwivedi and Dr. J.S. Singh who initiated me to take up the study of this Himalayan region. I must also express my sincere thanks to Dr. S.P. Singh, Dr. C. Shastri, Dr. Shekhar Pathak, Dr. Raghubir Chand, Mr. T.C. Uprati, Mr. I.L. Shah, Mr. Duli Chand, Mr. Mahesh Gururani, officials of the National Archives, New Delhi, State Archives, Lucknow, D.S.B. Campus Library, Naini Tal, and Anand Photographer, Naini Tal, and Mr. Surendra K. Singh the typist, whose effort has facilitated the culmination of this work. Cover photograph has kindly been supplied by Dr. Shekhar Pathak.

AJAY S. RAWAT

Contents

Preface   7

Chapter 1 GEO-HISTORICAL BACKGROUND   ... 11
Location and Extent   11
Geographical Regions   11
River Systems   12
Climate   14
Vegetation   14
Ethnical Background   15
Historical Perspective   16

Chapter 2 RULERS OF GARHWAL   ... 24
Kanak Pal, the Founder of Parmar
   Dynasty in Garhwal   29
Date of Accession of Kanak Pal   32

Chapter 3 PARMAR DYNASTY AND GURKHA
             INVASION   ... 35
Man Shah   41
Shyam Shah   42
Mahipat Shah   43
Prithvi Pat Shah   46
Fateh Shah   55
Pradip Shah   64
Lalit Shah or Lalipat Shah   66
Jai Krit Shah   67
Pradyumna Shah   70

Chapter 4 ADMINISTRATION OF THE RULERS   ... 79
Administration of Land Revenue   81
Trade   84

Judicial Administration   86
Army   87
Education   88
Maintenance of Temples   89

Chapter 5   FORMATION OF TEHRI GARHWAL
STATE AND ITS RULERS 1815-1949   ...   92

Chapter 6   ADMINISTRATION OF TEHRI
GARHWAL STATE   ...   106
Agriculture and Administration of Land
   Revenue   106
Forest Management   115
Preservation of Animal and Acquatic
   Life   123
Judicial Administration   126
Education   138
Medical   140
Communication   142
Local Self Government   143
Management of the Sources of Living   144

Chapter 7   POLITICAL MOVEMENT IN TEHRI
GARHWAL STATE   ...   152
1857 and Tehri Garhwal State   160
The Forest Uprising in Chandrabadni   163
The Rawain Incident   164
The Tehri Movement (1946)   171
The Saklana Uprising   171
Kirti Nagar Movement (1948)   172

Chapter 8   AN OVERVIEW   ...   179

Bibliography   ...   211

Index   ...   221

Plates   Between pages 192-93

1

Geo-Historical Background

Location and Extent

Garhwal at present comprises Chamoli, Dehradun, Pauri, Tehri and Uttarkashi districts. Its area is about 11,325 square miles. It is situated between 29°45′ N and 31°27′ N latitudes and 77°45′ E to 80°7′ E longitudes.[1] After the British occupation of Garhwal on 30th November 1815, it was divided into two parts, British Garhwal and Tehri Garhwal State. British Garhwal became a separate district under Kumaon Commissionery whereas in Tehri Garhwal State, the erstwhile Parmar rulers of Garhwal were reinstalled.[2] British Garhwal lay between 29°26′15″ and 31°5′30″ N latitudes and 78°12′ to 80°8′ E longitudes, with an area of 5,500 square miles.[3] Tehri Garhwal State was situated between 30°3′ and 31°18′ N latitudes and 77°49′ to 79°24′ E longitudes, with an area of 42,000 square miles.[4]

Geographical Regions

The mountainous region of Garhwal ranges in height from approximately 990 feet to more than 24,750 feet. A great contrast in elevations of deep valleys and mountainous peaks can be observed almost everywhere in the region. On the basis of altitude, complexity of physiographic features, geological chronology and structure, the region can be divided from south to north into three major parallel zones or regions as under:

1) The Outer Himalaya or the Sub-Himalaya or the Siwalik zone.
2) The Lesser or Lower or Middle Himalaya also known as 'Himachal'.
3) The Greater or Inner or Main or the Higher Himalaya, also known as 'Himadri'.

All these three major regions can be further divided into valleys and ranges. Besides these, we find the sub-mountain plains of Bhabar towards further south. Nearly half of the total mountainous area is included in the Lesser Himalaya, while the Siwalik zone is the smallest in area. The Outer Himalaya, as its very name signifies, is the outermost part of the mountainous chain.

The Siwalik Zone extends in a narrow varying width of about 4 to 18 miles, and its height above the sea level varies from 990 to 3,300 feet. Important towns like Dehradun, Rishikesh, and Kotdwara are situated in the Siwalik zone.

The Lesser Himalaya extends in a varying width of about 4 to 60 miles, between the valleys and the Siwalik range to the south and the Greater Himalaya to the north. An abrupt rise is to be observed in elevation which varies generally between 3,300 and 9,900 feet. Mussoorie, Tehri, Pauri, Uttarkashi, Lansdowne, Srinagar, Chamoli and Gopeshwar are the most important towns located in this zone.

The Greater Himalaya Zone has a varying width of about 24 to 45 miles, and it is maximum in the eastern and western corners of Chamoli district where it is about 42 to 45 miles in total. The altitude varies generally between 9,900 and 24,310 feet. In this region are situated some of the highest Himalayan peaks of which Nanda Devi (7,817 metres, or 25,645 feet) is the highest in India. Some of the other high peaks are Kamet (7,756 metres or 25,447 feet), Badrinath or Chaukhamba (7,138 metres or 23,420 feet), Trisul (7,120 metres or 23,360 feet), Dunagiri or Dronagiri (7,077 metres or 23,184 feet), Kedarnath (6,940 metres or 22,770 feet), and Gangotri (6,672 metres or 21,890 feet). Most of these peaks are situated in the eastern, western, and northern parts of Chamoli district.

River Systems

The river Ganga, alongwith its tributary Yamuna forms two small river systems viz the Yamuna system and the Ganga system. The major part of the region is drained by the Ganga system, whereas only a small section towards the west is drained by the Yamuna system.

The Yamuna system covers about half of the western part of Tehri Garhwal and about two-third of the western part of Dehradun. The river Yamuna rises from the Jamnotri glacier which is on the south-western slopes of the Bandarpunch peak. Tons, a major tributary of the Yamuna, which joins it below Kalsi in Dehradun district, originates from the Bandarpunch glacier. Asan, an important river of the Dun valley is also a tributary of the Yamuna.

The Ganga is termed as Bhagirathi upto the point where it meets its most important tributary, Alaknanda at Deoprayag, and from there on it acquires the name 'Ganga'. Bhagirathi takes its origin near Gomukh in the Gangotri glacier. The river Jahnavi or Janhavi also termed as 'Jadhganga' which originates in the Thag La region, just south of the international border, joins Bhagirathi as its northern most tributary about 7.2 miles west of Gangotri temple. Bhilangana or Bhilanganga, another important tributary of the Bhagirathi originates in the Kedarnath glacier zone in the extreme north of Tehri Garhwal district and meets the latter at Tehri town.

Alaknanda, also termed as Vishnuganga upto its point of confluence with Dhauliganga (west), rises from glaciers on the eastern slopes of Chaukhamba, and after flowing through a big gorge for a few miles, it meets its northernmost and the first important tributary, Saraswati at Mana village. Saraswati rises just south of the Mana Pass on the international border. The most important tributaries of Alaknanda from the north to south are: Dhauliganga west (rising from the Niti Pass region), Nandakini, Pindar and Mandakini. They join Alaknanda at Vishnuprayag, Nandaprayag, Karnaprayag and Rudraprayag respectively. These four 'Prayags' together with Deoprayag are famous in Garhwal as 'Panch Prayag' and are centres of great religious importance.[5] River Pindar originates from the Pindar glacier, just below the highest mountain complex of Nanda Devi. Mandakini rises from the southern slopes of Kedarnath peak and Nandakini from the glacier situated on the western slopes of Trisul.

Below Deoprayag, the Ganga has two important tributaries, Nayar or Naiyar, which drains a major portion of the Pauri Garhwal district, and the Song river, which after draining the south-eastern parts of Dehradun district meets the Ganga to its right above Raiwala junction. Another important river of the

Ganga system which does not join the main river within the U.P. Himalaya, is Ramganga or western Ramganga which drains the south-eastern portion of Garhwal.

Climate

A variety of climate from tropical to the polar can be seen in the region mainly because of the altitude and topographic complexity. Variations of weather and micro-climatic phenomena are sharp, fast and sometimes unpredictable, particularly in the rainy season. The principal determinants of weather and climatic conditions in the region include: (i) altitude and its topographic complexity, (ii) direction of the ridges and location on windward and leeward sides, (iii) degree of slope and its aspects, sunny or shady, (iv) intensity of forest cover, and (v) proximity to water bodies and glaciers.

On the basis of altitude and accompanying features, the region can be divided into eight kinds of broad climatic zones: (i) Warm tropical region (below 1980 feet), (ii) Cold tropical-subtropical region (1980-3960 feet), (iii) Warm temperate region (3960-5940 feet), (iv) Cool temperate region (5940-7920 feet), (v) Cold region (7920-9900 feet), (vi) Alpine region (9900-13200 feet), (vii) Glacial region (13200-15840 feet), and (viii) The perpetually frozen region (above 15840 feet). The glacial region is snow covered for 10 months a year except in July and August when the snow melts. The climate of the region can be divided into three well known seasons viz the rainy season, winter season, and summer season.[6]

Vegetation

The principal determinants of natural vegetation include, climate, soil, relief and biotic factors. Forests constitute the most valuable natural wealth of the region and this vegetation can be classified into the following zones.

1) *Tropical-Subtropical Forest Zone*: This zone is dominated by deciduous and sub-deciduous type of vegetation. Sal is the most significant species of this zone, which is found upto an altitude of above 4,290 feet. A few other species found in this zone include khair, sisso, semal, kanju and haldu.

2) *Sub-Temperate Zone*: The subtropical to temperate pine forests (with Chir Pine as the dominant coniferous tree), and

subtropical to temperate shrubs dominate at elevations varying from 2,970 feet to 6,930 feet.

3) *Temperate-Sub-Alpine Zone*: This zone extends generally between 4,950 feet and 10,890 feet altitude and is marked by the coniferous belt. The main species include various types of oak, deodar, blue pine, silver fir, spruce, cypress, kail and birch.

4) *The Alpine Zone*: It lies above 9,900 feet and Alpine forests and shrubs are found generally upto 13,860 feet altitude. With the increase in height, a gradual transition from larger flora to smaller mesophytic and xenophytic bushes and Alpine pastures can be observed, beyond which there is a lack of vegetal cover.

Ethnical Background

Kole is the first historically known race of Garhwal, which descended from the Munda ethnic group. Subsequently the Kirats, Khasas and the Sakas settled down in this terrain. Many other races, like the Tangana, Partagana, Naga and the Huns etc also came to this region and they inter-mixed with different waves of immigrants already settled here. Thus the contemporary society of Garhwal neither remained completely tribal nor transformed into a complete and class society. In the ancient times the powerful races and in the medieval as well as modern times, the powerful castes dominated the politics and economy. They were the decisive factors of local history. Naturally the less powerful races or castes had to fight or to surrender and be subjugated by the more powerful immigrants. Koles were defeated by the Kirats, Kirats by the Khasas and the Khasas were dominated by the people who came from the Indo-Gangetic plain.[7]

In the present social stratification of Garhwal, excluding castes from plains and immigrants from Tibet, three main castes are found, the Brahmins, the Rajputs and the Shilpkars. Shilpkars are the decendants of Koles and are supposed to be the autocthons of Garhwal. In the first category are placed—Koli, Tamta, Lwar, Auzis, Bhangi, etc and in the second group—Badi, Badai, Bhat, Mirasi and Hurkia etc.

Among the Rajputs again there are two groups—Asli Rajput or Kshatriya and Khas Rajput or Khasi-Jimdar. The first group of Rajputs is supposed to have migrated from the plains. These immigrant Rajputs came mostly as soldiers of fortune to seek service under the Hindu kings. The other category is from the indigenous racial group, the Khasas.[8]

In Garhwal amongst the Brahmins, the highest position in the social order is assigned to the Sarolas. The Gangaris are inferior to the Sarolas, but there is no marked line of difference between the two classes. The two sub-castes intermarry. Apart from the above mentioned classes, there is another group of Brahmins known as the Khas Brahmins. According to the 1901 Census Report, ". . . . Popular opinion considers Khas Brahmins and Rajputs as partly the original inhabitants of Kumaon and partly as degraded Brahmins and Rajputs."[9]

Historical Perspective

The earliest references regarding Garhwal and its pride spots are cited in the Skanda Purāna (Kedar Khand) and the Mahābhārata in the Van Parva. Skanda Purāna (Kedar Khand) defines the boundaries and extent of this holy land. It says that this heavenly abode of Kedar Khand is 50-yojan in length and 30-yojan in breadth.[10] It extends from Haridwar in the south upto perpetual snow in the north. On the west of it is the river Tamsa and in the east it is flanked by Baudhachal. Perpetual snow in the north means the Himalayas. The river Tamsa can be identified with the river Tons in Garhwal today. It is a major tributary of the river Yamuna and rises from the north-western slopes of Bandarpunch peak. Badhan is not only a pargana, but a mountain range too which demarcates Garhwal from Kumaon. This description of Kedar Khand to a great extent tallies with the expanse and area of modern Garhwal today.

In the Vanparva (Mahābhārata), where Dhaumya is narrating to Yudhisthira, the 'tirthas', i.e. pilgrimage centres of India, the name Gangadwara, i.e. Haridwar and Kankhala, the sacred spot in its proximity, have been referred.[11]

"O tiger among kings, 1 shall now describe those tirthas and sacred spots that lie to the North.

. . . O Yudhisthira the spot where Ganga rusheth past, cleaning the foremost of mountains, which is frequented by Gandharvas and Yakshas and Apsaras is called Gangadwara.

O king Sanatkumara regardeth the spot visited by Brahma-rishis as also the tirtha Kankhala (that is near it) as sacred."

As regards the name of the region in those days, it is possible that it must have been famous as Himvat. According to the Van Parva, when the Pandavas started off on their pilgrimage to Badrinath, Yudhishthira told Bhim to sojourn with Draupadi and others in Gangadwara until he returned from his journey to Badrinath, Gandhamadan, Kailash etc. But later it was decided that all of them should go and soon they arrived at Subahu Vishaya which was near Himvat.[12] There, they left behind their servants and goods and started on foot for Himvat Giri. While crossing the hills, studded with lakes, rivers and forests, they witnessed the country of Mlechha Gan.[13] In the end after visiting several places they reached the pilgrimage spots of Kailash, Badri, Gandhamadan, Vishala etc.[14] While perambulating in this sacred terrain, they saw the famous mountain peaks of Mainak, Mandar and Meru. After visiting these holy centres of Himvat, the Pandavas returned to Subahu Vishaya, from where they went back to their base camp via river Yamuna. In the description of their sacred wanderings, the name of Himvat has often been cited. On the basis of the above description and taking into account the places which are familiar like Badrinath, Gangadwara, etc it can be assumed that the hilly tract of Garhwal those days was known as Himvat.

The earliest ruling dynasty of Garhwal known to authentic history is of the Katyuris. The Katyuri Raja of Uttarakhand (Kumaon and Garhwal) was styled, "Sri Basdeo Giriraj Chakra Churamani", and the earliest traditions record that the possessions of the Joshimath Katyuris in Garhwal extended from the Sutlej as far as Gandaki and from the snow to the plains, including the whole of Rohilkhand.[15] Tradition gives the origin of their Raj at Joshimath in the north near Badrinath and a subsequent migration to Katyur valley in Almora district, where a city called Karthi-Keyapura was founded.[16]

The actual records of the Katyuris consist of only six inscriptions,* five of which are grants engraved on copper and one is a similar record inscribed on stone. The last belongs to the temple

*One copper plate inscription has been cited in the book 'Select Inscriptions', Volume II, edited by D.C. Sirkar. It is of the Katyuri king Latitsura of the year 854 A.D.

of Shiva at Vyaghreswar (the tiger lord) or Vakeswar (the lord of eloquence) situated at the junction of rivers Gomati and Sarju in the townwhip of Bageshwar in Almora district. It is supposed to be 1500 years old.[17] The slab on which the writing is inscribed is, unfortunately much mutilated especially in the right lower corner, where the date has been obliterated. Four of the other grants in the form of copper plates are preserved in the temple of Pandukeshwar near Badrinath.[18]

The Katyuris ruled Uttarakhand upto the 11th century and in certain pockets even after their decline. In Garhwal their disruption brought into existence many independent chiefs, fifty-two in number. One of the important principalities in that period was that of the Parmars, who held their sway over Chandpur Garhi* or fortress. Kanak Pal was the progenitor of this dynasty. Raja Ajay Pal, a scion of the Parmars in the 14th century is credited with having brought all the fifty-two of the independent chiefs under his rule. After his conquest, Ajay Pal's domain was recognised as GARHWAL owing to the exuberance of forts.[19] It is possible that after annexing all the principalities, Raja Ajay Pal must have become famous as 'Garhwala', i.e. the owner of forts, and with the passage of time his kingdom came to be known as Garhwal.

Dr. Shiv Prasad Dabral, with other historians of Garhwal history supports the tradition of nomenclaturing Garhwal, but at the same time he states that the word 'Garhwal' has been referred for the first time by Mola Ram somewhere around 1815. Mola Ram was a protagonist of Garhwali painting whose period ranges from 1743 to 1833.[20] But there is a copper plate inscription of Raja Man Shah of the year 1610 A.D. in the temple of Raghu-

---

*About the fortress Chandpur, Fuhrer has mentioned, " . . . . Chandpur fort is a fort which was the real seat of Kanak Pal, the legendary founder of the present Garhwal dynasty, whose descendant Ajai pal consolidated the Raj of Garhwal. The fort is situated on the peak of a promoutory formed by the bend of a stream flowing some 500 feet below it. The walls and some of the ruins of the dwelling houses are still standing. The former must have been very strongly built, as they consist of large slabs of cut stone, enclosing a space of about one and a half acre. There are also two flight of steps each formed of one solid block of stone, which are said to have quarried in the Dudha Toli Range."

(Fuhrer, A.: The Monumental Antiquities and Inscription in the N.W.P. and Oudh, p. 44).

nath ji at Deoprayag in which the word Garhwal has been referred. Then there is a copper plate inscription of Maharaja Fateh Shah of the year 1667 A.D. in which the word Garhwal has been mentioned again.[23] The inscription is a land grant endowed to some Balak Nath by Maharaja Fateh Shah. The great poet Bhushan has also referred the name Garhwal in a panegyrical poem eulogizing Maharaja Fateh Shah.[22]

Ajay Pal ruled Garhwal in the 14th century, but upto the 17th century we have no mention of the word 'Garhwal'. Owing to paucity of source material, one cannot arrive at a conclusion. However, it can be hypothesized that in coining the word 'Garhwal', the pretext must have been the same, i.e. Ajay Pal's consolidation of the fifty-two principalities, but the legend must have been metamorphosised in a later period. Since the progeny on the throne of Garhwal was of the Parmars even in the 17th century, it is possible that the then ruling king in order to glorify his ancestors' victory of the 14th century took it as a pride cause for naming his kingdom as Garhwal.

What was the name of this terrain before the reign of Ajay Pal; it is shrouded in oblivion. There are only allusions like the one by Atkinson. He is of the view that the ancient name of Kumaon and Garhwal was Khas-des, i.e., the country of the Khasas. Dr. D.C. Sirkar in his book, 'The Saka Pithas', states that Stri Rajya was located in Kumaon and Garhwal region of the Himalayas.[23] But they have given no historical proofs to corroborate their views.

About Stri Rajya, it was Hiuen Tsang who wrote that, "to the north of the country in the great snow mountains was the Suvarngotra country. The superior gold which it produced gave the country its name. This was the Eastern Women Country so called because it was reigned by a successor of woman. The husband of the queen was the king, but he did not administer the Government."[24] It is interesting to note that gold washing was a source of revenue during the rule of Parmar dynasty in Garhwal.[25] Further the progenitor of the Parmar dynasty, Kanak Pal was given the kingdom of Chandpur Garhi in dowry by some Raja Son Pal. Kanak Pal had come to Garhwal on pilgrimage, but after conjugal felicity, he settled down in Chandpur Garhi.[26] However, on the basis of these stray references no hypothesis can be developed. Dr. A.B.L. Awasthi is of the view that, "Brahmapura is identified with Garhwal and Kumaon".[27] But he too has not corroborated his view. About Brahmapura and also Govisana-it was the Chinese traveller Hiuen Tsang who has cited them in his accounts.[28] Cunningham[29] identifies Brahmapura with Lakhanpur in Kumaon, while Atkinson[30] thinks it refers to Barahat in Garhwal. However, both agree that the reference is in connection with the Katyuri kingdom of the Himalayas. Govisana[31] is placed near Kashipur in Naini Tal district.

Garhwal was ruled by the Parmars upto 1804. The same year in January according to A.R. Gill the Garhwali king Pradyumna Shah was defeated and killed by the Gurkhas in the battle of Khurbura.[32] The date of the battle of Khurbura as given by Hari Krishna Raturi is different. He states that at Khurbura, now part of Dehradun, Pradyumna Shah perished with most of his retainers after being defeated by the Gurkhas on 14th May, 1804.[33]

The Gurkhas ruled Garhwal upto 1815, when they in turn were defeated and driven away by the British forces. During the Gurkha rule, Sudarshan Shah, Raja Pradyumna Shah's son, entirely despaired of ever regaining his lost kingdom, had eventually taken abode in Bareilly. But after the Gurkha defeat, the portion of Garhwal (later came to be known as Tehri Garhwal State), west of river Alaknanda, except for Rawain, Jaunsar and Dehradun was restored to Raja Sudarshan Shah and confirmed through a Sunud No. XVI of 1815[34]. On 17th November 1815, Dehradun was annexed to Saharanpur district.[35]

The land on the east of Alaknanda was occupied by the Britishers and was known as British Garhwal. It was attached to the Kumaon Commissionery. On 4th March, 1820, a treaty was signed between Raja Sudarshan Shah and the British. According to it, the British accepted claim of the Raja and his scions over Tehri Garhwal State. Sudarshan Shah on the other hand pledged to extend help to the British during emergency. In 1824, the pargana of Rawain was added to Tehri Garhwal,[36] but Dehradun, Mussoorie and Jaunsar were retained in Saharanpur district,[37] and on 26th December, 1842, a resolution was passed that these areas would remain permanently with Saharanpur district.

Raja Sudarshan Shah on receiving the land to the west of

Alaknanda made Tehri his capital. It is situated at the confluence of the rivers Bhagirathi and Bhilangana, at an altitude of 2,328 feet above the sea level. During those days there was not even a village on the spot and the settlers were unwilling to come. He accordingly spent Rs. 700 in building thirty small houses for which tenants at length were found, each paying a rent of Rs. 3 a year. Such was the humble origin of Tehri.

It appears that one of the reasons why Sudarshan Shah chose Tehri as his capital was its strategic position. It is surrounded on three sides by the Bhagirathi and in the background there are steep hills. Probably he had nostalgic and religious reasons also for choosing the site. Srinagar, the previous capital of the Parmar kings has been referred as, 'Dhanush Tirth', (i.e. a pilgrimage centre in the shape of a bow) in Kedar Khand,[38] similarly Tehri situated at the confluence of the rivers Bhagirathi and Bhilangana is also recognized as another 'Dhanush Tirth' in Kedar Khand. It is really interesting to observe the phenomenon of a bow and arrow at the point where these two rivers meet in Tehri. The river Bhagirathi meanders across like a bow and its tributary joins it in the shape of an arrow.

REFERENCES

1. Toposheet 53/I.J.K.M.N.
2. Sankrityayan, Rahul: Garhwal, p. 236.
3. Atkinson, E.T.: NWP Gazetteer, Volume III, p. 239.
4. Walton, H.G.: British Garhwal, A Gazetteer, p. 209.
5. Rawat, Ajay Singh: Uttarakhand Ka Rajnitik Itihas, pp. 2-3.
6. Kaushik, S.D.: "Climatic zones and their related socio-economy in the Garhwal Himalaya"—*Geographical Review of India*, 1962, pp 24, 22-41.
7. Pathak, C.S.: Kumaon University and Kumaon: A Souvenir, p. 11.
8. Joshi, L.D.: The Khasa Family Law, p. 10.
9. Census of India, 1901, Volumes XVI, p. 216.
10. Bhattacharya Pd. Brijratna: Skanda Puranantargat Kedar Khand Grunth 27.

11. The Mahabharata of Krishna Dwarpayana Vyasa, translated by Pratap Chand Roy, Vol. II, Sabha Parva and Van Parva pp. 208-209.
12. The Mahabharata Volume II, edited by Vishnu S. Sukthankar, 1/141/7, pp. 24-29.
13. Ibid., 3/145/12.
14. Ibid., 3/145/15-18.
15. Rawat, Ajay Singh: op. cit., pp. 13-14.
16. Joshi, L.D.: op. cit., p. 28.
17. Journal of the Asiatic Society of Bengal, VII, 1056.
18. Atkinson, Edwin T.: Kumaon Hills (Reprint 1974), p. 470.
19. Raturi, H.K.: Garhwal Ka Itihas, p. 2.
20. Lal, Mukandi: Garhwal Painting, p. 15.
21. श्रो बदरी केदार (1) श्रीराम (1) श्री साके 1589 संवत् 1924 ज्येष्ठ मासे दिने 4 गते गुरु वासरे श्रीनग्र शुभ स्थाने श्री महाराजाधिराज फतेपति साही देवज्यूले भगापत्त लेखी दीनु छ (1)...
बालक नाथ जोगी को भागचद वाली दीनु (1)
गढ़वाल सन्तान ने बालक नाथ जोगी का संतान...
22. Fateh Prakash, edited by Thakur Shoor Beer Singh from the original manuscript, p. 3.
23. Sirkar, D.C.: The Saka Pithas, p. 96.
24. Watters, Thomas: On Yuang Chwang's Travels in India (A.D. 620-645), Volume I, p. 330.
25. Williams, G.R.C.: Historical and Statistical Memoirs of Dehradun.
26. Parmar, Pati Ram: Garhwal Ancient and Modern, p. 184.
27. Awasthi, A.B.L.: Studies in Skanda Purana, Part I, p. 48.
28. Beal, Samuel: Buddhist Records of the Western World (1884), Volume I, pp. 198-99.
29. Cunningham, A.: Ancient Geopraphy of India, p. 356.
30. Atkinson, E.T.: op. cit., Volume XI, p. 453.
31. Cunningham, A.: Archaeological Report (1871), Volume I, p. 251.
32. Gill, A.R.: Valley of the Doon. p. 7.
33. Raturi, H.K.: op. cit., p. 309.
34. Aicchison, C.U.: A Collection of Treaties Engagements and Sunuds Relating to India and Neighbouring Countries, Volume II, p. 58.

35. Walton, H.G.: Dehradun a Gazetteer, Volume I, p. 83.
36. Darshan, Bhakt: Garhwal ki Divangat Vibhutian, p. 139.
37. Dewar, Douglas: A Hand Book to the English Pre-Mutiny Records, p. 159.
38. Bhattacharya, Pd. Brijratna, op. cit., 184/1069/24.

2
Rulers of Garhwal

According to Atkinson there are four chronological lists of the Parmar rulers of Garhwal. The earliest one is that of Captain Hardwick (1796 A.D.). The second list is taken from an official report of the year 1849 A.D. and is the same as that accepted by Beckett, the settlement officer in an old report on Garhwal. It gives several details which are not found in other lists. A third list is given by William and differs in some respects from Beckett's list. The fourth was obtained by Atkinson through an Almora Pundit and may be called the Almora list.[1] These lists are given in Tables 1 to 4.

Raja Sudarshan Shah also prepared a list of his ancestors in his book 'Sabhasar', which has not been mentioned by Atkinson. Sudarshan Shah wrote Sabhasar in 1828 A.D. The original manuscript is in the dynastic collection of Thakur Shoor Beer Singh, Purana Durbar, Tehri.

Among the lists cited by Atkinson, the one prepared by Beckett appears to be most authentic and it tallies with the one prepared by Raja Sudarshan Shah of his ancestors.[3] Beckett was Assistant Commissioner of Garhwal and the land settlement which commenced in 1856 in Garhwal was launched by him.[2] In this settlement for the first time, a regular field measurement of the whole cultivated area was made. He was, therefore, in a better position to prepare an authentic list of the Parmar kings of Garhwal. It is interesting to observe that the chronology of the Parmar kings, which was sung by the bards also, to a great extent tallies with Beckett's list. In the present times, a scion, known by the name of Pingal Dass, of the bard family of the erstwhile Tehri State, sings it on ceremonial occasions. Pingal Dass resides in a village called Purola.[4]

Table 1. Hardwick's list of Garhwal rajas

Sl. No.	Name	No. of years reigned		Name	No. of years reigned
1.	Bhog Dunt, the first Raja between whose reign and Adey Pal, 900 years passed of which no record exists	900	32.	Lecheme Naat	69
			33.	Prem Naat	71
			34.	Saada Nand	65
			35.	Perma Nand	62
			56.	Maha Nand	63
2.	Adey Pal	50	37.	Sooka Nand	61
3.	His son Bejey Pal	60	38.	Subu Chand	59
4.	Laak Pal	55	39.	Terra Chand	44
5.	Dehrm Pal	65	40.	Maha Chand	52
6.	Kerrem Pal	70	41.	Goolab Chand	41
7.	Narain Deo	72	42.	Ram Narain	59
8.	Hurr Deo	45	43.	Govind Narain	35
9.	Govin Deo	49	44.	Lachmen Narain	37
10.	Ram Deo	51	45.	Jegget Narain	32
11.	Runjeet Deo	53	46.	Mataub Narain	25
12.	Inder Sain	35	47.	Sheetaub Narain	37
13.	Chunder Sain	39	48.	Anund Narain	42
14.	Mungal Sain	32	49.	Herry Narain	45
15.	Choora Mun	29	50.	Mahah Narain	33
16.	Chinta Mun	33	51.	Renjeet Narain	31
17.	Pooren Mun	27	52.	Raamro Narain	33
18.	Birkee Ban	79	53.	Christuroo	49
19.	Bir Ban	81	54.	Jegyaroo	42
20.	Soorey Ram	79	55.	Herroo	32
21.	Kerreg Singh	60	56.	Futteh Sah	39
22.	Sooret Singh	72	57.	Dooleb Sah	60
23.	Mahah Singh	75	58.	Purteet Sah	35
24.	Anoop Singh	59	59.	Lallet Sah who died in 1781 and left four sons, was succeeded by his eldest son	
25.	Pertaub Singh	29			
26.	Hurree Singh	39			
27.	Jaggen Naat	55			
28.	Bejjee Naat	65	60.	Jakert Sah, and was succeeded by his brother and the last Raja	2½
29.	Gokul Naat	54			
30.	Raam Naat	75			
31.	Goopee Naat	82	61.	Purdoo Man Sah	

Total number of years	3,374½

Table 2. Beckett's list of Garhwal rajas

Sl. No.	Name	Reign	Age at death	Year of death (A.D.)
1.	Kanak Pal	11	51	729
2.	Shyam Pal	26	60	725
3.	Padu Pal	31	45	756
4.	Abigat Pal	25	31	781
5.	Sigal Pal	20	24	797
6.	Ratna Pal	49	68	652
7.	Sali Pal	8	17	858
8.	Bidhi Pal	20	20	878
9.	Madan Pal I	17	22	895
10.	Bhagti Pal	25	31	920
11.	Jai Chand Pal	29	36	943
12.	Prithi Pal	24	46	973
13.	Madan Pal II	22	30	995
14.	Agasti Pal	20	33	1015
15.	Surati Pal	22	36	1037
16.	Jayant Singh Pal	19	30	1073
17.	Anant Pal I	16	24	1072
18.	Anand Pal I	12	20	1084
19.	Vibhag Pal	18	22	1102
20.	Subhajan Pal	14	20	1116
21.	Vikram Pal	15	24	1131
22.	Vichitra Pal	10	23	1141
23.	Hansa Pal	11	20	1152
24.	Som Pal	7	19	1159
25.	Kadil Pal	5	21	1164
26.	Kam Deo Pal	15	24	1179
27.	Salakhan Deo	18	30	1197
28.	Lakhan Pal	23	32	1220
29.	Anant Pal II	21	29	1241
30.	Purab Deo	19	33	1260
31.	Abhaya Deo	7	21	1271
32.	Jairam Deo	23	24	1290
33.	Asal Deo	9	21	1299
34.	Jagat Pal	12	19	1311
35.	Jit Pal	19	24	1330
36.	Anand Pal II	28	41	1358
37.	Ajal Pal	31	59	1389
38.	Kalyan Sah	9	40	1398
39.	Sundar Pal	15	35	1413

(Contd.)

Sl. No.	Name	Reign	Age at death	Year of death (A.D.)
40.	Hansdeo Pal	13	24	1426
41.	Bijai Pal	11	21	1437
42.	Sahaj Pal	36	45	1473
43.	Balbhadra Sah	25	41	1498
44.	Man Sah	20	29	1518
45.	Shyam Sah	9	31	1527
46.	Mahipat Sah	25	65	1552
47.	Prithi Sah	62	70	1614
48.	Medni Sah	46	62	1660
49.	Fateh Sah	48	21	1708
50.	Upendra Sah	1	22	1709
51.	Pradipt Sah	63	70	1772
52.	Lalipat Sah	8	30	1780
53.	Jaikarat Sah	6	23	1786
54.	Pradhman Sah	18	29	1804

Table 3. William's list of Garhwal rajas

Sl. No.	Name	Sl. No.	Name
1.	Kanak Pal	20.	Vibhog Pal II
2.	Bisheshwar Pal	21.	Gugyan Pal
3.	Sumat Pal	22.	Vikram Pal
4.	Poorun Pal	23.	Vichitra Pal
5.	Ameegat Pal	24.	Hans Pal
6.	Shuptee Pal	25.	Swarn Pal
7.	Retee Pal	26.	Kanteekri Pal
8.	Salwahan Pal	27.	Kamdeo Pal
9.	Mudun Pal	28.	Sulukshun Deo
10.	Bidhee Pal	29.	Mahalukshun Deo
11.	Bhugdat Pal	30.	Sut Pal
12.	Vibhog Pal	31.	Apoorub Deo
13.	Jeychander Pal	32.	Jay Deo
14.	Heerut Pal	33.	Jitang Pal
15.	Mudun Sahee	34.	Kalyan Pal
16.	Abeegut Pal	35.	Ajay Pal
17.	Sooruj Pal	36.	Anant Pal
18.	Jeyut Pal	37.	Sundar Pal
19.	Aneerudo Pal	38.	Sehj Pal

(Contd.)

Sl. No.	Name	Sl. No.	Name
39.	Vijey Pal	44.	Mahipati Sah
40.	Bahadur Pal	45.	Prithvi Sah
41.	Sital Sahai	46.	Medini Sah
42.	Man Sah	47.	Fateh Sah
43.	Sam Sah		

Table 4. Almora list of Garhwal rajas

Sl. No.	Name	Sl. No.	Name
1.	Bhagwan Pala	27.	Sona Pal 1209 AD
2.	Abhaya Pala	28.	Kanha Pal
3.	Bishesha Pala	29.	Sandhi Pal
4.	Karna Pala	30.	Sulakshana Pal
5.	Kshema Pala	31.	Lakshandeva Pal
6.	Vyakta Pala	32.	Alakshandeva Pal
7.	Suratha Pala	33.	Ananta Pal
8.	Jayati Pala	34.	Abhideva Pal
9.	Purana Pala	35.	Abhayadeva Pal
10.	Avyakta Pala	36.	Ajaya Pal
11.	Salivahan Pala	37.	Ajaya Deva Pal
12.	Sangita Pala	38.	Asok Pratapa Pal
13.	Mongita Pala	39.	Jayadeva Pala
14.	Ratna Pala	40.	Ganitadeva Pala
15.	Madana Pal I	41.	Jitarhdeva Pala
16.	Vidhi Pal	42.	Kalyana Pala
17.	Bhagdatta Pal	43.	Ana Pala
18.	Jayachandra Pal	44.	Dipanta Pala
19.	Kirthi Pal	45.	Priyanihara Pala
20.	Madan Pal II	46.	Sundara Pala
21.	Anibuddha Pal	47.	Sahaja Pala
22.	Vibhogita Pal	48.	Vijaya Pala II
23.	Subadhan Kot	49.	Balbhadra Sah
24.	Vikram Pal	50.	Sitala Sah
25.	Vijaya Pal	51.	Man Sah 1547 AD
26.	Hansa Pal	52.	Sama Sah

(Contd.)

Sl. No.	Name	Sl. No.	Name
53.	Duloram Sah 1580 AD	58.	Upendra Sah 1717 AD
54.	Garbhabhanjan Mahipati Sah 1625 AD	59.	Pradipt Sah 1717-72 AD
		60.	Lalat or Lalita Sah 1772-80 AD
55.	Prithi or Prithvi Sah 1640 to 1660 AD	61.	Pradhuman Sah 1785-1804 AD
56.	Medni Sah		
57.	Fateh or Fatehpat Sah 1684-1716 AD	62.	Sudarshan Sah 1815 AD
		63.	Bhuwani Sah

The progeny of the rulers of Garhwal claim their descent from the Parmar dynasty. Sudarshan Shah in his work 'Sabhasar' while dealing with the chronology of the Garhwali kings has stated clearly that he and his ancestors are of Parmar origin.[3]

Bhakt Darshan is also of the view that the progenitor of the Garhwali kings was a Parmar.[4] It is significant that the bard songs in Garhwal are known by the name of 'Pawada' or 'Pawara'. Shyam Parmar has observed that 'Pawaras' are popular wherever the Parmars had settled down, such as in Bihar, Malwa, Bundelkhand, Agra region and even in Maharashtra. He has further stated that they are known as 'Pawada' in Brij and Bhojpuri, 'Pawara' in Madhya Pradesh and U.P. and 'Pawade' or 'Pawada' in Maharashtra.[5] Dr. Satyendra agrees with this view and states that the chivalrous songs of the Parmars are known as 'Parmaras'.[6] Some of the famous 'Pawaras' of Garhwal are that of Madho Singh Bhandari, Garhu Sumyal, Jai Dev Parmar and Ramu Rawat.[7]

On the basis of 'Sabhasar', Bhakt Darshan and the prevalence of 'Pawaras' in Garhwal, it can be concluded that the rulers of Garhwal were Parmars.

Kanak Pal, the Founder of Parmar Dynasty in Garhwal

According to Beckett's list and the one given in 'Sabhasar', Kanak Pal was the founder of the dynasty. Atkinson states that a cadet of the Parmar house of Dharanagar came on pilgrimage to the holy places in the hills and visited Son Pal on his way. The latter was so pleased with the young prince that he gave him his daughter and part of 'Pargana' Chandpur as dowry.

He has mentioned further that the Dharanagar prince appears to be Kadil Pal of Beckett's list.[8] This alludes that Kanak Pal came to Chandpur in 1159 A.D. Bhakt Darshan is of the view that Kanak Pal came from Dharanagri to Garhwal in 888 A.D.[9] Dr. Patiram Parmar writes that in samvat 745, i.e. 688 A.D. Kanak Pal of the reigning family of Malwa arrived in Garhwal. As the tradition goes, Raja Kanak Pal on his arrival here was adopted as a successor to the Raja named Son Pal, who also gave him his daughter in marriage.[10] Nothing is known of Son Pal's dynasty. It appears that it was supplanted by the Kanak Pal family and possibly Son Pal must have been one of the several chieftains of Garhwal. In this regard Pandit Harikrishna Raturi, author of two books is of conflicting opinion. While in 'Garhwal Varnan' he states that Kanak Pal came to Garhwal in 688 A.D.[11], in 'Garhwal ka Itihas' he maintains that he came from Dharanagri in 888 A.D.[12]

The above authors have not given any corroborative evidences that Kanak Pal hailed from Dharanagri. Moreover in 1927, correspondence had taken place between Rai Bahadur Chakra Dhar Jayal, the diwan of erstwhile Tehri Garhwal State and the Dhar State authorities regarding an enquiry if Kanak Pal was in any way related to the royal family of Dhar State.[13] A reply from Dhar Durbar along with the report of the history officer of Dhar State was received in December 1927, in which it is clearly stated that there is no relationship between the Dhar State family and the Tehri Garhwal State.[14] All this correspondence is preserved in the dynastic collection of Thakur Shoor Beer Singh, Purana Durbar, Tehri.

It appears that Kanak Pal came from somewhere in Goojar Desh as is vividly evidenced by an ancient inscription which was discovered at Chandpur Garhi on the walls of a temple in 1940 and which has been referred to in the book 'Garhwal Jati Prakash'.[15] Goojar Desh comprised the states of Rajasthan, a part of Maharashtra, a part of Madhya Pradesh, Malwa and Gujarat.[16]

There is another important evidence which supports the view that the Parmars of Garhwal and their first ruler migrated to this region from the south of latitude 26°, i.e. the land of Mewar, Gujarat as well as Maharashtra. It is significant that the image

of Lord Ganesh is very popular with Garhwal's cultural and
social life. 'Kholi ka Ganesh', i.e. carvings or paintings of Lord
Ganesh on the main doorway of the houses, is supposed to be
an auspicious symbol in every Garhwali family and especially in
the royal blood. The peculiar feature of these paintings and carvings is, that the trunk is turned towards the right hand side. The
ancient statue of Lord Ganesh in a dancing posture at Joshimath,
so sacred to the royal family has got its trunk turned towards the
right hand side. We also find the right turned trunks on the wall
paintings and the wooden statue of Lord Ganesh on the gates of
Purana Durbar in Tehri. Purana Durbar was the first palace built
after the partitioning of Garhwal in 1815. The ancient statue of
Lord Ganesh worshipped with 'Sri Yantra' in the 'Sri Raj Rajeshwari Kotha' of Purna Darbar, its trunk is also turned towards
the right hand side.

This sculptural style of Lord Ganesh with the trunk towards the
right is a common feature in Rajasthan, Maharashtra, and Gujarat. In U.P. and the northern regions of India, the trunk of Lord
Ganesh is turned towards the left hand side as is prescribed by
Sukra Niti.[17] The Sukra flora represents the Upper Gangetic Plain,
the Himalayan regions as well as the humid deltaic and littoral
sections of Eastern India.[18] Thus the idol of Lord Ganesh in
Garhwal alludes that this sculptural style must have been introduced by the Parmars who had migrated from Goojar Desh.

The temples of Ād Badri, just adjacent to Chandpur Garhi,
indicate further that the Parmar kings of Garhwal came from
Goojar Desh. Dr. K.P. Nautiyal is of the view that ".... the
Ād Badri shrine in Garhwal has got resemblance with the Solanki
temples of Gujarat and Rajputana", and ".... almost every
sign of Ād Badri is attributed to the rulers of Garhwal". The
temples of this region were generally built between 9th and 13th
centuries.[19] This period coincides with the early Parmars, who
were ruling Chandpur in that era.

Although there is a similarity between the Solanki temples of
Gujarat and those of Chandpur Garhi, the influence in total is
not only of Gujarat but of the architectural style which was
popular throughout that vast area Goojar Desh in that period.

It is also significant that in Garhwal and Kumaon there are
many Rajput castes which trace their origin from Gujarat and

Rajasthan and many of them had come to Garhwal with Kanak Pal, e.g. Gorla Rawat, Bartwal, Rautela, Bagli Negi, Kala Bhandari etc.[20] Pandit Balkrishna Shastri has supported this view and he states that the Narwaris came from Masigarh in Gujarat.[21]

On the basis of the information referred above, it can be assumed that Kanak Pal, the founder of the Parmar dynasty in Garhwal came from somewhere in Goojar Desh; but to indicate a particular place in Goojar Desh, owing to lack of primary sources, would be erroneous. However the possibility of Kanak Pal's migration from Dharanagri of Gujarat in Goojar Desh can be ruled out. About Dharanagri in Malwa, as has been mentioned earlier, the authorities of Dhar State in December 1927 accepted that there was no relationship between the Tehri Garhwal State family and the Dhar State. As regards Gujarat, since 941 A.D. upto the fourteenth century, Gujarat was under the sway of the Solankis, and before them, the Chawras were ruling this area.[22] On the basis of the sources quoted hitherto, Kanak Pal had come to Garhwal before this period.

It can be hypothesized on the basis of similarity between the names in Abu and Garhwal that Kanak Pal could have come from Abu in Rajasthan or somewhere in the proximity. Chandpur Garhi in Garhwal was the name of Kanak Pal's domain and Chandrapuri is a place situated on the foothills of Mount Abu in Rajasthan. In Mt. Abu we find Gomukh as a holy place.[23] Gomukh is also in Uttarkashi district of Garhwal. Koteshwar is both in Abu[24] and in Garhwal. The Koteshwar of Garhwal is enroute from Tehri to Deoprayag. Both the Koteshwars are temples of Lord Siva. Rishikesh is also both in Garhwal and Abu.[25] Mandakini is a river in the Chamoli district of Garhwal. It is a tributary of the river Ganga. In Mount Abu there is a holy water pit known by the name of Mandakini.[26] This pit was dug by some Parmar king.

Date of Accession of Kanak Pal

There is a variation in the dates given by various authors as regards the date of accession of Kanak Pal in Chandpur. As has been mentioned earlier, there are three different views, Beckett, Dr. Pati Ram and Pandit Hari Krishna Raturi. Raturi in his book 'Garhwal Varnan' has stated 688 A.D. as the year of migration of

Kanak Pal from Dharanagri in Malwa to Garhwal. The authors have not evidenced their view and the year seems improbable, because the first king of the Parmars of Malwa was Upendra (Krishna Raj) and his period falls between 847 and 873 A.D.[27] Dr. Shiv Prasad Dabral and Rahul Sankrityayan have quoted the views of different authors only. Bhakt Darshan, and Pandit Hari Krishna Raturi (Garhwal ka Itihas) have stated the year 888 A.D., which seems more probable since the Parmars were ruling Mt. Abu in the 9th century. Pratipal Bhatia is of the view that the Parmars of Abu stand next only to the Parmars of Malwa in their political and cultural achievements and they ruled for almost the same period as their brethren in Malwa.[28] According to Atkinson, the Dharanagar prince is not Kanak Pal, but Kadil Pal of Beckett's list and his year of accession is 1159 A.D. Atkinson has cited the year from Cunningham, who assigns the founding of Chandpur to the year 1159 A.D.

However owing to paucity of source material it can only be hypothesized that Kanak Pal, the founder of the Parmar dynasty in Garhwal came from somewhere in Goojar Desh, probably Mount Abu, in the year 888 A.D. The account of the Parmar dynasty from Kanak Pal to the reign of Ajay Pal lacks in archaeological and other evidential details to analyze it. It seems that the actual history of this dynasty starts from the period of Ajay Pal, i.e., in the 14th century.

REFERENCES

1. Atkinson, E.T.: op. cit., Volume II, pp. 445-47.
2. Letter No. 133, Kumaon files, 2nd August 1859, State Archives, Lucknow.
3. Shah, Sudarshan: Sabhasar (original manuscript) p. 54.
4. Darshan, Bhakt: Garhwal ki Diwangat Vibhutian, p. 6.
5. Parmar, Shyam: Bhartiya Lok Sahitya, p. 106.
6. Satyendra: Brij Lok Sahitya Ka Adhyayan, p. 348.
7. Chatak, Govind: Garhwali Lok Gathaen, pp. 199-204.
8. Atkinson, E.T.: op. cit., Vol. II, p. 446.
9. Darshan, Bhakt: op. cit., pp. 5-8.
10. Parmar, Pati Ram: Garhwal Ancient and Modern, p. 189.

11. Raturi, Hari Krishna: Garhwal Varnan, pp. 9-10.
12. Raturi, Hari Krishna: Garhwal Ka Itihas, pp. 337-39.
13. Letter No. 560/C, dated 23rd May 1927 and endorsement No. 1839/50/26-27, dated 13th June 1927, from Tehri Garhwal State.
14. Report of the History Officer of Dhar State contained in letter No. 17, dated 22nd July, 1927 and D.O. No. 1004, dated 10th December 1927 from Dhar Darbar.
15. Shastri, Balkrishna Bhatt: Garhwal Jati Prakash, p. 24.
16. Munshi, K.M.: The Glory that was Goojar Desh, Part I, p. 8.
17. Sukra Niti, Slokas 168-70
18. Basu, Major B.D. (ed.): The Sacred Book of the Hindus, Vol. XVI, p. 160.
19. Nautiyal, K.P.: Archaeology of Kumaon, p. 98.
20. Tomar, Rudra Singh: Rudra Kshatriya Prakash, pp. 148-52.
21. Shastri, Balkrishna Bhatt: op. cit., pp. 131-45.
22. Reu, Vishveshwar Nath: Raja Bhoj, p. 232.
23. Muniraj, Shant Murti: Abu, pp. 271-72.
24. Ibid., p. 233.
25. Ibid., p. 263.
26. Ibid., p. 231.
27. Reu, Vishveshwar Nath, op. cit., p. 225,
28. Bhatia, Pratipal: The Parmars, p. 163.

3

Parmar Dynasty and Gurkha Invasion

The history of the Parmar dynasty from Kanak Pal upto the reign of Raja Ajay Pal lacks evidential details. Except for their names in the dynastic lists, there is no source material to analyse their account. Ajay Pal is the 37th in the list of the Parmar rulers from Kanak Pal and the date of his death given in the list by Beckett is Samvat 1446, i.e. 1389 A.D. He ruled for 31 years; this means he came to the throne in 1358 A.D. C. Mabel Duff is of the view that, he was the first king to transfer his capital from Chandpur Garhi to Srinagar in 1358 A.D.[1] Walton has stated, "Ajay Pal transferred the seat of Government from Chandpur to Devalgarh in the fourteenth century, and is held to be the first who attempted to bring the scattered states under one power."[2] Devalgarh is about 8 to 9 miles from Srinagar and before settling down in Srinagar, he must have sojourned there while battling with various chieftains of Garhwal to unify them under his power. Bhakt Dharshan has viewed that Raja Ajay Pal was the first king of the Parmar dynasty who conquered and subdued the various principalities, 52 in number and consolidated them into one kingdom. These 52 principalities were as follows:[3]

1) Chandpur Garh
2) Kandara Garh (of the Kandaras)
3) Deval Garh (Raja Deval's)
4) Nag Nath Garh (Nag dynasty)
5) Poli Garh (of the Bachwan Bishts)
6) Khar Garh (of the Khar caste)
7) Phalyan Garh (the Phalyan brahmins)

8) Bangar Garh (Nag Vanshi Ranas)
9) Kuili Garh (Sanjawans)
10) Bharpur Garh (Sanjawans)
11) Kujjari Garh (Sanjawans)
12) Sil Garh (Sanjawans)
13) Lodh Garh (of Lodi)
14) Raika Garh (of Ramolas)
15) Mungara Garh (Rawats)
16) Upu Garh (Chauhans)
17) Molya Garh (Ramolas)
18) Sankari Garh (Ranas)
19) Nala Garh (In Dehradun)
20) Rani Garh (Ranas)
21) Viralta Garh (Rawats)
22) Chaunda Garh (Chaundal caste)
23) Rani Garh (Khatis)
24) Tope Garh (Topewals)
25) Sri Guru Garh (Padiyar)
26) Lobha Garh (Lobhan Negis)
27) Badhan Garh (Badhan caste)
28) Dusholi Garh (Manwar king)
29) Dhauna Garh (Dhouniyals)
30) Langur Garh
31) Vag Garh (Vagli Negi)
32) Triya Garh (Triya caste)
33) Purasu Garh
34) Lodan Garh
35) Ratan Garh (Dhamoda caste)
36) Garhkot Garh (Bagarwal Bisht)
37) Garhtang Garh (Bhotiyas)
38) Van Garh
39) Bhardav Garh
40) Chaundkot Garh (Chaundkotis)
41) Nayal Garh (Nayals)
42) Ajmeer Garh (Payals)
43) Sawli Garh
44) Badalpur Garh
45) Sangela Garh (Sangela Bisht)
46) Gujaroo

47) Jaunt Garh
48) Jaunpur Garh
49) Champa Garh
50) Kara Garh
51) Bhuwana Garh
52) Kanda Garh (Rawats)

Ajay Pal was a great ruler. Poet Bharat in his work 'Mano-daya' has compared his different qualities with those of Krishna, Yudhisthira, Bhim, Kuber and Indra.[4] There are several primary sources to evidence his reign in Garhwal. In Devalgarh, the statue of Raja Ajay Pal is engraved on a wall in front of the temple of Lord Vishnu. Ajay Pal is seated in a lotus posture and he is donning a turban and ear rings. The following letters are engraved on the left hand side of the statue:

अजयपाल को धर्म पायो भण्डारी करो कू...

Then there are different ancient 'tantrik' manuscripts in the dynastic collection of Thakur Shoor Beer Singh of Tehri in which the name of Raja Ajay Pal has been referred to several times.

Ajay Pal, after establishing the kingdom of Garhwal built a residence for himself at Devalgarh where he installed the family deity, goddess Raj Rajeshwari. Devalgarh is the 'Pith', i.e. the seat of saint Satnath of the Gorakhnath Panth and Ajay Pal was also a disciple of this 'Panth' or sect. He is generally placed in the category of Raja Bhartri Hari and Gopi Chand, who were also followers of this sect. George W. Briggs in his book 'Gorakh-nath and the Kanphata Yogis', has stated that, "Raja Ajay Pal was the founder of one of the ten sects of Gorakh Panthis".[5] Ajay Pal held a reputed position in this religious order. His name also appears in the list of the 84 Siddhas[6] or the elevated souls. There is a very ancient 'tantrik' manuscript in the dynastic collec-tion of Thakur Shoor Beer Singh in which Raja Ajay Pal has been addressed as, 'Ādi Nath'.[7]

This clearly indicates the position of esteem held by Raja Ajay Pal amongst the Gorakhpanthis. Ajay Pal after vanquishing the 52 chieftains must have developed a revulsion for battles and bloodshed and he, therefore, joined the Nath Panth.

About the palace of Raja Ajay Pal at Srinagar, Fuhrer[8] has given the following description:

".... The palace of Raja Ajay Pal must have once displayed considerable architectural pretensions and extent, as its ruins even now cover some acres of land. It was built of large blocks of stones laid in mortar and had three grand fronts each four storeys high, with projecting porticoes profusely ornamented in the lower parts with elaborate sculptures. .... It is said that no woodwork whatever was used in its construction, and this is attested by the fact that the portions still remaining have none, the windows even to the lathing being of stone, while the only doorway left is of stone carved so as to exactly resemble wood. These doors are very massive and heavy and it must have taken immense labour to put them up". The palace is no longer there in Srinagar (its photograph is however still available in the dynastic collection of Colonel Yudh Beer Singh of Dehradun); but the description in itself speaks of Raja Ajay Pal's sway over Garhwal and confirms the view that Srinagar was the first capital of unified Garhwal.

Ajay Pal was succeeded by Kalyan Shah. From Kalyan Shah upto Bijay Pal we do not have any information about their rule in Garhwal, except that their names are mentioned in the list given by Beckett and the one referred to in 'Sabhasar'. According to Beckett, Kalyan Shah was succeeded by Sundar Pal, Sunder Pal by Hansdeo Pal and Hansdeo Pal by Bijai Pal. After Bijai Pal comes Sahaj Pal, the 42nd ruler of the dynasty, about whom we have sufficient inscriptional evidence as follows:

a) An inscription of 1605 Vikrami, i.e. 1548 A.D. on the stone door of the temple of Kshetra Pal at Deoprayag.

b) Another inscription of 1608 Vikrami, i.e., 1551 A.D. on a bell in the temple of Raghunathji at Deoprayag. This bell is supposed to be dedicated to the temple by Sahaj Pal.

On the basis of the inscription of 1548 A.D., it can be assumed that Sahaj Pal must have ascended the throne before 1548 A.D. Raturi is of the view that the last available date of Sahaj Pal is 1575 A.D. This alludes that Sahaj Pal ruled approximately from 1548 A.D. to 1575 A.D. The poet Bharat has highly eulogised Sahaj Pal and says that Garhwal was in a prosperous state during his reign.

Sahaj Pal was Akbar's contemporary; although the whole of Northern India was approximately under Akbar's sway, Garhwal

retained its independence. A.L. Srivastava has viewed that
". . . The relations of the Empire with a few other notable states
deserve notice. An important principality among them was that
of Srinagar Garhwal. It seems to have maintained some kind of
diplomatic intercourse with the Mughal Court, but otherwise it
retained its independence".[9]

A.L. Srivastava has not clarified the type of diplomatic relations
between Garhwal and the Mughal king. Abul Fazal in his work
Ain-i-Akbari while describing the Subah of Delhi has stated that,
". . . . its breadth from the Sarkar of Rewari to the Kumaon
Hills is 140 kos."[10] He further states that, ". . . . a part of the
northern mountains of this Subah is called Kumaon", and the
Sarkar of Kumaon contains 21 mahals. He has not mentioned
Garhwal anywhere in his work. From the account of Abul Fazal,
it is vividly indicated that Kumaon was a part of the Mughal
Empire, but Garhwal was not subjugated by the Mughals. From
Ferishta[11] we learn that at that time an impression of great wealth
of the hill states was generally prevalent amongst the Muslims.
He writes, "The Raja of Kumaon also possesses an extensive
dominion, and a considerable quantity of gold is procured by
washing the earth mounds in his country, which also contains
copper mines. His territory stretches to the north as far as Tibet
and on the south reaches to Sambhal, which is included in India.
. . . . The sources of the Jumna and of the Ganges are both to
be found within the Kumaon territory". This description of
Ferishta tallies more with Garhwal than Kumaon. In ancient
times Garhwal was celebrated for its mines of copper and lead,
and gold washing in the Bhagirathi, Alaknanda valleys and along
the Son Nadi in the Patli Dun was an important source of income.
Garhwal also contains the sources of the two rivers, Jamuna and
the Ganges.

After Sahaj Pal, Balbhadra Shah came to the helm of affairs.
He was the first ruler to have adopted the title of Shah. This
title is also used by Kalyan Shah, the 38th ruler of Beckett's list
and the immediate successor of Raja Ajay Pal, but it was only
after Balbhadra Shah that this surname was popularised by the
rulers of Garhwal. According to Bhakt Darshan, when Aurangzeb
defeated his brother Dara Shikoh, the latter is said to have taken
refuge in Srinagar Garhwal, but he was treacherously sent to

Delhi and for this act of prodition, the Raja was investitured with the title of Shah. But this view is sceptical since Aurangzeb ascended the Imperial throne in 1658 A.D. whereas both Kalyan Shah and Balbhadra Shah reigned during the later half of the 16th century.

Dr. Pati Ram Parmar is of the view that, a Bartwal from village Satera in Talla Nagpur is said to have been sent to Delhi on some state affairs. During his stay there, one of the female members of the royal seraglio fell seriously ill. The messenger of Garhwal implored to be allowed to diagnose her suffering through a thread tied to the wrist of the patient. On his success he asked for the title of Shah for his Raja, instead of the reward intended for him.

Walton has referred that, ". . . . a royal prince of the Delhi house came to Garhwal for a change of air. On his return, his account of his reception so pleased the Emperor that he bestowed the title of Shah upon the Raja. . . . The visit is said to have occurred in 1483 A.D."[12]

How far the traditions as revealed by the aforesaid authors are correct, cannot be said because the contemporary Muslim chronicles are silent about the incident. However it can be concluded that after conquering the 52 principalities and establishing the vast kingdom of Garhwal, which extended upto Sambhal in Moradabad district, and which was not under the sway of the Delhi Sultanate, Raja Ajay Pal must have been recognized as Shah, the Imperial Majesty. This also leads us to the conclusion that his immediate successor Kalyan Shah must have adopted this title on the above pretext. Ajay Pal did not change the cognomen of Pal to that of Shah though he had established his independent hegemony, because, he was already famous as Ajay Pal, and moreover, being a follower of the Gorakhnath sect, the title Shah must not have appealed to his saintly nature. After Kalyan Shah, the 38th ruler of Beckett's list, the subsequent rulers upto Balbhadra Shah, the 43rd ruler, must have also adopted this cognomen, but it took some time to come into vogue, since it was an alien name and, therefore, the surname Pal with their first name is more popular.

As mentioned earlier Sahaj Pal reigned upto 1575 A.D. Dabral maintains that Man Shah, the immediate successor of Balbhadra

Shah ascended the throne in 1591 A.D. This signifies that Balbhadra Shah, the successor of Sahaj Pal, ruled Garhwal from
1575 A.D. to 1591 A.D. Walton has mentioned that in 1581 A.D.
Balbhadra Shah fought a battle against the neighbouring kingdom of Kumaon at Gwaldum.[13] During those days Rudra Chand
(1565 to 1597 A.D.), a scion of the Chand dynasty, was ruling
Kumaon.[14] Dabral is of the view that this battle was waged
somewhere around 1590 and 1591 A.D. The year of the battle
cannot be fixed, but it certainly means that Balbhadra Shah was
ruling Garhwal during that period.

Man Shah

According to Beckett's list Balbhadra Shah was succeeded by
Man Shah. There are sufficient inscriptional evidences of his reign
which are as follows:

a) An inscription on the door of the temple of Kshetra Pal at
Deoprayag, dated 1665 Vikrami, i.e. 1608 A.D.

b) Another inscription in the temple of Raghunath ji at Deoprayag. It is of 1667 Vikrami, i.e. 1610 A.D.

Both the inscriptions are land grants conferred to the temples.

Apart from these inscriptions, there is another source of information about Man Shah's reign. In the book 'the Early
Travels in India, 1589 A.D. to 1619 A.D.' by Foster, a European
traveller, Finch has given lucid details of his tour in India from
1608 to 1611 A.D. He mentions the country of Garhwal and the
name of the ruler Raja Man Shah. He says that the very rich
and all powerful king Man Shah's kingdom lies in between the
Jumna and the Ganges. It is said that he takes his meals in big
golden utensils. The length of his domain is 300 kos and the
breadth 150 kos. One of the borders of his kingdom is 200 kos
from Agra.[15].

From the account of William Finch it can be assumed that
Raja Man Shah must have been on the throne of Garhwal upto
1611 A.D. and he must have ruled approximately from 1591 A.D.
to 1611 A.D.

During the reign of Man Shah, the king of Kumaon, Laxmi
Chand invaded Garhwal seven times, but was repulsed each time
with considerable loss.[16] In the seventh attack Laxmi Chand was

very badly defeated and his capital was occupied by Man Shah's general, Nandi.[17] Rahul Sankrityayan has also mentioned the conquest of the capital of the Chand king's Champawat by Nandi.[18] Bharat the court poet of Raja Man Shah has highly eulogised his intrepidity in his work 'Manodaya'. The original manuscript of Manodaya is not available now.

Pandit Shambhu Prasad Bahuguna has stated that the court poet Bharat of Raja Man Shah and Jyotik Rai of the Mughal Court are the same person.[19] This is not true; however it is interesting that the name of one Jyotik Rai appears in the inscription of 1608 A.D. of Raja Man Shah in the temple of Kshetra Pal at Deoprayag. But this Jyotik Rai has been addressed an 'Mathpati' or the chief priest of the temple. Moreover as Lt. Colonel Tod has stated that the Jyotik Rai of the Mughal Court was not one particular person, but it was a title conferred upon any courtesan, who used to be well versed in astronomy and astrology.[20]

Shyam Shah

Man Shah was succeeded by Shyam Shah, the 44th ruler of this dynasty. He was a famous king and his name is referred to in the 'Tuzuk-i-Jahangiri' or the memoirs of Jahangir. It is an account of the presentation of a horse and an elephant to Raja Shyam Shah of Garhwal by the Mughal Emperor.[21] "Raja Shyam Singh [Shah], Zemindar of Srinagar (in Garhwal) was given a horse and an elephant". There is also a copper plate inscription of Shyam Shah of Samvat 1672 i.e. 1615 A.D.,[22] which corroborates that Shyam Shah ruled Garhwal during the reign of the Mughal Emperor Jahangir. This copper plate inscription is in connection with the endowment of land to some Shivnath Jogi of the village Silasari.

As regards the fixation of the dates of Raja Shyam Shah's rule in Garhwal, Shiv Prasad Dabral has stated that he was on the throne from 1611 to 1630 A.D. Shyam Shah's predecessor was ruling Garhwal until 1611 A.D. which indicates that he must have come to the helm of affairs by 1612 A.D. The presentation of the horse and elephant by Jahangir was made in April 1621 after which there are no evidential details to indicate that Shyam Shah ruled after this period. Thus it can be assumed that Shyam

Shah ruled Garhwal approximately from 1612 to 1622 A.D. Raturi states that Shyam Shah died without any issue, so his uncle Mahipat Shah succeeded him.[23] Raturi has not given a definite date of Shyam Shah's death. Walton and other authors are also silent about the demise of Shyam Shah. Thus it can be assumed that Mahipat Shah must have been crowned somewhere around 1622 A.D.

Mahipat Shah

Mahipat Shah was famous in Garhwal as 'Garva Bhanjan', i.e. one who destroyed the pride of his enemies in the battle field. It is said that there were frequent tiffs between Garhwal and the neighbouring Kumaon region during his reign and he was successful in defeating his enemies. Andrade, a Jesuit missionary has mentioned his invasion of Tibet in 1624 A.D. He says that the Raja of Srinagar invaded Tibet at three points. One of his armies numbered 12 thousand men with 11 thousand muskets and 20 small pieces of artillery, the second army consisted of 20 thousand men and the third one was smaller to the former two. But as a heavy snow-storm broke on the mountains and the passes forming the lines of communication were held by the Tibetans who offered a desperate resistance at every point, the whole enterprise failed. The situation became normal and he left Mana.[24]

Raturi has also described Mahipat Shah's assault on Daba or Dapa in Tibet and he states that Mahipat Shah succeeded against the Tibetans.[25] Dabral has supported this view,[26] and he mentions that Mahipat Shah suppressed the bandits of Sirmor and taught them a good lesson. But the dates of these ventures have not been given by them.

Dabral is of the view that Mahipat Shah reigned from 1631 to 1635 A.D. Rahul Sankrityayan and others have given no particular dates. It is said that Mahipat Shah died while fighting against the Raja of Kumaon. As tradition goes, he was determined to end his life in this campaign since he had killed a few innocent Nagas (serpent gods), and then he had gouged out the eyes from the statue of Bharat in the temple of Bharat at Rishikesh. He was so contrite about his misdeeds that he wanted to finish his life on a battle field. However there is no account of the last battle fought by Mahipat Shah in the history of Kumaon

written by Badri Dutt Pande or Rahul Sankrityayan. It seems
that Mahipat Shah ruled from 1622 to 1631 A.D. From the aforesaid account of Andrade, it is evident that Mahipat Shah was
ruling Garhwal in 1624 A.D. There is another information which
supports the view about Mahipat Shah's rule in that period.
Atkinson has referred to an inscription of Mahipat Shah of the
year 1625 A.D., at Keshav Rai Ka Math, i.e. the monastery of
Keshav Rai at Srinagar in Garhwal. But when I visited the monastery in 1976, the inscription had been obliterated by then. The
inmates of the monastery told me that is was decipherable until
September 1972 after which it was effaced by vandals.

Apart from C' Wessels, Andrades journey to Tibet via Srinagar
Garhwal has also been confirmed by another author, Sir Edward
Maclagan[27] in his book, 'The Jesuits and the Great Mogul'. He
states that ". . . . on March 30, 1624, Father Antonio de Andrade
left Agra with a lay brother, Manual Marques, to follow the king,
Jahangir, on his journey to Kashmir. On reaching Delhi, however, he learnt of the projected departure of a band of Hindu
pilgrims to Badrinath in the Himalayas, and with characteristic
promptitude he decided to join them with a view to penetrating
beyond the mountains". Maclagan has mentioned that Andrade
was accompanied by Manual Marques. C' Wessels has also given
the name of Andrade's companion as Marques.[28]

From the account of Azevedo, another Jesuit missionary, who
visited Tsaprang, it is evidenced that Mahipat Shah died in 1631
A.D. Francis de Azevedo was appointed in 1627 A.D. to the Mogor
Mission by the 'Society of Jesus' at Agra. On June 28, he started
from Agra to Tsaprang, via Srinagar Garhwal. He was at Srinagar
in July 1631 A.D. and witnessed the funeral of the king. Thus it
can be construed that Mahipat Shah ruled from 1622 A.D. to
1631 A.D.

The aim of the Jesuits to visit Tsaprang was to spread Christianity. From their accounts it can be concluded that Mahipat
Shah was an independent ruler and could challenge the might of
the Mughals. Andrade has mentioned that no regard was paid
to Jahangir's decree[29] by the Garhwalis when Andrade was passing through Garhwal on his second visit to Tsaprang. The account
is as follows.

"Father Andrade started in advance on June 17 accompanied only by his old companion, Brother Marques, and a
Father Gonzales de Sousa. They had some troubles on the
road, especially at Srinagar, where no regard was paid to
the rescripts from Jahangir. . . . This was reached on 28th
August 1625."

Mahipat Shah had three brave generals in his army, Madho
Singh Bhandari, Rikhola Lodi and Banwari Dass. Rikhola Lodi
had led the Garhwali forces against Tibet, Sirmor and the southern boundary of Garhwal in the Doon valley. There is not much
information about Banwari Dass. Madho Singh Bhandari is the
most conspicuous name amongst the warriors of Garhwal and
Kumaon. There is a maxim about him in the hills:

एक सिंघ रेंदो बण, एक सिंघ गाय का
एक सिंघ माधो सिंघ और सिंघ काहे का

meaning thereby, that on this earth there are only three 'singhs',
one is the lion, the other is the cow's horn and the third is
Madho Singh.

His period falls in the reign of Mahipat Shah, Rani Karnavati
and Prithvi Pat Shah. Dabral has stated that Madho Singh Bhandari was dead by 1635 A.D. Bhakt Darshan is also of a similar view
and says that Madho Singh Bhandari died in action at Chotta
Chini in Tibet in 1635 A.D. This was the last battle fought by the
brave warrior. As tradition goes, he was fatally wounded in the
battle field owing to which the Garhwali troops were demoralized.
The Tibetans, who were scared by the very name of Madho
Singh Bhandari rejoiced at the predicament of the Garhwalis and
their sagging morale. When the news of the enemy camp reached
Madho Sihgh, he became worried about the life of his soldiers
and took a quick decision. Concomitantly he ordered his troops
to roast him alive and install him on a horse back so that the
Tibetans may not know about his death. The troops did as they
were told and the roasted body of Madho Singh seated on horse
back was taken out in a procession towards the enemy line. The
Tibetans thought he was alive and their rejoicing came to an
abrupt end. In the meantime the Garhwalis retreated from the
battle field in an organised manner. To commemorate the intre-

pidity and sacrifice of this brave warrior, 'Pawadas' are sung in his praise.

It is possible that Madho Singh Bhandari might have died in the battle of Chotta Chini, as has been mentiond by Dabral and Bhakt Darshan, but the battle must have been fought around or after 1640 A.D. and not 1635 A.D as referred to by the above authors. There is a copper plate inscription of Samvat 1697 i.e. 1640 A.D., issued by Maharani Karnawati on behalf of her son Maharaja Prithvi Pat Shah, confirming a grant of land to the Hatwal Brahmins of the village Haat in Chamoli district of Garhwal. Madho Singh Bhandari has been referred to as one of the witnesses in it.

Prithvi Pat Shah

Mahipat Shah was succeeded by Prithvi Pat Shah. From the accounts of the Jesuit missionary Azevedo, it is known that Prithvi Pat Shah was only seven years old when he became heir apparent.[30] Dabral is also of similar view and states that his mother had taken the reins of the State in her hands to look after his welfare and rule the kingdom on his behalf. Dabral has not mentioned the real name of this queen. He says that she was known by the name of 'Nak Katti Rani', i.e. a queen who chops off the noses. Her name was actually Karnavati as is evident from the copper plate inscription of 1640 A.D. mentioned earlier. Maharani Karnavati's name is also mentioned in an old manuscript, 'Sanwari Granth'. This manuscript, deals with 'tantra' and her name has been cited in a similar manner as in the copper plate inscription of 1640 A.D. She has been referred as, 'Maharani Mata Karnavati', i.e. queen mother Karnavati. The manuscript is in the dyanastic collection of Thakur Shoor Beer Singh of Purana Durbar, Tehri.

In this connection I may clarify an old misunderstanding and correct the mistake committed by G.R.C. Williams[31] and also by Atkinson. They have stated that Karnavati was the wife of Ajboo Kuwar or Kuwar Ajab Shah. Actually Maharani Karnavati was the consort of Maharaja Mahipat Shah, wheras Ajboo Kuwar was one of the nine sons of Prithvi Pat Shah.[32] This means that Ajboo Kuwar was the grandson of Maharani Karnavati and not her husband as has been pointed out by the foreign authors.

There is an interesting incident which speaks of Rani Karnavati's bravery and the reason she was nicknamed as 'Nak Katti Rani'. Niccolao Manucci, the author of 'Storia Do Mogor', has mentioned that, Shah Jahan deployed an army to invade Garhwal. In the battle that ensued the Mughal forces were defeated very badly and the noses of the survivors were chopped off.[33]

"The purpose that Shah Jahan had of fighting with the Rana was diverted to a campaign against the Hindu prince of Sirinaguer [Srinagar] which is in the midst of lofty mountains in the north, covered all over with snow. But it did not happen to him as he had hoped. To effect his purpose he despatched a general at the head of 30 thousand horsemen besides infantry. The prince allowed his enemy to penetrate into the mountains retiring as they advanced. When the soldiers of Shah Jahan had got a certain distance, he closed the roads, so that they could neither advance any farther nor retreat, and there was no way of deliverance for them. Finding himself in this danger, the general sent proposals for peace negotiations, but the Hindu prince returned the answer that his resolve to retreat was too late. Already the commander had a deficiency of supplies, and all his camp was in great confusion. He, therfore, requested the prince, permission to withdraw, and although the rajah could have destroyed everyone of them, he did not wish to do so. He sent to say that he would grant them their lives, but his soldiers required all their noses as a memorial of having given them a gift of their lives. Shah Jahan's soldiers finding themselves in such dreadful straits, rather than lose their lives were content to lose their noses. They abandoned their arms, throwing them down where they stood and issued one by one leaving their noses behind them on the spot. From this, Shah Jahan, out of shame, never again attempted to make war against the rajah and he gave an order that ever afterwards his prince should be spoken of as Nactirany (Nak-kati-rani)—that is to say 'cut nose' and until this day he is known by this name. The general, who could not endure coming back with his nose cut off, took poison, and put an end to his life before he got back to the plains."

Manucci has stated that a Garhwali prince routed the Mughal forces, but it was actually the queen, Rani Karnavati, who exhibited exemplary bravery and gave a crushing defeat to the Mughal army. 'Mughal Darbar ya Maasirul Umra', which is a translation from the original text has also related this incident and mentioned that it was a queen who was responsible for humiliating the Mughals. Manucci has not given the name of the general, but 'Mughal Darbar ya Maasirul Umra', has mentioned the name of the general also. He was known as Najabat Khan. In the narration it is stated that the widow of the king of Garhwal was ruling with the help of Dost Baig an artillery officer, who was in service since the time of her late husband. The queen was famous as 'Nak-katti-Rani', because she used to punish the insurgents by cutting their noses. The narration continues that the Mughal invaders under Najabat Khan were defeated by the Garhwali forces, thirty kos from Srinagar, the capital. In the battle some of the Mughal troops perished and some took to flight from the battle field. Najabat Khan was one of the survivors, who sustained by living on leaves and roots of trees. But he incurred the Emperor's displeasure for this shameful defeat and was demoted.[34]

Travernier has also recounted this incident, but he has mixed it with the period when Suleiman Shikoh took refuge in Garhwal.[35] "Aurangzeb ordered troops to advance towards the mountains of Srinagar in order to compel Raja Nakti Rani to put Suliman Shiko in his power. But the Raja being able with 1,000 men to defend all the entrances to his country which are narrow and difficult." Aurangzeb was defeated by the Garhwalis, he further recounts and thereupon "had recourse to ruse, seeing that force availed nothing."[36]

On the basis of Manucci, Travernier and Maasirul Umra, it can be concluded that the Mughals invaded Garhwal and were badly defeated. Further, the noses of all the survivors were chopped off owing to which Rani Karnawati earned the name of 'Nak-Katne-wali-Rani', i.e. a queen who chops off the noses and later, 'Nak-kate-Rani'. There is a difference in the description of Manucci and Maasirul Umra as regards the cutting of noses of the Mughal troops. Maasirul Umra has tried to draw a curtain upon the humiliation of the Mughal forces, but the statement that the Rani awarded punishment by cutting off noses indicates that she must have treated the Mughal forces in a similar manner. Manucci being an alien has candidly described the humiliation of the Mughal troops in Garhwal.

The date and year of the battle have not been accounted for by the above authors and it is not possible to fix the exact date owing to paucity of source material. However on the basis of the copper plate inscription of Rani Karnavati of the year 1640 A.D., it can be assumed that the Mughals must have invaded Garhwal around 1640 A.D. and also Rani Karnawati was ruling on behalf of Prithvi Pat Shah atleast upto that period. From the accounts of Manucci and others, as cited above, the Mughals were defeated by Rani Karnavati alias (Nak-kate-Rani) the ruler of Garhwal and not Prithvi Pat Shah. Thus the battle between the Garhwalis and the Mughals must have been fought during that period when Karnawati was ruling as his guardian. Prithvi Pat Shah ascended the throne in 1631 A.D. at the age of seven years. In 1640 A.D. he was only sixteen years and thus was not in a position to fight the Mughals on his own.

This period, which can easily be termed as a glorious era of the history of Garhwal, is also distinguished by another landmark.

In 1659 A.D. after the defeat of Dara Shikoh at the battle of Samugarh[37] on 29th May 1658, his son Suleiman Shikoh took refuge in Garhwal. According to Muntakhabu-l-Lubab,[38] "Suleiman Shikoh had sought refuge with the zamindar of Srinagar". Travernier has also referred to Suleiman Shikoh's escape to Garhwal, but he has mixed the two incidents in one, i.e. of 'Nak-kati-Rani' and of Suleiman Shikoh's taking refuge in Garhwal. He has stated,[39] "Aurangzeb ordered troops to advance towards the mountains of Srinagar in order to compel Raja Nakti Rani to put Suleiman Shikoh in his power. But the Raja . . . rendered all Aurangzeb's efforts futile who thereupon had recourse to ruse, seeing that force availed nothing." In the footnote, the translator V. Ball has mentioned that, "Sreenagar is the original Srinagar, the capital of Kashmir, and that the account is based upon hearsay".[40] As is well known, Srinagar was the capital of the kingdom of Garhwal and it was founded by Raja Ajay Pal in 1358 A.D. In Tuzuk-i-Jahangiri as cited earlier, Srinagar has been referred to for the kingdom of Garhwal. Manucci has also mentioned the name of Srinagar, the capital and the country of Srinagar for the Garhwal kingdom. The translator's foot note that the incident is hearsay cannot be accepted. According to Muntakhabu-1-Lubab it is vividly evidenced that Suleiman Shikoh took refuge in Garhwal. The view is further supported by Bernier, Manucci and Qanungo.

Aurangzeb sent messages to Prithvi Pat Shah to surrender the prince but his persuasion and threats were met with contempt. In the book 'Bernier's Voyage to the East Indies,' it is mentioned that,

> "He maketh the Raja Jesseinge write one letter after another to the Rajah Serenaguer promising him very great things, if he would surrender Suleiman Chekouh to him . . . The Rajah answers that he would rather lose his estate, than do so unworthy an action. And Aurangzeb, seeing his resolution, taketh the field and maketh directly to the hills . . . But the Rajah laughs at all that, neither hath he more cause to fear on that side. Aurangzebe may cut long enough, they are mountains inacessible to an army, and stones would be sufficient to stop the forces of four Hindustan, so that he was constrained to turn back again."[41]

Manucci has also mentioned the defiant attitude of the Raja of Garhwal. He wrote to Raja Jai Singh that on no account he could harm his reputation by making over to Aurangzeb anyone who had sought his protection. He was however thankful for Raja Jai Sing's friendship, as for Aurangzeb he needed neither his promises nor his menaces. He further wrote that he might inform the Mughal that he had no respect for either his power or his victories and let him recall to mind the occasion when his father Shah Jahan sent an army to Garhwal and the survivors of that army had their noses chopped off. In the end he has commented, "let him know that he who could cut off noses could equally cut off heads."

Aurangzeb then took recourse to ruse. Dr. Qanungo is of the view that when Jai Singh could not convince the king of Garhwal to surrender Suleiman Shikoh, he instigated a powerful Brahmin minister against him who tried to give him poison in the form of medicine. But the vigilant prince tested the adulterated medicine on a cat and was saved. When the king came to know about his minister's treachery he got him beheaded. Later Jai Singh inspired the Garhwali prince Medni Shah to emulate Aurangzeb and revolt against his father.

Afterwards Suleiman Shikoh was surrendered to Aurangzeb somewhere around December 1660 A.D. because according to Dr. Qanungo he was brought before Aurangzeb on 5th January, 1661 A.D. Bernier has mentioned that, ". . . of Dara's family, there now remained Soliman Chekouh, whom it would not have been easy to draw from Serenaguer if the Raja had been faithful to his engagements. But the intrigues of Jesseingue, the promises and threats of Aurengzebe, the death of Dara and the hostile preparations of the neighbouring Rajahs, shook the resolution of this pusillanimous protector."[42]

Bernier has not detailed the circumstances in which Suleiman Shikoh was surrendered and from his account it appears that Prithvi Pat Shah had to yield to the circumstances. But during the surrender it seems he was away from Srinagar the capital of Garhwal. Bernier in his description has referred to the "hostile preparations of the neighbouring Rajahs," and Walton has mentioned that "during the reign of Pirthvi Shah the aggressions of the Kumaonis continued under the leadership of the then Raja Baz Bahadur who had already fought on the side of Khalel Ullah against the Garhwalis".[43] It is possible that the neighbouring Raja of Kumaon must have launched an attack on the borders of Garhwal and during that period Prithvi Pat Shah had to move from Srinagar the capital to thwart the invasions of the Kumaonis. Moreover it seems that Medni Shah was banished from Garhwal owing to his misdeed. He had to leave Srinagar for Delhi on this issue where he died in 1662 A.D. His death in Delhi is corroborated by the 'farman' which Aurangzeb sent to Prithvi Pat Shah in 1662 A.D.[44] In the 'farman' it is stated,

"Exalted amongst the nobles Prithi Singh, the Raja of Srinagar, having the hopes of benign favours, should know that recently Medni Singh, the son of Raja Prithi Singh has passed away. He [the Raja] should have all the patience and toleration. A robe of honour having been awarded to him, for conferring favours and making him distinguished, is hereby sent along with the farman. It has been enjoined that he [the Raja] should be thankful to the Emperor and be always firm in adopting the right path of obedience and submission. The prosperity of the Empire shall be considered by him the best means for fulfilling his hopes and desires and welfare of his present and future."

This farman is preserved in the U.P. State Archives, Lucknow.

Further the penitence of Raja Prithvi Pat Shah about his son's treachery indicates his innocence as regards the surrender of Suleiman Shikoh. Manucci has stated,

> "The aged Rajah of Srinagar felt greatly the vileness of the deed carried out by his only son and so great was his sorrow that in short space he ended his days under the disgrace, saying he would sooner have lost his territory and all his wealth than that his son should be guilty of such an act of infamy."[45]

According to the sources of local history, the tradition goes that when Prithvi Pat Shah sentenced his minister to death, the other ministers, officials and all the members of the family became hostile to him. Medni Shah on the advice of his ministers revolted against his father and tried to seize power. Concomitantly, Aurangzeb sent Kunwar Ram Singh, son of Mirza Raja Jai Singh, to Srinagar Garhwal to persuade the authorities to hand over Suleiman Shikoh to him. When Ram Singh met Prithvi Pat Shah, he refused to comply and told him that he will protect the Mughal prince until he lives. Then Kunwar Ram Singh and Medni Shah, who were friends, tried to hatch a conspiracy against Suleiman Shikoh. But before they could take any action against him he came to know about their motive and slipped away in the night with the intention of escaping to Tibet. Unfortunately he lost his way in the hills and was betrayed by the villagers. They informed Medni Shah about his whereabouts who got him arrested and handed him over to Ram Singh.[46]

Prithvi Pat Shah was not only a brave and independent ruler but also a liberal and religiously tolerant. Maclagan is of the view that he permitted Father Ceschi to build a church at Srinagar and also allotted him some land for an orchard. Father Ceschi was nominated for service in Abyssinia, but difficulties of travelling intervened and ultimately he was sent to Agra in 1648 A.D. He was subsequently invited to Srinagar in Garhwal.[47]

Manucci has supported this view and stated that, "The Rajah was a great friend of the Jesuit Fathers and had accorded leave to build churches and allowed everyone who chose to profess the religion of Christ. I knew two Italian priests, great friends of this Rajah, Father Etanilao Malpique and Father Chesco."[48] In the footnote it has been mentioned that, "about 1648 Father Stanislaus Malpique or Malpia, a Jesuit, received permission to build a Church from the Raja of Srinagar Garhwal". Malpique was at Agra in 1656 A.D. When Manucci arrived there he met father Malpique.

Shiv Prasad Dabral and local historians have stated that Prithvi Pat Shah ruled upto 1660 A.D. This view is not correct, as the farman that Aurangzeb sent to Prithvi Pat Shah about his son Medni Shah's death was of the year 1662 A.D. Then there is another farman of the year 1665 A.D. of Aurangzeb which he sent to Fateh Shah the ruler of Garhwal on his grand-father Prithvi Pat Shah's death. The translation of the farman is as follows:

"Raja Fateh Singh having hopes of benign favours should know that recently the news of the death of Raja Prithi Singh, his grand-father has been delivered to the imperial court and his nomination as the successor to the deceased. Therefore, he is declared by the Emperor, the Raja of the country of Srinagar. For elevating his position a robe of honour and a dagger studded with jewels, awarded to him, are sent hereby, along with the farman. He [the Raja] should be grateful for benign favours and always be firm in adopting the right path of obedience and services. The performance of Imperial services, in the best possible manners should be deemed by him the best means for fulfilling his hopes and desires and the welfare of his present and future. As a farman has previously been issued to the deceased to march on the Zamindar of Kumaon from the side of Srinagar to fight for his mahals, kill and plunder the area to the maximum; it has further been enjoined upon him to enter the country of that refractory Zamindar for plundering and capturing his mahals. The act will make him a favourite of the Empire."[49]

It appears that Prithvi Pat Shah was alive upto 1667 A.D. The

Government of India had invited the Chinese attention to a copper plate inscription of that year which bears the seal of Raja Prithvi Pat Shah of Garhwal, in support of their case regarding the boundary dispute about Nilang. Both Ram Gopal[50] and Shanta Kumar[51] have cited this inscription. Then there is another copper plate inscription of Maharaja Fateh Shah, the grandson of Prithvi Pat Shah of Jyestha, Samvat 1724, i.e., 1667 A.D. In this copper plate also the royal seal is of Maharaja Prithvi Pat Shah, though it has been issued by Fateh Shah. It runs in favour of some priest, Balaknath of the Gorakhnath cave in Srinagar, the capital of Garhwal. The inscription mentions the land grant which was bestowed upon Balaknath and his progeny.

From the inscriptions cited above, it is obvious that Prithvi Pat Shah was alive upto 1667 A.D. It seems that he abdicated the throne in 1665 A.D. in favour of his grandson, Fateh Shah since he had banished his son Medni Shah from Garhwal. When the Mughal court received the information that Fateh Shah has been crowned as king of Garhwal, Aurangzeb must have conceived that Prithvi Pat Shah is dead because Aurangzeb who had himself seized power by interning his father could never have imagined that one can abdicate the throne in favour of his grandson. Moreover from the time of Qutubuddin Aibak to Aurangzeb there are several examples in Muslim history of treachery and blood-shed to capture power, and Aurangzeb, who was brought up in this environment, thought that Fateh Shah could have ascended the throne only after Prithvi Pat Shah's death.

The farmans issued by the Mughal Emperor to the Rajas of Garhwal, Prithvi Pat Shah and Fateh Shah, are couched in the phraseology as if the kings of Garhwal had accepted the suzerainty of the Mughal Emperor. It is not substantiated by realities; Garhwal was absolutely independent during the medieval period as has been brought out by earlier cited proofs. Moreover the defeat of the Mughal army during the rule of Shah Jahan and the very fact that Suleiman Shikoh took refuge in Garhwal shows, that the king of Garhwal was not under the Mughal Emperor and that the fugitive prince thought him capable to withstand the threats of the Mughal Court. These farmans are just a ruse to illustrate the suzerainty of the Mughal Emperor in the hills and particularly in the latter case to browbeat and allure the young king to his subjugation. What he could not achieve on the battle field during the rule of Prithvi Pat Shah, he tried to attain in the reign of Fateh Shah with the help of this farman. The farman of 1665 A.D. was also aimed at resuscitating the influence of Aurangzeb in Kumaon with the help of the Garhwali king.

Raja Prithvi Pat Shah was a great builder. He got a township, Prithvi Pur in the Doon valley built after his name. His mother Karnawati had established the village Karanpur in Dehradun, and several tanks and canals were constructed by her in Dehradun and in Garhwal. The construction of the Rajpur canal of Dehradun is also attributed to her for irrigating the land between Dehra and Rajpur. A palace in Navada was also built during her reign. G.R.C. Williams has mentioned that Ajboo Kuwar was the governor of Nawada. On reading this account, as has been pointed out earlier, Atkinson committed the mistake of stating that Rani Karnawati was the consort of Ajboo Kuwar.

There are several primary sources of account of the reign of Raja Prithvi Pat Shah. Apart from the two farmans of Aurangzeb and two inscriptions of Raja Prithvi Pat Shah cited already, the following other sources are also available:

1) 'Nishan' of Dara Shikoh sent to Prithvi Pat Shah dated 15th May 1547, as has been quoted in the book 'Mughal Farmans' (1540 A.D. to 1706 A.D.) Volume I, edited by Dr. K.P. Srivastava.[52]

2) Inscription in the monastery of Madho Dass in Laxmi Narayan temple of the year 1642 A.D. at the village Bhaktiana, just adjacent to Srinagar. The inscription is in the outer portion of the main temple wall.

3) Inscription of the year 1664 A.D. on the southern door of the temple of Raghunathji in Deoprayag.

4) An inscription on the western doorway of the temple of Raghunathji in Deoprayag. This inscription is also of 1664 A.D.

Fateh Shah

Walton is of the view that Prithvi Shah was succeeded by Medni Shah, of whose reign he states further, "we have no record except references in the annals of Kumaon to aggressions made

on Garhwal". According to him Medni Shah was succeeded by
Fateh Shah in 1684 A.D. Dabral has relied on Walton's information and has stated that Medni Shah ruled from 1660 A.D. to
1684 A.D. But as has been mentioned earlier, Medni Shah after
the surrender of Suleiman Shikoh aroused the wrath of his father
Prithvi Pat Shah and was banished from Garhwal. He died in
exile in Delhi in 1662 A.D. which is confirmed by the 'farman' of
Aurangzeb sent to Prithvi Pat Shah and which has been quoted
already. Thus Medni Shah did not rule Garhwal as has been incorrectly referred to by the gazetteers and the authors of Garhwali history.

Prithvi Pat Shah was succeeded by Fateh Shah at the age of
33, which is evident from his portrait* in the dynastic collection
of Thakur Shoor Beer Singh. In the painting Fateh Shah is
mounted on a horse and is giving a very stately look. So the belief
that Fateh Shah came to the throne at the age of seven years
and that his mother was ruling as his guardian as stated by
Pandit Harikrishna Raturi and Dabral is not correct. Prithvi
Pat Shah had abdicated in his favour in 1665 A.D. and Fateh Shah
must have been installed as the ruler of Garhwal only when he
had attained adulthood.

Fateh Shah was a brave warrior. G.R.C. Williams is of the view
that he invaded Saharanpur and established a township named
Fateh Pur in Haraura Pargana. Walton has stated that Fateh
Shah in 1692 A.D. led a memorable attack from Dehradun on
Saharanpur, which was repelled with great difficulty by Sayyed
Ali, the imperial general. Fateh Shah is also credited with the
extension of his power into Tibet.[53] Rahul Sankrityayan[54] and
Fateh Prakash[55] have supported the view that Fateh Shah invad-
ed Tibet and his sword and armour were preserved for a long
time in the monastery at Daba.

Dabral and Bhakt Darshan are of the opinion that Fateh Shah
invaded Sirmor in 1692 A.D. and conquered a large part of the
country in Paunta and Jaunsar region. The year of invasion as
mentioned by these authors is not correct, because the animosity
between Fateh Shah and the Raja of Sirmor Nahan is regarded as

---

*The age of Fateh Shah at the time of accession has been mentioned by
the artist of the portrait.

the prelude to the famous battle of Bhangani, which was fought between Fateh Shah and Guru Gobind Singh. In the 'Sikh Itihas', written by Thakur Deshraj it is mentioned that the ruler of Sirmor Nahan feared Fateh Shah so much that he sought the help of Guru Gobind Singh to reconcile matters. Guru Gobind Singh persuaded Fateh Shah in friendliness to restore good relations with the Raja of Sirmor and return the portion of his kingdom which had been wrested by him.[56] Bhagat Laxman Singh has stated that the Guru was successful in establishing congenial relationship between Fateh Shah and the Raja of Sirmor Nahan, Medni Prakash. "In those days the Guru settled a long standing boundary dispute between Raja Medni Prakash of Nahan and Raja Fateh Shah of Srinagar, Garhwal.[57]

Fateh Shah and Guru Gobind Singh were good friends, but later on they fought a battle against each other at Bhangani. The cause of the battle, according to Surinder Singh Johar, was the refusal of presents sent by Guru Gobind Singh to Fateh Shah on his daughter's nuptial ceremony with the son of Raja Bhim Chand of Kohlur. "Dewan Nand Chand while presenting the gifts, told the Raja that Guru Gobind Singh had presented jewellery worth Rs. one lakh to Fateh Shah's daughter. Raja Bhim Chand was much enraged and was filled with anger that his son's father-in-law was friendly to the Guru, who was his bitter enemy. He threatened to refuse his daughter in marriage for his son, if he accepted the Guru's gifts. Message was sent to Raja Fateh Shah, who was much perplexed and replied that is was a great sin to fight against the Guru, who was in friendship with him. At this reply Bhim Chand was infuriated and ordered his drum to be beaten which was a signal for departure. He declared that the marriage of his son with the daughter of Fateh Shah was cancelled. Fateh Shah had no alternative but to capitulate to the wishes of Raja Bhim Chand.[58]

Bhim Chand was annoyed with Guru Gobind Singh, because the latter had refused to lend Bhim Chand his elephant. Anil Chandra Banerjee has expressed his view that in 1685 A.D., the Guru went to Paonta at the invitation of Medni Prakash, the ruler of Nahan. The background is not quite clear, but it seems, he has further commented, forces were at work. Bhim Chand the ruler of Kohlur, within whose territories Anandpur was situated, appears to have been perturbed by the Guru's interest in military matters. Sikh penetration into the hill region had begun in the early years of the pontificate of Hargobind, and the Sikhs had participated in military operations on more than one occasion. As a result of this suspicion an atmosphere of confrontation developed on small issues like Bhim Chand's desire to take an elephant from the Guru. The climax was Bhim Chand's demand of tribute from the Guru as a mark of his political subordination. The tension in Kohlur attracted the attention of Medni Prakash, the ruler of the neighbouring State of Nahan, who presumably desired to strengthen himself against his rival Fateh Shah, the ruler of Garhwal by installing the Guru in his own territoriy. Thus the Guru's presence though unwelcome in Kohlur was probably supposed in Nahan to be an accession to its strength.[59]

According to 'Vichitra Natak', the autobiography of Guru Gobind Singh, the famous battle between Fateh Shah and Guru Gobind Singh was fought at Bhangani, a village six miles from Paonta, the residence of Guru Gobind Singh. The original manuscript is in the dynastic collection of Thakur Shoor Beer Singh of Tehri and its Hindi version has been published by Shiromani Gurudwara Prabandhak Committee. The 'Vichitra Natak' gives no explanation of the transfer of residence to Paonta, it merely says that "afterwards I left home and went to the place called Paonta". Guru Gobind Singh has further mentioned, "in Paonta which is a beautiful place I enjoyed myself on the banks of the Jamuna and saw amusements of different kinds. There I killed many tigers and bears, and Fateh Shah who was the king became annoyed with me without any reason".[60]

Dr. Fauja Singh is of the view that the battle of Bhangani was the first of so many battles fought by Guru Gobind Singh and to connect it with the story of the return and refusal of the presents sent by the Guru on the occasion of Fateh Shah's daughter's marriage is not correct.[61]

On the basis of the statement of Guru Gobind Singh in his autobiography that Fateh Shah fought with him for no obvious reasons, and Dr. Fauja Singh's view, it can be concluded that the refusal of presents could not have been the pretext for the battle of Bhangani; Guru Gobind has nowhere in his accounts mentioned the name of Raja Bhim Chand. However it is difficult to believe that Fateh Shah suddenly took military measures without any reason. It seems that among the possible grievances of Fateh Shah was the presence of the Guru's armed camp near his territory. When Guru Gobind Singh made himself conspicuous by hunting big game, the news must have reached Srinagar and Fateh Shah, swayed with the idea that the Guru might settle down permanently at Paonta, launched an attack. Moreover Paonta occupied a strategic position guarding the only convenient route connecting Nahan and Garhwal. It is also not unlikely that his subjects suffered sometimes from the lawless activities of the Guru's followers. The Guru's statement that Fateh Shah "came to blows with me", shows that he was a direct target of the Raja's wrath.

The battle ended without any consequences as has been pointed out by Raturi. Guru Gobind Singh has mentioned at several places in the 'Vichitra Natak' that Fateh Shah was defeated by him. Anil Chandra Banerjee has stated on the basis of 'Vichitra Natak' that Guru Gobind Singh was victorious. "The Guru's account in the 'Vichitra Natak', is not clear enough in respect of details, but the Guru himself fought in the field, and there is no doubt that he won a complete victory". But the victory has not been substantiated by annexation of territory. The Sikh Review corroborates the fact that there was no occupation of territory by Guru Gobind Singh.[62] In his autobiography Guru Gobind Singh too has nowhere referred to annexation of any territory within the Garhwali kingdom.

Anil Chandra Banerjee has further stated that the Guru was not prepared to take unnecessary risks by allowing his reckless followers to march into Garhwal, nor did he consider it wise to continue his residence at Paonta. That he took this decision after the battle with the Garhwali king shows that the result of the battle was far from the expectations of the Guru. He thought it expedient only to enter into an understanding with Bhim Chand and return to Makhowal. All this happended in 1688 A.D.

During Fateh Shah's reign there were several invasions on Garhwal by the Kumaonis. Bhakt Darshan is of the view that Fateh Shah had fought a number of battles against Kumaon, but without any conclusive results. Walton has expressed that

the invasion by Kumaon, which commenced in the reign of
Prithvi Pat Shah was carried vigorously in the reign of his successor Fateh Shah. Gyan Chand of Kumaon, who came to the
throne in 1698 A.D., inaugurated his reign in the traditional
manner with a raid upon the fertile Pindar valley, which was laid
waste as far as Tharali. The next year he crossed the Ramganga
and plundered Sabli, Khatli and Sainchar; an attack which was
returned in 1701 A.D. by the Garhwalis, who overran Chaukot
and Giwar in Kumaon. From this period onwards the relations
between Garhwal and Kumaon took the form of raids and
counter-raids across the border. In 1703 A.D. the Kumaonis were
successful against the Garhwalis in a battle fought at Duduli,
just above Melchauri. In 1707 A.D. another great expedition was
undertaken towards Garhwal, and this time the Kumaon forces
took possession of Juniyagarh in Bichla Chaukot, and again
passing Panduwakhal and Dewaliphal passes penetrated as far
as Chandpur and razed the old fort to the ground. The next
Kumaoni Raja, Jagat Chand plundered Lohba and garrisoned
the fort of Lohbagarh at the head of the Panduwakhal pass, and
in the following year he pushed in through Badhan and Lohba
and uniting his forces at Simli, near the confluence of the Pindar
and the Alaknanda, proceeded down the valley as far as Srinagar.
Walton has further mentioned that the Raja of Kumaon occupied Srinagar and the Garhwali Raja fled to Dehradun. Fateh
Shah appears to have returned very soon, for in 1710 A.D. his
troops were again mobilized in Badhan.

Walton's account of the invasions on Garhwal seems to be
exaggerated. It is possible that there must have been bickerings
between the neighbouring chiefs, and encroachment upon each
other's territory or an attack led by the Kumaoni Raja, but not
a series of invasions as have been described by him. He has
mentioned that the old fort of Chandpur (the original feudal
state of the Parmars before they became masters of Garhwal)
was razed to the ground. But approximately after 200 years,
Fuhrer witnessed this ancient fort as has been mentioned by him
in 1891 A.D.[63] Moreover, if Garhwal would have been invaded
several times during the reign of Fateh Shah, then it would have
been in a shambles. But as is evidenced by the writing of the
contemporary literatis, Garhwal was in a prosperous state during

the rule of Fateh Shah. Bhakt Darshan is of the view that Fateh Shah's era was one of the most glorious periods in the history of Garhwal and he was a great patron of art and literature. Tradition has it that like Vikramaditya and Akbar he too had nine illustrious figures ('Navratna') in his court, who were Sureshanand Barthwal, Revatram Dhasmana, Rudridutt Kimothi, Hari Dutt Nautiyal, Vasavanand Bahuguna, Shashidhur Dangwal, Sahdev Chandola, Kirti Ram Khanthola and Hari Dutt Thapliyal. The following ancient and panegyrical works of his period are available today:

1) 'Fateh Shah Karna Granth', by Jatadhar or Jatashankar. The original manuscript is preserved in the Ved Shala Library of Pandit Chakradhar Shastri at Deoprayag.

2) 'Fateh Prakash', by Ratan Kavi or Kshem Ram. The original manuscript is in the dynastic collection of Thakur Shoor Beer Singh and he has edited and published it from Bharat Prakashan Mandir, Aligarh in 1961. Both authors were the court poets of Fateh Shah.

3) 'Vrit Vichar' by Kavi Raj Sukhdev Misra. This manuscript is in the dynastic collection of Thakur Shoor Beer Singh.

4) 'Vrit Kaumudi' or 'Chhandsar Pingal', by Mati Ram. The original manuscript is also in the dynastic collection of Thakur Shoor Beer Singh. A few pages of the manuscript are also available in the 'Nagari Pracharani Sabha', Varanasi.

Ratan Kavi has eulogised the glory of Fateh Shah, and also the splendour of his kingdom Srinagar Garhwal. He has further commented that in Garhwal there was perfect law and order owing to which people did not lock their houses.

Kavi Raj Sukhdev Misra, the most celebrated scholar of the period in his work 'Vrit Vichar' has praised Fateh Shah's gallantry. The poem is a point to point description of the portrait available of Maharaja Fateh Shah.

Bhushan has also eulogised Fateh Shah. Thakur Shoor Beer Singh has quoted the poet in the introduction of the book 'Fateh Prakash' edited by him. Mati Ram's famous work, 'Vrit Kaumudi' or 'Chhandsar Pingal' is replete with the praise of Fateh Shah. He has compared his generosity with that of Shivaji. The original collection is in the dynastic collection of Thakur Shoor Beer Singh. Dabral has also cited these lines stating that they have been taken from the original manuscript 'Vrit Kaumudi' which was composed in the year Samvat 1785 i.e. 1728 A.D. Dabral has committed a mistake in noting down the year. In the manuscript itself the year of composition of 'Vrit Kaumudi' has been given as Samvat 1758 i.e. 1701 A.D. Dr. Satyendra has also extracted it from the original manuscript and referred it in the research journal of Agra University'.[64] Thus on the basis of the above panegyrial works, it can be assumed that Fateh Shah was a brave warrior, and during his rule Garhwal was in a prosperous stage.

Bhakt Darshan is of the view that Fateh Shah was a great patron of painting and music. There is however no record corroborating the view that there was any musician of eminence in his court. As regards his patronage to painting, Ananda K. Coomaraswamy mentions,[65] "At the close of the seventeenth century two Hindu painters from the Mughal court, viz. Shyam Dass and Har Dass accompanied Suleiman Shikoh to Garhwal. It is possible that these painters got patronage during the reign of Fateh Shah which might have given birth to the Garhwali school of painting. Mola Ram, the grandson of Har Dass who lived from 1760 to 1833 was a protagonist of this school of art. This school was more Rajput than Mughal".[66]

Fateh Shah had great reverence for the 'Nath Panth' as is evident from the 'Tamra Patra' (which has been cited already) of Samvat 1724, i.e. 1667 A.D., issued by him in favour of one Balak Nath Jogi. This saint Balak Nath had achieved great fame amongst the 'Siddhas' of northern India.[67] He had also invited the Sikh Guru Ram Rai to his kingdom and built a Gurudwara in Dehradun. Fateh Shah then made an endowment of 3 villages, Khurbura, Rajpur and Chamsari to Guru Ram Rai. Later his grandson, Pradip Shah added a further grant of 4 villages, viz. Dhumawala, Mujanwala, Panditwari and Dhantawala to the Gurudwara.

There are several land grants of Fateh Shah which he endowed to temples. Some of these copper plate inscriptions are still available which are detailed below:

1) A copper plate inscription of the year 1667 A.D. issued by him in favour of Balak Nath Jogi, which has been cited earlier.

2) A copper plate inscription of Samvat 1757, i.e. 1700 A.D.

the copy of which is available in the dynastic collection of Thakur Shoor Beer Singh. This is a temple grant of the Raj Rajeshwari temple in Devalgarh Mandal.

3) An inscription of the year 1706 A.D. This is famous as the 'Bindakoti Tamra Patra'. It is not only a temple grant, but also mentions that a part of the income derived from the land bestowed would be used for maintaining a 'dharamshala', where pilgrims and the poor shall get free food.

4) An inscription of the year 1710 A.D.

5) An inscription of the year 1715 A.D. which is a land grant to the monastery of the disciples of the Nath Panth. This inscription is in the dynastic collection of Thakur Shoor Beer Singh. Some words of the inscription cannot be deciphered.

There is also a numismatic evidence of the reign of Fateh Shah. Dabral and Raturi have given the photographs of the coins issued during his reign.

The inscription of the year 1715 A.D. is quite important, since the date of Fateh Shah's demise can be calculated with its help. There are different versions furnished by various authors as regards the death of Fateh Shah.

In Backett's list it is Samvat 1765, i.e. 1708 A.D. Dr. Pati Ram and Shiv Prasad Dabral have relied on the date given by Walton, who states that Fateh Shah died in 1716 A.D. Raturi and Rahul Sankrityayan have fixed the date of his demise to a later period i.e. 1749 A.D. Bhakt Darshan says that Fateh Shah died in 1715 A.D.

According to the copper plate inscription of 1715 A.D. of Fateh Shah it is obvious that he was ruling upto this year. After this copper plate inscription we do not find any evidence of his reign in the form of inscriptions, edicts etc. It is possible that Fateh Shah died in 1715 A.D. There is a copper plate inscription of Samvat 1773 i.e. 1716 A.D. of Pradip Shah's reign in the dynastic collection of Thakur Shoor Beer Singh. On the basis of this inscription it is obvious that by 1716 A.D. Fateh Shah was dead. The period between the issue of the two copper plate inscriptions, i.e. of Fateh Shah 1715 A.D. and of Pradip Shah 1716 A.D. is one year, one month and seven days. It is possible

that Fateh Shah died after the copper plate inscription of the
year 1715 A.D. was issued. Now the question arises—who ruled
between the time that elapsed between Fateh Shah's death and
Pradip Shah's accession to the throne. It must have been a short
span, about a year approximately. Bhakt Darshan is of the
opinion that Fateh Shah was succeeded by his son Dalip Shah.
Dabral has only cited the views of different authors. Walton
states that after Fateh Shah's death his son Dalip Shah came to
the throne in 1716 A.D.

Fateh Shah must have been succeeded by Upendra Shah as is
evident from Beckett's list. There is a portrait of Upendra Shah
also in the dynastic collection amongst the portraits of the other
Garhwali kings, which further indicates his status as a ruler.
Moreover the 'Bindakoti Tamra Patra', which has been cited
already, varifies his succession. This inscription of 1706 A.D. shows
that Upendra Shah was the eldest son of Fateh Shah and Dalip
Shah was his second son. Amongst the witnesses in the inscription, the names of Fateh Shah's sons Upendra Shah, Dalip Shah,
Madhukar Shah and Pahar Shah have been referred to. Upendra
Shah's name is first in the order which shows that he was the
eldest son. Thus according to the principle of primogeniture prevalent amongst the Rajputs, Upendra Shah, and not Dalip Shah,
must have succeeded Fateh Shah.

Pradip Shah

Fateh Shah was succeeded by Upendra Shah, who ruled for
about a year. After Upendra Shah, Pradip Shah ascended the
throne in 1716 A.D. Raturi is of the view that Pradip Shah ruled
for 30 years and his age at the time of death was 63. Dabral has
stated that Pradip shah was only five years old at the time of
accession, and the queen mother was his guardian. However, the
kingdom was managed by some Puran Mal or Puriya Naithani.
Dabral has concocted a story that Pradip Shah was a minor just
as Raturi has done in the case of Fateh Shah. After Prithvi Pat
Shah there has been no king in independent Garhwal, who ascended the throne as a minor. It is quite possible that Puriya Naithani
was an important official during Pradip Shah's rule who might
have wielded some influence owing to his position. But to state
that he was managing the affairs of the kingdom solely is a jaun-

diced view. If Pradip Shah was a minor when he ascended the throne in 1716 A.D., the copper plate inscription issued the same year, should have been in the form as the one issued by Maharani Karnawati in 1640 A.D. (which has been cited already) as guardian on behalf of her son Prithvi Pat Shah. The inscription of 1716 A.D., in no way indicates that Pradip Shah was a minor and his mother was his guardian. The name of Puriya Naithani also has not been mentioned.

Dabral has mentioned that three copper plate inscriptions of the years, 1725, 1734, and 1755 A.D. are available. But he has not referred to the source of their availability and the details of these inscriptions. Apart from these inscriptions another grant of Pradip Shah of the year 1716. A.D., which has been cited already is available. Together with the aforesaid primary sources, two coins of the reign of Pradip Shah are available in the State Museum, Lucknow. Rahul has stated that inscriptions upto the year 1772 A.D. are available, but he has not given the particular years and the number of inscriptions available.

The period of Pradip Shah is notable from the view point that congenial relationships were established between Kumaon and Garhwal during his reign. Batten has stated that in the years 1744-48 A.D., the Rohillas invaded Kumaon twice under their leaders Najib Khan and Pienda Khan. Though their stay was short, Batten has further commented, "It's ill results to the province are well and bitterly remembered, and it's mischevious, though religiously zealous, character is still attested by the noseless idols and trunkless elephants of some of the Kumaoni temples."[68] When Pradip Shah got information about the attack, he sent his forces to help the Kumaoni king, Kalyan Chand. The joint forces of Garhwal and Kumaon gave a stiff resistance to the Rohillas, but they could not check the invasion effectively and they had to come to a peace settlement with them. The Rohillas demanded three lakh rupees in cash from the ruler of Kumaon. This amount was advanced by Pradip Shah to Kalyan Chand as a loan. Thus, the situation was saved and Rohillas returned to their country.[69]

Later Najib Khan invaded Garhwal also in 1757 A.D. The Garhwalis were defeated, and Najib Khan established his authority in the Dun. But on 31st October 1770 A.D. the Dun region was retrieved by the Garhwali forces. Pradip Shah's reign heralded a period of prosperity in Garhwal. G.R.C. Williams is of the view that, ". . . the period of his (Pradip's) accession was still one of peace and prosperity".[70] Pradip Shah ruled Garhwal upto the end of the year 1772 A.D., as has been evidenced by Rahul who states that inscriptions of Pradip Shah upto this year are available.

Lalit Shah or Lalipat Shah

Pradip Shah was succeeded by Lalit Shah who ascended the throne of Garhwal on 29th Mangsir, Samvat 1829, i.e. December 1772 A.D. There are two coins of Lalit Shah in the State Museum, Lucknow. W.H. Valentine has also displayed these coins in his book 'The Copper Coins of India', and has stated that Lalit Shah ruled from Samvat 1828 to Samvat 1837, i.e. 1771 to 1780 A.D.[71] But as is evidenced from the death of Pradip Shah, Lalit Shah came to the throne in 1772 A.D. During his reign the Sikhs ravaged Dun in 1775 A.D. and 1778 A.D. but as he was embroiled in a battle against Kumaon during that period, he could not counter the Sikh marauders during the second attack. Walton is of the view that "Lalit Shah was however less fortunate in his administration of Dehradun, where affairs rapidly proceeded from bad to worse."

Lalit Shah's reign is marked with internal dissensions in the neighbouring region of Kumaon between two rival factions, the claimants to the throne and a few officials of the late king, Raja Deep Chand. In this turbulent state, some Kunwar Mohan Singh, who was also known as Mohan Singh Rautela, proclaimed himself the ruler of Kumaon in 1777 A.D. But the ministers of the late king, especially Joshis, who were hostile to Mohan Singh joined hands with Lalit Shah the ruler of Garhwal, and helped him in entering Kumaon with a big force. Mohan Singh was defeated and he left Kumaon in 1779 A.D. Lalit Shah took advantage of the situation and placed his second son Pradyumna Shah on the throne of Kumaon with the help of Harsh Deo Joshi who was given the office of the Prime Minister of Pradyumna Shah as a reward for his services. Later Pradyumna Shah acquired the family name Chand of the Kumaoni kings and declared himself to be the adopted son of Raja Deep Chand.

Jai Krit Shah

Lalit Shah died immediately after his victory over Kumaon. After installing his son Pradyumna Shah, he was on his way back when he died of malaria at Dulri in August 1780. Thereafter he was succeeded by his eldest son, Jai Krit Shah, the step-brother of Pradyumna Shah.

The two brothers, Jai Krit Shah, the ruler of Garhwal and Pradyumna Shah, alias Pradyumna Chand were not on good terms. It is said that Jai Krit Shah even conspired with Mohan Singh, who was in exile, to oust Pradyumna Shah from Kumaon. Walton is of the view that the Garhwal Raja Jai Krit Shah demanded an acknowledgement of his seniority by right of birth, which the Kumaon Raja Pradyumna Chand refused on the ground that Kumaon had never acknowledged the supermacy of Garhwal and that he was bound to maintain the dignity of the throne to which he had succeeded. It seems that Pradyumna Shah foiled the intrigue of Jai Krit Shah by invading Garhwal. Mola Ram, a contemporary poet and painter, has mentioned that Pradyumna Shah looted Devalgarh first and then launched an attack on Srinagar the capital.[72] But he has not mentioned the dates of the invasion. It seems that the attack must have been launched in 1780 A.D. after Jai Krit Shah's accession to the throne.

Disorder was rife in Garhwal during his reign and squabbles erupted in a virulent form within the kingdom. Amongst the officials there were two factions, one was led by the Khanduri community and the other by the Dobhals. Kripa Ram Dobhal, a powerful minister was the root cause of this dissension. He had virtually captured power and whoever resisted him, was hanged to death. Gradually opposition started building against him and members of the Negi clan revolted openly. They invited Ghamand Singh Mian the Governor of Dehradun to Srinagar, who killed Kripa Ram in the court and arrested the members of his clique. Concomitantly he looted the treasury of Srinagar, the capital on the pretext of advancing the pay and arrears of the soldiers. In the meantime the Sikhs also raided Dehradun and the Bhabhar and advanced as far as Salan. Taking advantage of the situation, Ghamand Singh seized power and in this act of treachery he was supported by one Ajab Ram.

Mola Ram states that Jai Krit Shah was reduced to a state of helplessness in the prevailing circumstances and called him for counsel. Later he told him to write a letter on behalf of Jai Krit Shah to Jagat Prakash, the king of Sirmor to help him against the recalcitrants. Jagat Prakash acceded to the request and immediately marched towards Garhwal. Enroute the combined forces of Kumaon and of the insurgents under the command of Vijay Ram Negi tried to hamper the progress of the Sirmor king, but were defeated badly in the battle of Kaprauli, near Srinagar. After this primary success, Jagat Prakash entered Srinagar, where he defeated and killed Ghamand Singh. Subsequently Jai Krit Shah was reinstalled as king of Garhwal after which Jagat Prakash returned to his kingdom.[73]

Mola Ram has not given the dates of the incident from the time when bickerings started between the Dobhals and the Khanduris to the uprising of Ghamand Singh and his subsequent defeat by Jagat Prakash. It is possible that the series of incidents must have commenced since 1780 A.D. after the invasion of Srinagar by Pradyumna Shah and continued upto the year 1781 A.D.

Dabral has stated that after Jagat Prakash left for Sirmor, Jai Krit Shah went to the temple of the family deity Raj Rajeshwari at Devalgarh to propitiate her against his misfortunes. Concomitantly Pradyumna Shah was informed about the king's absence from the capital by the invidious ministers of Garhwal. Pradyumna Shah immediately launched an attack on Garhwal and defeated Jai Krit Shah. Pradyumna Shah stayed in Srinagar for three years after which he returned to Kumaon.

On his return Jai Krit Shah took the reins of the kingdom in his hands. But again he had to face fresh troubles and this time he was betrayed by his own man, Dhani Ram. Jai Krit Shah was extremely frustrated by this set back and in sheer desperation he went to the temple of Raghunathji at Deoprayag to end his life. The king who was always a failure in life was successful in the end; on the fourth day he died in the premises of the temple. His four queens also perished with him in the pyre and before dying threw a curse on Pradyumna Shah and the unfaithful ministers.

Dabral has not mentioned the date of invasion of Pradyumna Shah and it appears that he did not stay in Srinagar for three years after defeating Jai Krit Shah. The motive of his stay too has not been indicated by Dabral. Jagat Prakash left Srinagar as has been hypothesized earlier in the year 1781 A.D., so the invasion must have been launched in the period following his departure the same year. There is a possibility that Pradyumna Shah stayed in Srinagar for some time for a few months or a year approximately from 1781 to 1782 A.D. with the intention of consolidating his rule in Garhwal, but owing to possible disturbances in Kumaon he had to leave Srinagar. However it does not appear logical as Dabral has mentioned that Pradyumna Shah spent three years in Garhwal. It is too long a period in which there would have been revolt against Pradyumna Shah and he could have been ousted from Kumaon. His departure to Kumaon as has been referred to by Dabral certainly indicates that there was some sort of insurgency there. As it is, Kumaon had already been disturbed by internal dissensions in the recent past. It seems that Pradyumna Shah's motive was to become the ruler of both Kumaon and Garhwal and in the initial years he attempted to bring Garhwal under his sway. But later the internal turmoil distracted his ambition and he was forced to concentrate on Kumaon only.

It can thus be concluded that Jai Krit Shah was reinstated as the ruler of Garhwal in 1782 A.D. after which he tried to consolidate his kingdom as is vividly evidenced by a letter of 1784 A.D., which he wrote to Kardar Gajey Singh Negi of Taknore. There was a boundary dispute between the two kingdoms of Bushehar and Garhwal regarding Nilang. In the above mentioned letter of 1784 A.D., which has been quoted by Shanta Kumar[74] and Ram Gopal,[75] Jai Krit Shah had stated that some land had been given in Nilang to the Jadhs of that area for agricultural purposes at a rent of Rs. 20 in the past. This document was also shown to the Tibetan representative at the boundary discussion in 1926 between India and Tibet, and it was accepted by them.

There is a probability that during the lean period of Jai Krit Shah, when he was embroiled in border disputes with Kumaon, Nilang was occupied by the king of Bushehar. Later when Jai Krit Shah was reinstated, he retrieved it with the intention of consolidating his kingdom.

Jai Krit Shah ruled upto 1785 A.D. The authors of Garhwal

history have given different dates of Jai Krit Shah's reign. Raturi states that he ruled from 1791 to 1797 A.D. Mukandi Lal[76] as 1780-1785 A.D. and according to Beckett's list it is 1780-1786. A.D. Walton has not given the date of Jai Krit Shah's demise and the other authors have quoted the view of the aforesaid writers. The dates given by Mukandi Lal and Beckett are approximately the same and are more probable. Raturi's view that he ruled from 1791 to 1797 A.D. has not been substantiated by any evidence. Moreover the letter of 1784 A.D. by Jai Krit Shah, which was quoted by the Indian Government during the boundary discussions in 1926, is a clear indication that they ear of accession of Jai Krit Shah as given by Raturi is incorrect. Jai Krit Shah ascended the throne in 1780 A.D. and was ruling upto 1781 A.D. as has been mentioned earlier, and from 1785 A.D. onwards there is enough evidence to substantiate that Pradyumna Shah had come to the helm of affairs. Thus it can be concluded that Jai Krit Shah ruled from 1780 to 1781 A.D. and from 1782 to 1785 A.D.

Pradyumna Shah

After Jai Krit Shah's demise, Pradyumna Shah left Kumaon and took over the reins of the Government in Garhwal. He established himself as ruler in 1785 A.D. B.D. Pande has mentioned that since that year, Harsh Deo Joshi managed the affairs of Kumaon on behalf of Pradyumna Shah; whereas Walton maintains that Pradyumna Shan transferred the throne of Kumaon to his brother Parakram Shah, but Parakram was feeble and unpopular, and Mohan Singh Rautela made good his re-entry into Kumaon in 1786 A.D. Of the two postulations, B.D. Pande's statement is more valid, because the contemporary author Mola Ram has not mentioned that Parakram Shah ever ruled Kumaon. Mola Ram, the protagonist of Garhwal school of painting, was Pradyumna Shah's contemporary and in the same period he wrote two books, 'Garh Rajya Vansha Kavya', which in a tottered condition is with Dr. Shiv Prasad Dabral; and the other 'Ganika Natak', or 'Garh Gita Sangram' of 1800 A.D. The original manuscript of this is in the dynastic collection of Thakur Shoor Beer Singh.*

*'Ganika Natak' of Mola Ram has been edited by this writer and is published from Naini Tal.

Mohan Singh with the help of his brother Lal Singh and Parakram Shah soon staged a come back. He invaded Kumaon and defeated Harsh Deo Joshi in the battle of Pali Gaon in 1786 A.D. But his hold over Kumaon was ephemeral. Two years later Harsh Deo Joshi retaliated with a strong force and assailed Kumaon. He defeated and arrested Mohan Singh. Later he got him murdered so that there would be no strong claimant to the throne. After that Harsh Deo Joshi requested Pradyumna Shah to rule Kumaon. But on visualizing the disturbed conditions there, he declined the offer. Parakram Shah also discouraged him from going to Kumaon since he was interested in installing Mohan Singh's son as ruler there. Walton has remarked that, "after unsuccessfully offering the vacant throne to Pradyumna Shah, Harsh Deo Joshi set up a *roi faineant* in the person of Shiv Singh Rautela while keeping all real power in the hands of the Joshis and their adherents. Before, however their government was firmly established in Almora, the capital of Kumaon, they were driven out by Lal Singh, the brother of Mohan Singh, who placed on the throne his nephew, Mahendra Singh under the style of Mahendra Chand. Lal Singh took the place of Harsh Deo as regent, and aided by the machinations of Parakram Shah banished, imprisoned or executed the leaders of the Joshi faction". Harsh Deo Joshi took refuge in Srinagar, where Pradyumna Shah bestowed a fiefdom on him in the proximity of Paidulsyun.

Pradyumna Shah did not stay in peace since the time he returned from Kumaon. At Srinagar problems were created by his younger brother Parakram Shah owing to his dissipated life style and lust for power. Mola Ram, the contemporary author, has given a vivid account of the exploits of Parakram Shah in his work 'Ganika Natak' or 'Garh Gita Sangram'. According to him, Parakram Shah stooped down to the level of kidnapping his 'ganika' or mistress without any reason. He also intrigued against the faithful ministers of Pradyumna Shah, particularly the Khanduri brothers, Rama and Dharni. Later on these brothers were murdered and Parakram Shah was held responsible for the heinous crime. But Pradyumna took no action against him. He was even conspiring against Pradyumna Shah's family, his wife and children. In the prevailing disorder, the situation deteriorated fast and Pradyumna Shah virtually became a prisoner in the hands of Parakram Shah. This resulted in a family feud between the heir apparent, Kunwar Sudarshan Shah and his uncle Parakram Shah. The officials also supported different factions and anarchy prevailed in Garhwal. For the Gurkhas, who were interested in annexing Garhwal, it was an opportune moment to intervene. They, therefore, sent their 'vakil' or ambassador to Garhwal on the pretext of patching up differences between Parakram Shah and Sudarshan Shah.[77] The incident must have occurred in 1800 A.D., because Mola Ram wrote the play 'Ganika Natak' in this year.

Prior to the political wranglings cited above, Garhwal had been invaded by the Gurkhas in 1791 A.D. Harsh Deo Joshi had invited the Gurkhas to Kumaon and with his help they set forth an expedition in 1790 A.D. and speedily occupied Almora. Next year preparations were made for the invasion of Garhwal and the Gurkhas penetrated as far as Langurgarhi, a strong fortress about 10 miles off the location now occupied by Lansdowne. Langurgarhi defied all their attempts for over a year when news of the Chinese invasion of Nepal reached the besiegers, they were compelled to raise the siege to meet this new danger. All the Gurkha troops were withdrawn from Kumaon and Garhwal, while the traitor, Harsh Deo Joshi was left as governor in Almora. The Garhwali king was however so impressed by this show of Gurkha power that he agreed to pay a yearly tribute of Rs.25,000 and to keep an agent at the court of Kathmandu.

The Gurkhas, having settled their disputes with Garhwal and China, returned to Almora, and Harsh Deo Joshi found himself out of employment and an object of suspicion to his masters. He fled to Srinagar court in the hope of inducing the Garhwal Raja to intervene on behalf of Padam Singh, who claimed the throne of Kumaon. Pradyumna Shah however wisely refused to interfere again in Kumaon affairs. Padam Singh, therefore, returned to the plains, but Harsh Deo remained at Srinagar.

Ever since the siege of Langurgarhi was raised in 1791-1792 A.D. small bands of Gurkhas periodically plundered the border parganas, which they were taught to look upon as their lawful prey. The prisoners made in these expeditions were sold as slaves, the villages were burnt and the country made desolate. The Garhwalis on their part made bloody reprisals and a border warfare ensued. Several fresh attempts were made to capture Langurgarhi by the Gurkhas, but all of them proved unsuccessful. Finally, the Gurkhas, under their leaders Amar Singh Thapa, Hastidal Chautariya and Bam Shah made a decisive attempt to conquer Garhwal. In February 1803 the Gurkhas launched an attack on Srinagar. The Garhwalis fought with great intrepidity but were badly outnumbered and lost ground. After being defeated, Pradyumna Shah crossed the river Alaknanda with his army and retreated towards Uttarkashi. The Gurkhas were in pursuit and defeated him again at Barahat, i.e. Uttarkashi. Pradyumna Shah then fled towards the plains, the Gurkhas still pursuing him. He offered resistance to them at Chamuwa, now known as Chamba but was defeated. After losing this battle Pradyumna Shah escaped to Dehradun. Later he sought the help of Ram Dayal Singh, the Gujar Raja of Landhura and made a final attempt to regain his kingdom. A battle was fought at Khurbura, now part of Dehradun in which Pradyumna perished with most of his retainers.[78] The Gurkhas then gave a royal funeral to Pradyumna Shah at Haridwar. A.R. Gill has cited the date of the battle of Khurbura as January 1804.[79] Raturi states that this battle was fought on 14th May 1804. Evidently the date given by Raturi is more reliable, because Hari Krishna Raturi was the 'diwan' of the erstwhile Tehri Garhwal State during the rule of Raja Kirti Shah and he must have got the information from the Durbar. This date was important for the Garhwali kings, because on that day Garhwal was subjugated to the Gurkha yoke. As such the information available from the Durbar should be authentic.

Pradyumna Shah was a brave king and he died in the battle field like a true warrior. To defend his kingdom, he tried to muster a large army against the Gurkha forces as has been pointed out by Dabral. He states that Pradyumna Shah sold all his valuables and the costly throne at Saharanpur to raise an army of 12 thousand soldiers, but unfortunately he lost.

Several causes can be attributed to the defeat of this gallant king. Garhwal, as has been mentioned earlier, was plagued by perpetual turmoils from the time of Raja Jai Krit Shah and this was sapping the vitality of the kingdom. Nature also caused havoc in the form of a famine before the Gurkha onslaught. Raturi has stated that Garhwal was marred by a famine in Samvat 1851 and 1852, i.e. 1794 A.D. and 1795 A.D. This famine is still notoriously known as 'ekawani-bawani', i.e. 51-52, in Garhwal, and 'bawani' has become a synonym for famine in Garhwal since that year. Garhwal was yet to recover from this devastation that it was struck by an earthquake. Trebeck and Moorcraft, who were in Srinagar Garhwal in February 1819, have stated that,

> "Garhwal was conquered by the Gurkhas in 1804, and the capital about the same time was visited by the natural calamities of an earthquake and an inundation. It had not recovered from these disasters at the time of our visit, and more than half the city was in ruins".[80]

B.D. Pande has written about this earthquake, that it was felt for seven days and nights continuously.

Apart from the political intrigues and natural calamities that had plagued Garhwal, the discomfiture of Pradyumna Shah as regards the intrigues of his younger brother Parakram Shah and the treachery of Harsh Deo Joshi and Mola Ram were also responsible for the Garhwal's disaster in 1804. About Harsh Deo Joshi's insidious behaviour of inviting the Gurkhas to attack Kumaon and then Garhwal has been already mentioned. Mola Ram was also responsible for instigating the Gurkhas to invade Garhwal as he has stated in his book 'Ganika'.[81]

About the rule of Pradyumna Shah, three dates have been given. Beckett states that he ruled from 1786 A.D. to 1804 A.D. Raturi is of the view that he ruled from 1797 A.D. to 1804 A.D., and Mukandi Lal[82] has fixed his period from 1785 to 1804 A.D. The period fixation as quoted by Mukandi Lal is authentic and it tallies with the date given by the State Museum, Lucknow. There are nine coins of Pradyumna Shah in the State Museum, Lucknow and on their basis, it has been stated that Pradyumna Shah ruled from 1785 A.D. to 1804 A.D. Thus the date of accession given by Raturi as 1797 A.D. is obviously not correct. Moreover in the dynastic collection of Thakur Shoor Beer Singh, there is a copper plate inscription of 1788 A.D. which vividly indicates that Pradyumna Shah had ascended the throne by 1788 A.D. i.e. much before 1797 A.D. It can thus be concluded that Pradyumna Shah ruled from 1785 A.D. to 1804 A.D.

REFERENCES

1. Duff, C. Mabel: The Chronology of India from the Earlier Times to the Beginning of the 16th Century, p. 225.
2. Walton, H.G.: British Garhwal, a Gazetteer, p. 114.
3. Shastri, Balkrishna Bhatt: Garhwal Jati Prakash, pp. 8-10.
4. Dabral, Shiv Prasad: Uttrakhand Ka Rajnitik Tatha Sanskritik Itihas, Volume IV, p. 210.
5. Briggs, George W.: Gorakhnath and the Kanphata Yogis, p. 74.
6. Yogi, Bhambhut Nath: Navnath tatha Goraksh Stvanjali, p. 8.
7. Sanwari Granth: Original manuscript, p. 24.
8. Fuhrer, A.: The Monumental Antiquities and Inscription in the N.W. P. and Oudh, Allahabad 1891, p. 46.
9. Srivastava, A.L.: Akbar the Great, Volume 2, p. 232.
10. Fazal, Abul: The Ain-i-Akbari, translated by Colonel H.S. Jarrett, Volume II, p. 283.
11. Ferishta, Mehomed Karim (Translated by Briggs) History of the Rise of the Mohomedan Power in India till the year A.D. 612, Vol. IV, pp. 549-50.

    Trebeck and Moorcraft who visited Srinagar, Garhwal in February 1819 have stated that, ". . . . gold is found in the sand of the river, particularly after a heavy fall of snow or rain in the neighbouring mountains." (Moorcraft and Trebeck—Travels in Hindustan, Vol. 1, p. 7.)
12. Walton, H.G.: British Garhwal, a Gazetteer, p. 115.
13. Walton, H.G.: Almora Gazetteer, p. 174.
14. Walton, H.G.: British Garhwal, a Gazetteer, p. 115.
15. Foster, Williams: The Early Travels in India, 1583 A.D. to 1619 A.D., p. 181.
16. Walton, H.G.: British Garhwal, a Gazetteer, p. 115.
17. Pande, Badri Dutt: Kumaon Ka Itihas, p. 273.
18. Sankrityayan, Rahul: Garhwal, p. 132.
19. Bahuguna, Shambhu Prasad: 'Virat Hridaya' in *Tripathaga*, September 1956, p. 105.
20. Todd, James: Annals and Antiquities of Rajasthan, Volume II, p, 1211.
21. The Tuzuk-i-Jahangiri: Edited by Henry Beveridge, Translated by Alexander Rogers, p. 202.

22. Rawat, Ajay Singh: Uttarakhand Ka Rajnitik Itihas, p. 63.
23. Raturi, H.K.: Garhwal Ka Itihas, p. 382.
24. C' Wessels: Early Jesuit Travellers in Central Asia 1603-1721 A.D., p. 96.
25. Raturi, H.K.: Garhwal Ka Itihas, p. 378.
26. Dabral, Shiv Prasad: op. cit., p. 257.
27. Maclagan, Sir Edward: The Jesuits and the Great Mogul, p. 343.
28. C' Wessels: op. cit., p. 97.
29. Maclagan, Sir.Edward: op. cit., p. 345.
30. C' Wessels: op. cit., p. 96.
31. Williams, G.R.C.: Historical and Statistical Memoirs of Dehradun, para 182-83.
32. 'Abhilekh Gar Register' No. 4, Tehri, pp. 492-94.
33. Manucci, Niccolao: Storia Do Mogor or Mogul India (1653-1708) Volume I, pp. 215-16.
34. Mughal Durbar Ya Maasirul Umra, Vol. III, pp. 492-94.
35. Travernier, Jean Baptiste: Travels in India, Vol. I, p. 364.
36. Ibid., op. cit., Vol. 1, p. 364.
37. Qanungo, Kalika Ranjan: Dara Shikoh (In Hindi) pp. 118-125.
38. Elliot and Dowson: The History of India as told by its own Historians, Vol. VII, p. 245.
39. Travernier, Jean Baptiste: op. cit., Vol. I, p. 364.
40. Ibid., p. 364.
41. Bernier's Voyage to the East Indies, p. 75.
42. Bernier, Francois: Travel, in the Mogul Empire, pp. 104-105.
43. Walton, H.G.: British Garhwal, a Gazetteer, p. 117.
44. Farman of Abuzzafar Muhi-ud-Din Muhummed Aurangzeb of the year 1673 A.H./1662 A.D.
45. Manucci, Niccolao: op. cit., Volume I, p. 381.
46. Raturi, H.K.: Garhwal Ka Itihas, pp. 386-88.
47. Maclagan, Sir Edward: op. cit., pp. 107-109.
48. Manucci, Niccolao: op. cit., p. 381.
49. Farman of Abuzzafar Muhi-ud-Din Muhummed Aurangzeb of the year 1675 A.N./1665 A.D.
50. Gopal, Ram: India China Tibet Triangle, p. 127.
51. Kumar, Shanta: Himalaya Par Lal Chhaya, p. 152.

52. Srivastava, K.P.: Mughal Farmans (1540 A.D. to 1706 A.D.), Volume I, pp. 53-54.
53. Walton, H.G.: British Garhwal a Gazetteer, p. 118.
54. Sankrityayan, Rahul: Garhwal, p. 149.
55. Kavi, Ratan: Fateh Prakash, p. 2.
56. Deshraj, Thakur: Sikh Itihas, pp. 177-78.
57. Laxman, Bhagat: A Short Sketch of the Life and Works of Guru Gobind Singh, p. 60
58. Johar, Surinder Singh: Guru Gobind Singh a Biography, pp. 90-91.
59. Banerjee, Anil Chandra: Guru Nanak to Guru Gobind Singh, p. 199.
60. Singh, Guru Gobind: Vichitra Natak, p. 297 (Original manuscript) Hindi publication, p. 45.
61. *The Sikh Review*, Volume XIV-XV, p. 48.
62. *The Sikh Review*, Volume, XIV-XV, p. 50.
63. Fuhrer, A.: The Monumental Antiquities and Inscriptions in the N.W.P. and Oudh, Vol, II, p. 44.
64. Bhartiya Sahitya (Agra University) Vol. IV, October 1956, p. 189.
65. Coomaraswamy, Ananda K.: Catalogue of the Indian Collections in the Museum of Fine Arts Boston, Part V, Rajput Painting, p. 17.
66. Coomaraswamy, Ananda K.: Catalogue of the Indian Collections in the Museum of Fine Arts Boston, Part VI, Mughal Painting, p. 12.
67. Mandir Ghot Siddha: Amar Sandesh tatha Baba Balak Nath Ki Jeevani, p. 47.
68. Batten, J.H.: A Few notes on the Subject of the Kumaon and Rohilkhand Turaee, *Journal of Asiatic Society of Bengal* XIII, Pt. 2, 1844, p. 898.
69. Pande, B.D.: Kumaon Ka Itihas, p. 328.
70. Williams, G.R.C.: Historical and Statistical Memoirs of Dehradun, Para, 94.
71. Valentine, W.H.: The Copper Coins of India, p. 226.
72. Ram, Mola: Garh Rajya Vansha Kavya (original manuscript) It is in the collection of Dr. Shiv Prasad Dabral of Dogadda and is in a tattered condition.
73. Ram, Mola: Garh Rajya Vansh Kavya (original manuscript).

74. Kumar, Shanta: Himalaya Par Lal Chhaya, p. 155.
75. Gopal, Ram: India China Tibet Triangle, p. 144.
76. Lal, Mukandi, Garhwal Painting, p. 21.
77. Rawat, Ajay Singh (ed.) Ganika or Garh Geeta Sangram of Mola Ram, p. 25.
78. Parmar, Pati Ram: Garhwal Ancient and Modern, p. 199.
79. Gill, A.R.: Valley of the Doon, p. 7.
80. Moorcraft and Trebeck: Travels in Hindustan. Vol. I, p. 6.
81. Rawat, Ajay Singh (ed.): op. cit., p. 83.
82. Lal, Mukandi: op. cit., p. 16.

4

Administration of the Rulers

The Government consisted of a simple monarchy, but the power of the sovereign was, in fact, far from absolute, being ever controlled in a greater or less degree by the will of the aristocracy.[1] In the 'Kothar Inscription'[2] it is mentioned that the religious head wielded a great influence over the king and Mola Ram has referred him as 'Ojha Guru', in his works.[3] According to G.R.C. Williams, the various ministers of the king were the, 'Diwan', 'Duftari', 'Wazir', 'Faujdar' and 'Negi'. Traill is of the view that the chief offices of the kingdom were the office of the, 'Diwan', 'Duftari', 'Bhandari', 'Wazir' 'Faujdar', 'Negi' and 'Thokdar'.[4]

It seems that the different officials during the reign of the Parmars were as follows:

Mukhtar: He was also known as the 'Wazir', and his duties were that of a prime minister.

Duftari: It appears that he was the director of the government offices and was stationed in the capital. His assistants were known as 'Pargana Duftaris' and their offices were located in every pargana (subdivisional) headquarter. Mola Ram is of the view that the 'Duftari' was a medium through which the king issued orders and announced the appointments of officials; their transfer orders and also their retirement. If an individual was to be convicted or in the case of investituring honour, the orders were issued by the office of the 'Duftari'.[5] A general record of the arable lands of the country, their extent, appropriation etc. was kept in the office of the 'Duftari'. To render these accounts more complete the corresponding deputies maintained the records.

Faujdar: Every pargana had one 'Faujdar'. The number of parganas in Garhwal however are not known. 'Faujdars' were like military Governors who administered the parganas. Their duty was to maintain peace, collect revenue and defend the frontiers of the kingdom. During the time of war, it were the 'Faujdars' who mustered troops to help their king.

Goldar: The various security chiefs in the capital were known as 'Goldars'. They had the power to appoint their own soldiers and were responsible for the security of the royal treasury and the other offices in the capital.

Thokdar: The revenue in the parganas was collected mainly by the 'Thokdars' who were like feudal lords[6] and their titles were hereditary. They were also known as 'Sayanas'. The latter, again, appointed one of the proprietors of each village, under the designation of 'Padhan', to levy and account directly for its cess. The remuneration of the 'Sayana' consisted of a trifling 'Nazrana' (offerings) from each village in the pargana, and of offerings from the 'Padhans' on certain festivals and on occasion of births and marriages in their own families. They were also entitled to a leg of every goat killed by the 'Padhans' in their divisions, and enjoyed a portion of rent free land in their own village. The dues of 'Padhans' were exactly similar, but were leviable only from their own tenants.

In the reserved districts, the royal domains were managed by the 'Wazirs' and 'Bhandaris' (the treasurers) and the rents of the alienated villages were collected by the grantees. No establishment of 'Sayanas' existed in the parganas.[7]

Negi: It appears that some individuals who were given the status of a 'thokdar' and were assigned the revenue of certain villages for their distinguished services to the king were known as 'Negis'. However, the actual occupancy in the land, frequently became vested in the descendants of such sort of assignees.

Diwan: He was the 'Wazir' and this title was prevalent in the neighbouring region of Kumaon. From the works of Mola Ram it appears that there were some petty officials in the kingdom also like the 'Chund', 'Chakar' and 'Chopedar'. 'Chund' was a messenger of the royal court who carried information from one place to the other. 'Chakars' were the orderlies of the royal court and the royal household. 'Chopedar' used to accompany the king and wielded the silver umbrella over his royal highness.[8]

The chief priest was an important official in the kingdom and was known as the 'Jyotik Rai' as is evident from the inscription of the temple of Kshetra Pal, dated 1608 A.D. which has already been referred in Chapter 3. The chief priest was well versed in astronomy and astrology.

Administration of Land Revenue

Under the Parmar kings, the proprietary right in land was vested in the sovereign and was inalienable. The paramount property in the soil though rested with the sovereign, its right however was only theoretically acknowledged by the subjects, but its practical existence was also deducible from the unrestricted power of alienation which the sovereign always possessed in the land. These tenures (of the occupant Zamindars) were never indefeasible, and as they were derived from royal grants either traditional or existing they could be abrograted at the will of the sovereign even without allegations of default against the holder and without reservation in his favour. When a provision in land was called for to reward military services or to remunerate the heirs of those slain in battle, it was usually made at the expenses of the existing rights.[9]

Pandit Badri Dutt Pande has mentioned that the king could transfer his proprietary right in the following circumstances:[10]

a) He could donate land to the Brahmins for their erudition and this act was known as 'Sankalp' or 'Vishnupreet'.
b) The king rewarded the brave with land for their gallantry and the process of investituring was known as 'Raut'.
c) The king also gave land to the officers in the form of fiefs in lieu of their salaries.

G.R.C. Williams[11] is of the view that "the land revenue was paid partly in kind, partly in money, generally in proportion of one half of the produce of the soil or its value. The land revenue was spent mostly in payment of troops. Very little money reached the royal coffers after the deductions necessary to meet the local expenditure. . . Money was spent on court musicians and dancing girls. A further alienation of the land revenue arose from constant donations to Brahmins and endowment of temples in successive reigns."

The land, i.e. 'Thath' which was bestowed upon different people

were known as 'Thathvans'. Although they had complete owner-
ship over the land, they could not expel the peasants already
settled within the territory given to them. The peasants who had
settled in the area possessed by the 'thathvans', were known as
'khaikars'. So long the 'khaikar' paid the revenue regularly, he
could not be removed from the land tilled by him. Apart from
the revenue, the 'khaikar' used to present various gifts to the
'thathvan' as a mark of fealty and esteem.[12]

The land which the 'thathvan' cultivated himself, he could settle
new families there and these new settlers were known as 'khai-
neys.[13] Amongst them, the 'thathvan' could categorize certain
families as temporary settlers and these families were known as
'sirtans'.[14]

However as Pauw has remarked, the land in the interior seldom
changed proprietors and the greater part of the occupants derived
their claims to the soil solely from the prescription of long established and undisturbed possession and this remark also applied
to many individuals, particularly Brahmins, whose ancestors,
having originally obtained estates on grants, not conveying any
property in the soil, their descendants, had subsequently, by the
migration of actual occupants, come into full possession of both
land and produce. Of grants which did not convey property in
the soil, but were only assignments of revenue, the most common
were those which were made as remuneration for the fulfillment
of public offices known as 'Negichari', 'Kaminchari', 'Jaidad', etc.,
and those made for the endowment of religious establishments.[15]

The main source of income was the land revenue, i.e. 'Sirti'
and the assessment was made in accordance with the fertility of
the land. One third, i.e. 'tihar' and half, i.e. 'adhela' of the total
yield used to be the normal land tax. In the capital the Duftari's
office used to maintain a record of the cultivated land and the
land was measured according to the amount of seed sown in a
particular plot.[16]

Other Sources of Income

G.R.C Williams is of the view that the revenue of the whole
kingdom barely exceeded five lakhs, including the income from
all sources, exports, imports, land revenue, mines and gold washing.[17] Captain Hardwicke who reached Srinagar, the capital of

the kingdom of Garhwal on 29th April, 1796, has mentioned in his narrative that, ". . . the annual revenue of this country, if the Rajah's word is to be taken, does not exceed 5 lacs and 6 thousand, rupees. This includes duties on exports and imports, the produce in grain, working of mines and washing of gold."[18] The description that Hardwicke and Williams have given is of those days when Garhwal was infested with various problems like that of succession, Gurkha inroads and famines. Those days the population in Garhwal had reduced to a great extent, e.g., as George William Traill has pointed out in his 'Statistical Sketch of Kumaon', that in 1821, the number of families in Srinagar, the capital of Garhwal was 562.[19]

Traill has further mentioned in the report that a portion of the most fertile land in the neighbourhood of the capital was retained for the exclusive supply of grain to the Raja, being cultivated at his own expense, but the principal source of the ordinary revenue of the sovereign, consisted in the frequent offerings presented by his subjects at the several Hindu festivals, and on occasions of extraordinary disbursement, such as marriage of the reigning prince, or of his son or daughter, a general import was levied to defray them, from all the assigned land of the country.[20]

Other sources of income for the king and his kingdom were:

Revenue from Gold Washing: The fiscal management of gold washing was extremely simple. Each gold washer paid 100 rupees a year to the government for the privilege of search without reference to the quantity of gold dust found.[21] The different places where gold dust was sought were Karnprayag, Paikhunda, Deoprayag, Rishikesh and Lakerghat.[22]

Mining: Iron, copper and lead mining were also important sources of income. Iron was produced in several parts of the country but the important mines were at Chandpur, Belungh, Bichan and Cholah. At Desauli, east of Srinagar was a lead mine, the whole produce of this went to the ruler, and the people, who worked it, were kept in constant pay, though their labour was required only for eight months out of twelve and sometimes not so long, the quantity of ore extracted being in proportion to the demand the Raja had for it. As a greater encouragement to the people who undertook the working of those mines, and in consideration of the injury to which their health was exposed, small portions of land were given to them on the produce of which no tax was levied.[23]

Copper was produced in many parts, the principal mines being at Nagpur and Dhanpur.[24] These copper mines worked only eight months in the year.[25]

Trade

Trade was of two types, one with Tibet and the other with the plains. Imports from Tibet were rock salt, borax, musk in pods, hawks and slaves from the area bordering Badrinath.[26] These items together with sheep wool blankets from Paikhunda in Garhwal, called 'punkhees' were supplied to Rohilkhand. Duties averaging six per cent of the value of the merchandize were levied at the passes on all imports and certain exports.[27]

Traill[28] in his report, 'Statistical Sketch of Kumaon', has mentioned that,

"The traffic of the province is divided into two branches, first the sale of the produce of the hills, and secondly, the carrying trade with Tartary; this latter again passes through two hands, the Bhotias, who hold direct intercourse with the Tartars, and the hill traders, who furnish returns and receive the Tartar merchandize in barter, the nature of the former of these transactions will be reserved for a separate article.

"The migratory habits of the Zamindars of the southern pergunnas, have given rise to a very general diffusion of commercial enterprise among them, and every individual possessed of a small capital, either singly or jointly with others, engages in traffic. With an investment composed of iron, copper, ginger, turmeric and other hill roots and drugs, the adventurer proceeds to the nearest mart in the plains, and there receives in barter for his merchandise, coarse chintz, cotton cloth, gur, tobacco, coloured glass beads and hardware, which in return, after supplying the wants of himself and friends, is disposed of at the villages in the midland and northern pergunnas or is reserved for sale till a fair occurs in the neighbourhood. Those again, whose credit or resources are more considerable enter eagerly into the Tartar trade. The imports from the plains are, in this case, the same as above enumerated, as fine manufacturers or expensive articles are only brought up when previously bespoke, from the Bhotias they receive in exachange, partly cash and partly Tartar and Bhote productions. The latter comprise hawks, musk, pankhis (coarse camlets), wax, masi (frankincense), kutki and a variety of other roots and drugs. The Tartar products consist of borax, salt, gold dust and chawr tails. The zeal and industry evinced by this class of traders, in the execution of commissions is very great, as they frequently proceed in person as far as Ferukhabad and Lucknow in search of articles required for them."

About the Tibetan trade, Captain Thomas Hardwicke has mentioned in his narrative that,

". . . . at the different 'ghats' or passes into the mountains, duties on imports and some kinds of exports are levied, which according to the best information I could obtain, is on an average about six per cent on their value, but on some particular articles, an additional duty is laid. The pass at Kotdwara is rented by an officer called 'Hakem', who pays annually to the Rajah twelve thousand rupees."

Pilgrim Trade

The furnishing of supply to the pilgrims who annually visited the shrine of Badrinath was also an important source of income. Statistics available of the year 1820 indicate that the pilgrims who reached Badrinath that year were 27,000 while many thousands turned back from the fear of cholera. As compared to Badrinath a lesser number of pilgrims visited Kedarnath. Traill[29] has mentioned that, "the receipts and disbursements of this temple may be taken at one third of those of Badrinath." Pauw[30] has remarked about the pilgrim routes that,

". . . . the pilgrim route enters Garhwal at Lakshman Jhula on the Ganges about 20 miles above Hardwar. It thence follows the valley pretty closely to Deoprayag, Srinagar and Rudraprayag. At this place pilgrims to Kedarnath proceed up the Mandakini to Gupt Kashi and Kedarnath, returning down the valley to Ukhimath whence the road begins to ascend. Throughout the whole length of this route, shops kept by villagers or by professional banjaras are opened every year to furnish supplies to the pilgrims at the halting places ('chattis')."

Judicial Administration

In the interior, justice was administered in civil and petty criminal cases by Faujdars, or Governors, while cases of magnitude, and those originating in the capital or neighbourhood, were determined in the Raja's court. Private arbitration or 'Panchayat' was frequently resorted to, more particularly for the adjustment of mutual accounts among traders or for the division of family property among heirs. Claims, when nearly balanced, were sometimes decided by lot in the following manner; the names of the parties were written in separate slips of paper, these were then rolled up, and laid in front of an idol in a temple, the priest of which was then employed to take up one of the rolled slips, and he whose name appeared, gained the cause.

Criminal offences of magnitude, were tried at the seat of Government, and accusations would be proved or rebutted by ordeal. The usual punishments for almost every degree of crime were fines or confiscations, and even murder was rarely visited with death, the convict, if a Rajput, being heavily mulcted, and if a Brahmin, banished. Treason was, however, generally punished capitally. The mode of inflicting capital punishment was either by hanging or beheading. In petty thefts, restitution and fine were commonly the only penalties inflicted, and in those of magnitude, the offender was sometimes subjected to the loss of a hand or of his nose. Crimes of the latter description were however extremely rare in the hills and did not call for severe enactments.[31]

Adultery with a woman of lower class was a petty misdemeanour punishable by fine, but if the adulteress happened to be a lady of rank, the rule was to cut off her nose and kill her lover. To make the punishment more signal, its infliction was left to the injured husband,[32] who, by the custom of the country, and by the existing principles of honour, was authorized and required to wash off the stain on his name by the blood of the offending parties, and no lapse of time, from the commission or discovery of the crime, proved a bar to the exaction of this revenge. Convicts were occasionally condemned to labour on the private lands of the Raja, to whom they, from that period became hereditary slaves.

Traill[33] has mentioned that three forms of ordeal were in common use: first, the 'Gola Deep' which consisted in receiving in the palms of the hands, and carrying to a certain distance, a red hot bar of iron. Second was the 'Karai Deep' in which the hand was plunged into a vessel of boiling oil, in which case the test of truth was the absence of marks of burning on the hand. Third was the, 'Tarazu ka Deep', in which the person undergoing the ordeal was weighed at night against stones, which were then carefully deposited under lock and key with the seal of the superintending officer. On the following morning, after a variety of ceremonies, the appellant was again weighed, and the substantiation of his cause depended on his proving heavier than on the preceding evening.

Army

Ferishta[34] has given a brief description of the Garhwali army. In his account he has stated, 'the Raja of Kumaon', but his mention of the fact that the sources of Jumna and Ganges are within the Kumaon territory clearly indicates that his description is of the kingdom of Garhwal. He has written that,

"the Raja of Kumaon also possesses an extensive dominion and a considerable quantity of gold which is procured by washing the earth mounds in his country, which also contains copper mines. His territory stretches to the north as far as Thibet, and on the south reaches to Sumbhal, which is included in India. He retains in pay an army of 80 thousand men, both cavalry and infantry, and commands great respect from the emperor of Dehly. His treasures too are vast. . . . . The sources of the Jumna and Ganges are both to be found within the Kumaon territory."

G.R.C. Williams, whose description is of the lean period of Garhwal has mentioned[35] that the standing army consisted of not more than five thousand infantry, a motely force armed after the fashion of the place to which each division belonged with match locks, bows and arrows or swords and bucklers. But the sword was the peculiar weapon of the hill warrior. One thousand men, he has stated further, were quartered at the capital, the rest were scattered in various directions to assist in collecting land revenue. Dress, discipline and regularity in paying them, were treated with regard by the Government.

The forces were maintained much in same principle as in the plains. Certain lands were assigned for their payment, under the management of the Commanders who conducted the civil as well as military administration of each district, superintending the collections, dispensing justice in civil and petty criminal cases, and referring those of importance to the Wazir at Srinagar.

From the account of Mola Ram[36] it can be stated that the weapons used by the Garhwali soldiers were, 'teer Kaman' (bow and arrow), 'bhala' (lance), swords, daggers, axe and guns. The soldiers used 'sar' (head gear) and 'kavach rani' (armour) to protect themselves. In the initial stages Garhwali army constituted of Garhwali soldiers only and their batallions were known as 'Lobha', 'Badhan' and 'Salan', according to the regions they hailed from. Later, Hindus and Muslims from the plains were also recruited. The recruitment was done through the Faujdars. A sound physique with knowledge of archery, sword fencing and shooting were the essential qualifications for the soldiers.

Education

There were no public institutions of the nature of schools, and private tuition was almost confined to the upper classes. The teachers were commonly Brahmins, who imparted to their scholars merely knowledge of reading, writing and accounts. The children of respectable Brahmins were taught Sanskrit and were occasionally sent to Benares to complete their studies, where they passed through the usual course of Hindu education consisting theology, astronomy, astrology, jurisprudence and sometimes medicine.[37]

The Garhwali kings were patrons of art and literature. Many poets and writers whose works have been referred to in Chapter 3 flourished during the rule of the Parmar kings in Garhwal. Amongst these literatis, the names of Jatadhar, Ratan Kavi, Kavi Raj Sukhdev Misra are most illustrious. A new school of painting also evolved during the Parmar epoch in Garhwal. As early as 1916, Dr. Coomaraswamy spoke of Garhwali painting in his work 'Rajput Painting'. Mukandi Lal is of the view that "the most remarkable thing about the Garhwali Painting is that they offer to indicate that the Mughal School of Painting evolved into Pahari Painting of which the Garhwali School is a branch."[38]

The Garhwal School of Painting has an extraordinary charm and grace. The foundation of this School of Painting was laid in Garhwal as far back as the second half of the seventeenth century. The founders of the Garhwal School, Sham Dass and Har Dass, father and son came to the court of Prithvi Pat Shah at Srinagar, the capital of Garhwal with the refugee prince Suleiman Shikoh, son of Aurangzeb's brother, Dara Shikoh. Sham Dass and Har Dass belonged to the Mughal School of Painting. In the fourth generation was born Mola Ram (1743-1833 A.D.), the greatest artist of the Garhwali School.[39] His descendants still live in Srinagar (Garhwal).

The Garhwali School like other 'Pahari' (Hill) schools of Kangra, Chamba, Jammu, Mandi, etc., is one of the offshoots of the Rajput School. But the Garhwali school excels other 'Pahari' schools in the treatment of women. Here they stand out more slender and charming.

Maintenance of Temples

Most of the land grant inscriptions which are available to this day are endowments to the temples. The revenue obtained from the land was used for the maintenance of temples.

In Garhwal 170 villages were endowed to the temple of Badrinath. Apart from this there were several charitable endowments for distribution of food to pilgrims proceeding to Kedarnath and Badrinath which were also supported by lands exclusively assigned for this purpose.[40]

REFERENCES

1. Asiatic Researches, Volume XVI, p. 168.
2. *Tripathaga*, September 1956.
3. Ram, Mola: Garh Rajya Vansh Kavya (Original manuscript), p. 35 ba.
4. Asiatic Researches, Volume XVI, p. 168.

5. Ram, Mola: Ibid., p. 40 a.
6. Stowell, V.A.: A Manual of the Land Tenures in Kumaon Division, p. 121.
7. Asiatic Researches, Volume XVI, p. 174.
8. Rawat, Ajay Singh: Uttrakhand Ka Rajnitik Itihas, p. 97.
9. Pauw, E.K.: Report on the Tenth Settlement of the Garhwal District, p. 32.
10. Pande, B.D.: Kumaon Ka Itihas, pp. 370-71.
11. Williams, G.R.C.: Historical and Statistical Memoirs of Dehradun, paras 224-25.
12. Pauw, E.K.: op. cit., p. 32.
13. Stowell, V.A.: op. cit., p. 34.
14. Ibid., p. 5.
15. Pauw, E.K.: op. cit., pp. 32-33.
16. Personal Communication with the denizens of Garhwal.
17. Williams, G.R.C.: op. cit., para 223.
18. Asiatic Researches, Volume VI, p. 339.
19. Asiatic Researches, Volume XVI, p. 148.
20. Ibid., p. 169.
21. Williams, G.R.C.: op. cit., para 226.
22. Asiatic Researches, Volume VI, p. 340.
23. Ibid., p. 341.
24. Ibid., p. 157.
25. Williams, G.R.C.: op. cit., para 230.
26. Asiatic Researches, Volume VI, p. 34.
27. Williams, G.R.C.: op. cit., para 230.
28. Asiatic Researches, Volume XVI, p. 193.
29. Ibid., p. 167.
30. Pauw, E.K.: op. cit., p. 32.
31. Asiatic Researches, Volume XVI, pp. 170-71.
32. Williams, G.R.C.: op. cit., para 233.
33. Asiatic Researches, Volume XVI, pp. 172-73.
34. History of the Rise of the Mahomedan Power in India, translated from the original Persian of Mahomed Karim Ferishta by John Briggs, Volume (IV), pp. 549-50.
35. Williams, G.R.C.: op. cit., paras 231-32.
36. Dabral, Shiv Prasad: Uttrakhand Ka Itihas, Volume (IV) p. 508.

37. Asiatic Researches, Volume XVI, p. 164.
38. Lal, Mukandi: Garhwal Painting, p. 27.
39. Ram, Mola: *Ganika* (edited by Ajay Singh Rawat) pp. 13-14.
40. Asiatic Researches, Volume XVI, pp. 166-67.

5

Formation of Tehri Garhwal State and Its Rulers 1815-1949

The Gurkhas ruled Garhwal until 1815 A.D. when at last they were defeated and driven away by the British forces. Sudarshan Shah, the heir apparent of Raja Pradyumna Shah, entirely despaired of ever regaining his lost kingdom had eventually settled down in Bareilly. He stayed in Bareilly from 1809 to 1811 A.D. where he was acquainted with Captain Hyder Young Hearsey, a brave and enterprising young Anglo Indian soldier of fortune whose state Kareli lay a few miles from the town.[1] It is said that he contracted a bargain with Raja Sudarshan Shah who is alleged to have sold the parganas of Doon and Chandi to him for a paltry sum of Rs. 3,005.

"I Raja Sudarshan Sah, son of Raja Hurdut Sah, grandson of Alup Sah, do hereby solemnly declare that whereas pergunnas Doon and Chandee were settled on my ancestors (without their being any coparency rights with any other person) by the firmans of his Majesty Emperor Aurangzeb (may God shed Heavenly lustre on his grave) at this present time being in a sound and healthy state of mind, and not being swayed by the false persuasions of others, but of my own free will and accord do hereby sell the above pergunnas, with all the rights accruing therefrom, such as revenue, sawer, fire wood and all the other zamindari rights together with the Imperial Firmans, to Captain Hearsey, in consideration of Rupees 3005 (three thousand and five) the half of which will amount to Rupees 1502-8-0 (one thousand five hundred and two rupees eight annas only). I hereby acknowledge to have received the whole of the aforesaid sum in full from Captain Hearsey. The whole sum has been paid by him and I have received and made use of it. I also acknowledge to have put Captain Hearsey in possession of the above pergunnas together with the Imperial Firmans relating to them. Nothing is due to me from him, not a dam not a diram. If I or any of my successors or heirs should set up a claim for any balance of the above mentioned sum, it should be rejected as false, and no cognisance whatsoever should be taken of it, I myself alone am responsible for this act. With this view I have executed the deed in order that it may serve both as a deed of sale and receipt for the above mentioned sum of money, also that it may be made use of as documentary evidence in case of any litigation."

Written this day, the 22nd June 1811, corresponding to the 30th Jumadul Saul 1226 A.M. and 17th Asad Fush and Bekramjeet Sunwat 1818.

(Signed and sealed)

Raja Sudarshan Sah

Witnessed by:

(signed) Chunie Lal, Moonshee, son of Diara Sahaie
Thakoor Das, incharge of office records.[2]

There are cogent grounds to reject the validity of this deed because firstly the names of the predecessors of Raja Sudarshan Shah have been stated incorrectly and secondly no sane person would dispose off two parganas for a paltry sum of Rs. 3,005 and that too, those parganas which were extremely fertile.

The British Government also did not believe Hearsey as is evident from the book. 'The Hearsey, Five Generations of an Anglo Indian Family'. The author is of the view, ". . . . it does not appear to be fully genuine in view of the wrong names of the ancestors of Raja Sudarshan Shah and also when the contents are compared with the draft of the deed of sale executed by Hearsey in favour of Hon'ble East India Company."[3]

Atkinson has also supported the above view, ". . . . it was

rightly held by both the Raja and the Government that as the conditions precedent to the grant had not been fulfilled, Major Hearsey had no claim, legal or moral".[4]

The Gurkha War ended in 1815 and at the termination of the war, the portions of Garhwal situated to the west of Alaknanda except for the parganas of Rawain and Dehradun were restored to Raja Sudarshan Shah,[5] and was confirmed through a 'Sunud' No. XIV, dated 4th March.[6] In July 1815 the Company Government directed the principal inhabitants of the parganas lying to the east of Alaknanda as far as Rudraprayag and to the east of the Mandakini above that point, to consider themselves under the authority of the Commissioner of Kumaon; and thereafter the tract remained a portion of his jurisdiction.[7] In common parlance this tract was known as Garhwal district or British Garhwal.

Traill, the Assistant Commissioner of Kumaon, was sent to Garhwal to introduce the British authority in that province and to conclude a settlement of the land revenue. It was subsequently suggested that "Rawain, the barren and rocky country between Nagpur and Jaunsar Bawar, containing the headquarters of the Tons, the Jumna and the Bhagirathi be handed over to the Raja of Garhwal", and though it was doubted whether the mild control of the Raja would impose a sufficient restraint on the predatory habits of the inhabitants, it was ultimately resolved to let him make the attempt.[8]

In 1816, Traill brought to the notice of the Government the difficulty that might arise if more precise words were not used in defining the boundary between British and Tehri Garhwal. Although pargana Nagpur was clearly intended to be included in the portion of the territory retained by the British, the loose use of Alaknanda and Mandakini rivers as the boundary in the negotiations of the period would cut off some valuable portions of that pargana, including the 'pattis' of Bamsu and Maikhanda and the mines near Dhanoli, which lay to the west of these rivers. In fact in 1823 the Raja laid claim to the villages lying to the west of the Mandakini on those very grounds, but it was ruled that the term Nagpur as used in the negotiation included all the subdivisions then within its established limits.

In 1818 Traill complained of the disorderly state of the Rawain pargana, the inhabitants of which being relieved from the fear of both the Gurkhas and the British had taken to their old occupation of plundering the pilgrims of Gangotri and Kedarnath.[9] In 1824, the pargana of Rawain was thus ceded to Tehri Garhwal and on 26th December 1842, the political agency of Tehri Garhwal State was given to the Commissioner of Kumaon. Hitherto a British official in Dehradun was working as the political agent of the State.[10] On the same date, 26th December 1842, a resolution was also passed that Dehradun, Mussoorie and Jaunsar shall remain permanently with Saharanpur District.[11]

Sudarshan Shah on receiving the terrain towards the west of Alaknanda, made Tehri his capital. It is situated on the left bank of the river Bhagirathi, 2328 feet above sea level. Those days there was no village on the spot and the settlers were unwilling to come. He accordingly allotted Rs. 700 to build thirty small houses for which tenants at length were found, each paying a rent of Rs. 3 a year. Such was the humble origin of Tehri.[12]

One of the reasons why Sudarshan Shah chose Tehri as the capital was its strategic position. Tehri is surrounded on three sides by the Bhagirathi and on the background there are steep hills. Probably he had nostalgic and religious reasons also for that site. Srinagar, the previous capital of the Parmar kings has been referred as 'Dhanush Tirth' (i.e. a pilgrimage centre in the shape of a bow and arrow) in Kedar Khand.[13] Similarly Tehri, situated at the confluence of the Bhagirathi and Bhilangana is also recognized as 'Dhanush Tirth' in the Kedar Khand.[14]

In Tehri, the phenomenon of a bow and arrow can be observed at the confluence of these two rivers. The river Bhagirathi meanders across like a bow and its tributary joins it in the shape of an arrow.

Sudarshan Shah had a very amiable nature and soon succeeded in establishing his hold over his subjects particularly as they had passed through a very bad phase. The kingdom of Raja Sudarshan Shah, Tehri Garhwal State was one of the many so-called native states of India, subordinate to the British Government, and the Raja was bound to give assistance and supplies when called upon to do so by the British authorities and to furnish facilities to the British for trading in his kingdom and the countries beyond.

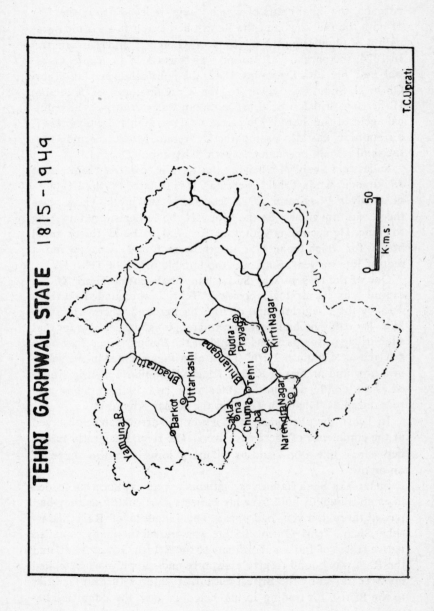

During the struggle of 1857, the Raja helped the British with men and money and kept 200 of his soldiers ready at the hills of Rajpur until the end of the struggle. It is said that the Nawab of Najibabad tried to persuade him to join hands against the British but Sudarshan Shah refused flatly and remained loyal to his British masters. In consideration of his loyalty and services the British are said to have intended to give him the Bijnor region but he demanded instead the Dun valley and Srinagar in British Garhwal which had formerly formed part of his ancestor's kingdom. Negotiations in this respect had not moved far, when Sudarshan Shah died in June 1859, and the matter was dropped for ever.[15]

Raja Sudarshan Shah is supposed to have been a good administrator, a learned scholar, well versed in Sanskrit poetry and also a poet.[16] A contemporary poet, probably a protege of the Raja, wrote, 'Sudarshanodayam Kavyam', in Sanskrit, in his patron's praise.

Sudarshan Shah's erudition is evidenced from his work, 'Sabhasar' which is in seven volumes. Three of these are with Thakur Shoor Beer Singh of Purana Durbar, Tehri; three are preserved in the State Library of Tehri Garhwal State, which is now known as Suman Library, and one volume is with Sri Jiwanand Sriyal of Nail Chami in Tehri Garhwal. 'Sabhasar' as has been stated earlier is important from the view point that it has dealt with the dynastic list of the Parmar kings of Garhwal. His work has covered a wide range from romanticism to personal character. It also throws light on the British attitude.

Raja Sudarshan Shah was a good hunter. Mola Ram has cited one of the incidents of his marksmanship. Once a British officer named Fridon accompanied the Raja on a tiger shoot. This officer was riding an elephant when a tiger pounced on him. The hunting party was petrified on witnessing the tiger's attack. Sudarshan Shah maintained his calm and shot the tiger. The Raja's bravery was highly appreciated by the British authorities in Calcutta.[17]

Apart from his initial residence in Tehri, Sudarshan Shah in 1848 started the construction of the palace of Purana Durbar in Tehri. This palace was the residence of the rulers, Raja Bhawani Shah and Raja Pratap Shah. Later when Kirti Shah became the ruler, he built a new palace for himself in Tehri in 1880-81. This new palace was known as the Naya Durbar. Purana Durbar came in the share of Kunwar Vichitra Shah, younger brother of Raja Kirti Shah.[18]

Rahul Sankrityayan is of the view that Sudarshan Shah died on 7th June 1859.[19] He had no male issue which fact gave rise to intrigues in the royal family over the question of succession.* Rizvi has stated that the Raja himself during his life time had favoured the cause of Bhawani Shah as his successor but his queen was in the favour of another claimant, Sher Shah. Soon after his death, Sher Shah with the queen's help declared himself the king and she herself took control of the royal treasury. In order to obtain recognition from the British Government over his claim, he got his step brothers as well as the nobility of the State to tender a petition in his favour to the Commissioner of Kumaon, within whose jurisdiction the State came. This document was signed by 106 men and even Bhawani Shah was forced to sign it and relinquish his claim in favour of Sher Shah. However, Bhawani Shah's wives rose to the occasion and extricated him out of this predicament. Concomitantly the Commissioner of Kumaon intervened and visited Tehri. Further he told Sher Shah to give up his claim in lieu of pargana Jaunpur which he could keep as his personal 'jagir' (fief) and for his relinquishment he would be given the status of a minister. Sher Shah did not agree and threatened to rebel. He was, therefore, taken away from Tehri on the pretext of hunting and was kept as a captive in Dehradun.[20]

Bhawani Shah thus ascended the throne. He was a man of saintly habits and had a philosophical bent of mind; he loved solitude and spent his time in visiting holy places. During the early part of his reign, the inhabitants of pargana Jaunpur rebelled against the Raja, probably at the instance of Sher Shah and his supporters, but it dwindled out as soon as news arrived that the British troops from Dehradun were on their way to crush the insurgency. The denizens of pargana Rawain also revol-

---

*However according to the Tehri Garhwal State records it seems that a son named Surjan Shah was born who died at an early age. (Tehri Garhwal State Records, File No. G-30-8/Tehri, Letter No. C-59 of 12-2-1927).

ted during his reign but he succeeded in subduing this uprising. Bhawani Shah died in 1871 and was succeeded by his eldest son, Pratap Shah.[21]

Pratap Shah ruled from 1871 to 1886.[22] He was a young man of 21 at the time of his accession. Pratap Shah built a new township, named Pratap Nagar, on a hill top near Tehri. Realizing the necessity of providing educational facilities to his subjects, the Raja established a school (now Pratap Intermediate College) at Tehri in 1883. It was then known as the Anglo Vernacular Middle School. Raja Pratap Shah was the first ruler who introduced English education in his State. He was a lover of music and was extremely fond of hunting. He also tried to improve the forest, judicial and police administration.[23]

During his rule several public uprisings occurred. The first of these was launched by the people of 'patti' Khas of Pratap Nagar tahsil but was soon suppressed by the Raja. Next was the Basar revolt of 1882 which was led by one Lachmu Kathait who although a 'faujdar' of the Raja supported the people of Rajgaon of patti Kaimar-Basar in tahsil Pratap Nagar. The people of that place had come to the capital to offer the Raja traditional presents on the occasion of his safe return from England. But they were harassed by the Raja's men and were made to wait in Tehri unnecessarily for a whole month. Lachmu Kathait who hailed from the same village and at that time happened to be in the capital became their spokesman. For his temerity he was dismissed from service and his property was confiscated. He then proceeded to Naini Tal and lodged a complaint against the Raja. The Governor of the province who happened to be there directed the Commissioner of Kumaon to probe into the matter. The Commissioner of Kumaon went to Pauri, the district headquarter of British Garhwal. In the meantime some 14,000 men from different parts of Tehri Garhwal assembled and proceeded to Pauri. The Raja on visualizing the state of affairs intercepted the procession mid way and made a compromise. He reduced the land tax of the people and conferred marks of honour on Lachmu Kathait and restored him his property.[24]

After this revolt the Raja had to face another problem in 1886 when some of the villagers from the neighbouring areas of Tehri rallied at the capital to protest against the misdeeds of his officials. Unfortunately before the king could take any dicision, he expired. The crowd then dispersed at the appeal of Rani Guleri, his widow.[25]

After Pratap Shah's death his son succeeded him. He was a boy of only 12 years and his mother Rajmata Guleri, appointed Vikram Singh, an uncle of the Raja as his regent. But the people did not like him and within a year there were signs of a revolt. The queen mother thus took the administration in her own hands and appointed a council of regency comprising three members for her help.

The young prince was educated first at Bareilly and then at Mayo College Ajmer. He was an extraordinarily brilliant student. While at Ajmer he got 3 gold medals and 11 silver medals besides several other prizes. In one of the examinations, he scored 8776 marks out of 10000, more than 87 per cent marks.[26]

In 1892, Kirti Shah came of age and took the reins of the kingdom in his own hands. The same year he was married to one of the grand daughters of Rana Jang Bahadur, the prime minister of Nepal. The dignity of a companion of the Star of India was conferred on him on 31st December 1898 and on 9th November 1901, he was made a Knight Commander of the same order.

Raja Kirti Shah took keen interest in the administration and welfare of his subjects, and his reign is, therefore, marked by several notable achievements. In 1891, the Anglo Vernacular Middle School of Tehri was raised to a High School and then it was known as Pratap High School. The Hewett Sanskrit Pathshala in Tehri was started by him and he opened several primary schools in the villages. Those days he donated Rs. 13,000 to Government High School, Srinagar for the construction of a hostel. He was a pioneer to bring electricity to Tehri, and waterworks were also constructed. He established a Municipal Board for Tehri town and several improvements were made in the functioning of courts, the forest department and other important offices of the State. He opened a leprosy centre at Uttarkashi, and several health centres were started in the State. He established a printing press at Tehri and an agriculture bank for the benefit of cultivators. A clock tower was erected in the capital town of Tehri and a new township Kirti Nagar was founded. He also established a miners and sappers force by reorganising the State military. This force was used in peaceful times for the construction of roads and bridges.[27]

Raja Kirti Shah was a man of versatile talents. He had a good command over Sanskrit, Hindi, Urdu, French and English. He was well versed in astrology, astronomy, and had imported a large telescope for an observatory established by him. He was an expert electrician. It is said that he invented the Hindi typewriter, but gave the copywright to a company. On visualizing his exceptional qualities, Lord Lansdowne commented in the Viceroy's Durbar in 1892 at Agra that the rulers of India should make Raja Kirti Shah as their ideal and try to achieve his standards.[28]

Kirti Shah had a religious leaning. He had perused the scriptures of all religions and on one occasion he organised a conference at Tehri of the followers of different religions. In this direction he was inspired by Swami Ram Tirth whom he not only encouraged but also extended pecuniary assistance to attend the World Religious Conference in Japan. Raja Kirti Shah died on 25th April, 1913.[29]

The rule of Raja Bhawani Shah, Pratap Shah and Kirti Shah is marked by natural calamities in the form of famines. The first famine which struck this area was in 1867. This year the spring crops were destroyed by drought. Grain was thus purchased from the southern parts of the State and sold in the famine stricken area. People generally purchased food grains in cash or in the form of labour. The people were however relieved from this distress with the harvesting of an excellent autumn crop.

The famine of 1877 is traditionally held to be the worst in this region. Relief works and poor houses were started and the village head-men were charged with the duty of bringing destitutes to these homes. Those employed in relief works were given tickets in lieu of wages and these tickets were exchanged for foodgrains kept with the traders.

After the famine of 1877, conditions in the State were smooth until 1889 when a dry spell in autumn coupled with a severe cholera epidemic and followed by an almost total loss of the spring crop of 1890 completely impoverished large sections of the people. Foodgrains were imported from the plains and loans were advanced to the people to enable them to purchase the same. This distress continued till 1892. In 1891, the Kharif crop suffered a loss of 50 per cent and the Rabi crop of 1892 also sustained a loss of 25 per cent. Herculean efforts were made to relieve the people and loans were again advanced to the people and relief grain shops were opened.

There were minor spells of localized scarcities again in 1894 and 1895; and in 1896 general famine conditions prevailed and necessitated opening of relief works and granting of loans. In 1902, the scarcity was again confined to certain parts of the district and it was met by giving advances to the traders for importing foodgrains from plains, cash grants for the support of village destitutes and opening of relief works.

In 1907, scanty and ill distributed rains were followed by a poor Kharif crop. The winter rains also failed, yielding only 40 per cent of the Rabi harvest in 1908. Gratuitous relief was immediately provided by the State to the people in the form of distribution of cash advances for sustenance and import of grains from the plains, opening of grain shops and the starting of civil works. The famine of 1908, it is said was the worst since 1877.[30]

Kirti Shah was succeeded by Narendra Shah who was then a minor.[31] During his minority the administration of the State was looked after by a regency council under the presidency of his mother. Like his father he was an educated prince and got his schooling at Mayo Collage, Ajmer. Duing his last years in Mayo College, Narendra Shah offered his personal services for the First World War, but pending correspondence on the subject, delayed the matter and the war ended.[32] However during the war years, a lot of wood was supplied by the Tehri Garhwal State to the British. From 1939 to 42, the total amount of wood supplied was 1,43,66,831 c.ft.[33] While a minor, His Highness was made a lieutenant by the British Government and a Kaiser-i-Hind Medal was awarded to Her Highness the dowager queen in recognition of the war services.[34]

On 4th October 1919, Raja Narendra Shah was coronated. He ruled for approximately 27 years and like his father, he had a knack for politics and took active interest in the administration of his State. He started his development plan from the forest department by sending young officials for training to the Forest

College, Dehradun and inviting foreign experts to improve the forest management of the State.

He founded a new township, Narendra Nagar, to which he shifted the seat of his Government and constructed the Kirti Nagar-Tehri motor road as well as a motor road from Muni-ki-Reti (near Rishikesh) to Narendra Nagar. He got the civil laws of the State compiled in a work named the Narendra Hindu Law in 1918, got a revenue settlement made of the entire land in 1924 and a forest settlement in 1927-28. The 'munar-bandi', fixation of the limits of the forests extended them very close to the villages, leaving practically no forest area for the use of the inhabitants.[35] This resulted in a serious revolt known as the Rawain dhandak or the rebellion of Rawain. This revolt has been discussed in detail in the chapter, 'Political Movements in Tehri Garhwal State'.

To disseminate education in the State a number of primary schools were opened and the Pratap High School was raised to an Intermediate College in 1940. He also extended financial assistance to bright students for studying abroad. To commemorate the memory of Raja Kirti Shah, he donated one lakh rupees and announced a financial grant of 6 thousand rupees annually to the Benares Hindu University in 1933 owing to which, Sir Kirti Shah chair of Industrial Chemistry started there.

Raja Narendra Shah tried to improve the medical facilities in his State by supplying latest equipments to the hospitals of Tehri, Uttarkashi, Deoprayag and Raj Garhi. The British were very pleased with his administration and conferred on him the title of K.C.S.I. and Benares Hindu University honoured him with the degree of L.L.D.[36]

Narendra Shah died in a car accident on 22nd September 1950, but he had relinquished the throne in favour of his son on 26th May, 1946. He was succeeded by his elder son, H.H. Manvendra Shah who ruled from October 1946 to 1st August 1949 when the State integrated with the Indian Union.[37]

REFERENCES

1. Gill, A.R.: Valley of the Doon, p. 8.
2. Ibid., pp. 8-9.

3. Pearse, Col. Hugh: Five Generations of an Anglo Indian Family, p. 61.
4. Atkinson, Edwin T.: Himalayan Districts of the N.W. Provinces of India (1884 edition), Volume II, p. 680.
5. Walton, H.G.: op. cit., p. 130.
6. Aitchison, C.U.: A Collection of Treaties, Engagements and Sunuds Relating to India and the Neighbouring Countries, Volume II, pp. 27-29.
7. Walton, H.G.: op. cit., p. 130.
8. Ibid., p. 130.
9. Ibid., p. 130.
10. Darshan, Bhakt: Garhwal Ki Divangat Vibhutian, p. 139.
11. Dewar, Douglas: A Hand Book to the English Pre-Mutiny Records, p. 164.
12. Williams, G.R.C.: op. cit., p. 130.
13. Bhattacharya, Pandit Brijratna: Skand Purāntargata Kedar Khand, 184/1069/24.
14. Ibid., 140/795-797, 80/1-7.
15. Rizvi, S.A.A.: Gazetteer of India, Uttar Prashed, Tehri Garhwal, p. 49.
16. Rawat, Ajay S.: Uttrakhand Ka Rajnitik Itihas, p. 91.
17. Ibid., p. 92.
18. Personal Communication, Thakur Shoor Beer Singh, Purana Durbar, Tehri.
19. Sankrityayan, Rahul: Garhwal, p. 247.
20. Rizvi, S.A.A.: op. cit., pp. 49-50.
21. Raturi, H.K.: Garhwal Ka Itihas, pp. 475-76.
22. Sankrityayan, Rahul: op. cit., p. 247.
23. Raturi, H.K.: op. cit., pp. 76-77.
24. Rizvi, S.A.A.: op. cit., p. 50.
25. Ibid., p. 50.
26. Personal Communication, Thakur Shoor Beer Singh, Purana Durbar, Tehri.
27. Darshan, Bhakt: op. cit., pp. 187-89.
28. Ibid., pp. 187-90.
29. Ibid., pp. 191-92.
30. Rizvi, S.A.A.: op. cit., pp. 98-99.
31. Sankrityayan, Rahul: op. cit., p. 247.
32. India and the War, Illustrated (1914-18), Parts I and II, p. 279.

33. Raturi, Padma Dutt: War Effort of Tehri Garhwal State Forest Department (1939-42), p. 633.
34. India and the War, Illustrated (1914-18), Parts I and II, p. 279.
35. Zila Tehri Garhwal Ke Bandobast Report, p. 7.
36. Pande, Badri Dutt: Kumaon Ka Itihas, p. 322.
37. Personal Communication, Thakur Shoor Beer Singh, Purana Durbar, Tehri.

6

Administration of Tehri Garhwal State

Tehri Garhwal State was one of the sovereign States in the Punjab States Agency.* It enjoyed full powers paying no tribute. The hereditary titles of the Raja were, 'His Highness' and 'Maharaja' and he was entitled to a dynastic salute of 11 guns** and a return visit from H.E., the Viceroy.[1]

The administration of the State was carried out chiefly in accordance with the old system of governing the State and in adherence with the requirements of the various Indian Acts.[2]

Agriculture and Administration of Land Revenue

Almost the whole State was an agricultural country and forests were in plentiful.[3] Statistics available of the years, 1938-39[4] and 1945-46[5] indicate that cultivation covered about 350 square miles, forest area about 2,775 square miles; grassy alpine and snow area about 1,375 square miles. The cultivator on the whole had a satisfactory yield from the land. He earned from his produce of grain and potatoes and also from his live stock, the price of which rose to a high level.

Practically, most of the State territory was a hilly terrain except-

*From 1st September 1943, the States connection from the Political Agent, Punjab Hill States, was transferred directly to the Hon'ble President for the Punjab States.

**On the occasion of Delhi Durbar held on 1st January 1877, Raja Pratap Shah was granted a personal salute of 11 guns which was subsequently changed in 1878 to a permanent salute.

(Tehri Garhwal State Records, File No. G-30-8, Letter No. C-59, dated 12th February, 1927).

ing, the sub-mountain area below Narendra Nagar. Being in the Himalayan region and interspersed with high mountains and numerous shallow streams, the region had no extensive level tracts for purposes of mechanised cultivation. Finer soils were only to be found in the river valleys where they widened out. Through the centuries, people had carved out terraces, which rose one above the other on the hill sides wherever the terrain had been found to be arable, and such flat strips were used for cultivation. The practice of cutting and burning the shrubs and bushes in certain areas, and then using such patches for raising crops for a year or two and letting them remain fallow again for a number of years to let shrubs and bushes grow up, and repeating the cycle thereby was a common practice. This type of sporadic activity was called 'katil' cultivation.

With the passage of time, on account of the increasing population* and the resultant pressure on the land, the need for more foodgrains extended the cultivation even to those hill sides which, in the past, could not be reclaimed, terraced and cultivated. Thus the demand for 'nayabad', literally new cultivation or land hitherto uncultivated was ever increasing.

Figures for the area of culturable land in the region are not available. In the past, the unassessed area was classed as old fallow (fallow land of more than 3 years standing), culturable waste and unculturable waste. Land which was previously measured but was found to be out of cultivation at the time of the settlements was termed 'benap' (unmeasured) and included land under forests, pastures and grazing grounds.[6]

The type of agriculture practised in the district depended on the elevation of land from the sea level, nature of soil and climatic factors such as rainfall, temperature and snowfall. The position of the fields in relation to sunshine and the availability of irrigation facilities also determined agricultural operations.

Rainfall provided the major source of water for irrigation. The average rainfall for Tehri was 29 inches and Narendra Nagar 103 inches. The region abounds in big and small rivers and they

*According to the Census of 1941, the population was 4,00,189 (The Annual Administration Report of Tehri Garhwal State, for the year 1945-46, p. 1).

also provided an important source of irrigation. In comparison with big rivers, the smaller ones were generally more useful. The small rivulets mostly dried out in the season when water was needed most for irrigating fields but even so they constituted an important source of water supply. Water was carried to the fields through 'guls' (channels) cut along the contour of the land surface. The length of the 'gul' varied according to the height of the field to be irrigated, and the course and water content of such streams. The headwork consisted of a small temporary dam laid acorss the stream through which water was canalised into the 'gul'. These guls were also used to run 'gharats' (water mills) and the amount of water in a stream or 'gul' was generally estimated according to the number of 'gharats' it was capable of turning.

Early Land Settlements

Practically nothing is known about the revenue administration in this area until the commencement of the 19th century. According to Hardwick who visited the area at that time, land revenue was realized by the ruler both in cash and in kind and amounted to about half the produce.

After his restoration, Sudarshan Shah got a settlement made for Tehri Garhwal State in 1823. Measurement of land was not undertaken and no village records were prepared. Land revenue was based on the quantity of seed sown. His successor, Bhawani Shah got a settlement done in 1860. In this settlement also land was not measured and no village records were prepared. The next settlement was made in 1873 by Pratap Shah. This settlement was also like the previous two settlements. The cultivators were not given the right to alienate their holdings by way of sale or mortgage but were considered hereditary tenants who could sublet their holdings to the Sirtans* and could also get their land cultivated on partnership basis. They could also give a portion of their land to the 'Kul Purohit', the family priest. In this settlement the entire area was distributed among different 'thoks', 'parganas' and 'pattis'. Measurement of land was however undertaken though not entrusted to the care of the settlement officer, but to

---

*Stowell has defined 'Sirtan' as tenant at will. (Stowell, V.A.: A Manual of the Land Tenures of Kumaon Division, p. vii).

different individuals, 'patti' or 'thok' wise. The procedure of land measurement is not known. After the settlement, 'Kardars' and State officials were charged with the responsibility of collection of land revenue. Each Kardar was handed over a 'patta' on his appointment and this 'patta' contained detailed instructions. Kardars were appointed annually and the 'patta' of those against whom there were public complaints were not renewed. Kardars were like Patwaris except for the fact that their tenure was for one year whereas Patwaris were permanent State employees.[7]

It seems that the settlement of 1873-76 was generally welcomed by the cultivators. A census of people, houses, cattle, sheep, goats and gharats (water mills) was also carried out. Land revenue in this settlement was assessed at the rate of one rupee per unit of area requiring one 'don' (30 seers) of seed for sowing it. The smallest unit of weight used in the settlement was 'patha' which equalled 2 seers, 16 pathas equalling one don.

The highest unit of weight was 'jyula'. They were of two types, one was the 'chakra jyula' and the other was known as 'sāmānya jyula'. According to the 'chakra jyula' of measurement, one jyula was = 16 dons = 12 maunds = 480 seers of seed. In the sāmānya jyula, one jyula was = 4 dons = 3 maunds = 120 seers of seed.[8]

No serious measure however appears to have been undertaken until 1903 for preparing village maps and khasras or field statement on the basis of actual measurement. Nor any attempt seems to have been made to clearly define and demarcate the boundaries of the villages until that year. In 1903, the then ruler Kirti Shah, undertook a proper settlement and village maps were prepared in respect of the villages falling within the parganas Bhilang, Chandrabadni, Pratap Nagar and Kirti Nagar. No such detailed settlement appears to have been carried out with respect to parganas Narendra Nagar, Uttarkashi, Udaipur, Jaunpur and Rawain. In this settlement, records of village boundaries and population were prepared and land revenue was assessed on the estimated area of holdings as fixed in the earlier settlement of 1873. Assessment was also made on the basis of 'dons', and 'pathas'. The cultivated land was classified in this settlement into four classes, viz. sera (irrigated), ukhar (land adjacent to the villages), awwal ukhar doyam and ukhar soyam. This classification of ukhar, awwal, doyam and soyam was based upon fertility. Another feature of this settlement was the change in the mode of assessing 'bishah', which was a sort of a tax.

To meet the expenses of the court, a cess of $12\frac{1}{2}\%$ was realized from the land revenue. This tax was taken in kind and was known as 'bishah'. It was started by Raja Sudarshan Shah.[9] During famines or other calamities 'bishah' was not levied on the peasants, but later on 4 times the amount was realized from them during good harvest. This tax was then known as 'Chaubara Naqadi'. In the settlement of 1903, an alteration was made. Henceforth 'bishah' was realized in the form of cash. That year in particular, the land revenue assessed came to Rs. 1,11,791 and 'bishah' amounted to Rs. 13,975.

The next settlement was ordered in 1916 by the then ruler Narendra Shah and it was completed in 1924.[10] In 1918 a revision was made. This settlement was done under the supervision of a regular settlement officer. 'Amins' measured all the fields and prepared maps and khasras on the spot. Plots were numbered on the maps and in the khasra; classification of the soil fields was recorded. Different categories of the land taken were talaon, upraon, ukhar awwal and ukhar soyam which are explained below:

i) *Talaon*:
   (a) Awwal—permanently irrigated land.
   (b) Doyam—intermittently irrigated land relying mainly on rivulets and rain.
ii) *Upraon*: Dry terraced land (upland) first class (awwal) and second class (doyam).
iii) *Ukhar awwal*:
   (a) Land adjoining the village area which was adequately manured and fertile.
   (b) Land adjacent to the villages which was also manured but was comparatively less fertile.
iv) *Ukhar doyam*: Land near the villages which was rugged.
v) *Ukhar soyam*:
   (a) Ijran—inferior terraced land cultivated intermittently.
   (b) Katil—unterraced inferior land cultivated intermittently.

For the first time an area unit of measurement, equal to 4,800 square yards or 20 nalis was adopted for assessing land revenue. A census of human beings and cattle was also conducted. In this settlement upraon doyam land was taken to be the standard. One nali of irrigated, upraon awwal and ijran land was deemed respectively equal to 3, 1½ and 3/4 of standard land. No assessment circles were however formed, instead the patti was adopted as the unit of assessment. At the close of the settlement in 1924, total revenue of the State rose to Rs. 3,09,280 from Rs. 1,11, 791 in 1903. In the settlement adhoc increases were affected on the assessment made in 1903, taking into consideration factors like location of villages, the classes of soil and extent of irrigated land in it, the rate of yield, the general economic condition of the cultivators, availability of pastures and the extent of damage caused by wild animals. After the adhoc increases in the assessment, villages were placed into 3 classes. Each village came to have a different revenue rate and villages having about equal revenue rates were classified together. An important feature of this settlement was the abolition of the levy 'bishah'.

The revenue settlement of 1916 which was completed in 1924 was the first settlement in Tehri State which seems to be scientific and which was more or less the same as in the neighbouring region of British Garhwal and Kumaon. The classification of land, talaon, upraon, ijran, katil etc. was also similar. In certain respects however this settlement was more practical than the settlements of Kumaon and British Garhwal since factors like the general economic condition of the cultivators, availability of pastures and the extent of damage caused by wild animals were taken into consideration. An important reform was also implemented by abolishing 'bishah'.

Detailed reports of the settlement prior to the year 1916 are not available, but it can be assumed that the revenue settlements from the time of restoration of Raja Sudarshan Shah upto 1903 were very sketchy. No serious attempts were made for preparing village maps and khasra on the basis of actual measurement before 1903. Then upto 1916, additional levy on the land revenue like 'bishah' and 'chaubara naqdi' were extorted from the cultivators to meet the expenses of the court which was unjust. But the measures adopted to relieve the famine stricken people those days alludes the administrative capabilities to an extent and the humanitarian approach of the kings. In 1877 e.g., during the reign of Pratap Shah when Tehri Garhwal State was hit by a famine, food relief depots were opened immediately in different places and land revenue was exempted that year.[11] Similarly in 1918-19, when famine gripped the lower parts of Tehri Garhwal State owing to the failure of Kharif crop and Rabi crop was also not prospective, 'takavi' loans amounting to Rs. 3,00,000 were advanced to the people. A poor house was also opened at Tehri where the crippled and the poor were fed at the Durbar's expenses.[12]

It is most remarkable that both in British Garhwal and Tehri Garhwal State during the last three decades of the 19th century, immigration had increased owing to the excellent system of famine relief.[13] Against other natural calamities also the State took keen interest in relieving the people, e.g. in 1938 during the land slide in the villages of Piplogi and Ramoli, in which 30 lives were lost and property worth about Rs. 10,000 was destroyed. His Highness Raja Narendra Shah personally visited the scene of the land slide disaster and helped and sympathized with the people.[14]

In 1943 it was felt that the time was ripe to revise the last land settlement by conducting Revisional Settlement operations.[15] The operations were started in June 1944 and a good progress was made upto the end of the year. About 1700 villages were re-surveyed, and for about 1000 villages records prepared by the Amins were attested by the Assistant Settlement Officers and for about 670 villages the assessment work was completely finished by the Settlement Officer.

In addition to its main task, the Settlement Department was also entrusted with the mutation work which was done by the Land Records Office and with the disposal of applications for new land, 20,455 mutation files were attested and 2024 applications for land were disposed off during the year by the department and 7861 'tanaza' (disputed) cases were heard and decision was given.

The quinquennial cattle census was conducted during the year to synchronize with that of U.P. The total livestock returns amounted to 5,27,319 animals against 5,16,660 animal returns during the last census of 1940. The chief reason for this enormous decrease was the export of animals to the neighbouring districts of Dehradun and British Garhwal where the prices of livestock soared very high due to war conditions.

The total revenue taken during different years, data of which only is available is shown below:

1903	Rs. 1,11,791
1923	Rs. 3,09,279
1943	Rs. 3,60,647
1944	Rs. 3,61,175
1945	Rs. 3,62,000

The increase in the revenue for the years 1943-45[16] as compared to the other years was partly due to the new cultivation and partly owing to the conversion of dry land into irrigated land.

Land Tenures

The land tenures in Tehri Garhwal State were similar to those prevalent in Kumaon or British Garhwal except that in Tehri State all the proprietary rights were vested in the ruler and were inalienable. There were certain exceptions however, the Saklanas* of village Saklana were 'hissedars', proprietors and later on the direct relations of the King were also made 'hissedar' in 1941. The tenures were mainly of three types, 'Maurusidar', possessing hereditary rights, the 'Khaikar', under proprietary rights and the 'Sirtan', tenant at will. The Khaikars held land from Maurusidars and the Sirtans from both the Khaikars and Maurusidars.[17] The Maurusidar was an agent of the Government for the collection of revenue and other dues. He enjoyed full rights by sale or otherwise of the land he owned with the permission of the hissedar. He could not however, secure cultivatory possession or in

---

Saklana Estate: It was a feudatory State situated in the west of Tehri State, with an area of 70 square miles. The owners or 'muafidars' paid an annual quit rent to the Raja of Tehri. During the Gurkha war their ancestors had rendered important services to the British and in lieu of that service they were given this estate. The muafidars had powers to try all civil, rent and revenue suits arising in their own villages, and exercised powers as Second Class Magistrates. Cases in which the muafidars were personally interested were transferred by the Commissioner of Kumaon as Agent for Tehri State, to competent courts in British districts.

(Walton, H.G.: British Garhwal, A Gazetteer, p. 214).

any way interfere with the Khaikars or their land or cultivation. All that he could do was to collect the State revenue together with the amount of 'malikana' dues. The Khaikars paid the land revenue, and in addition, 10% thereon as malikana to the Maurusidars. The land revenue was paid to the Government and the amount of malikana was retained by the Maurusidar. The Khaikar paid a fixed rent for his holding to the Maurusidar who had no right to eject him unless he himself surrendered the holding. His interest was heritable but not transferable. The other tenure holders were those sub-tenants who had been settled on the estates by the Maurusidars and had become Khaikars and could not be ejected. The Sirtans, literally meaning tenants who paid Sirti or Government revenue were divided into two categories, the descendants of old cultivators who paid a fixed rent to the Khaikars or the Maurusidars, and those tenants whose rent was not settled with the Maurusidar or Khaikars. The Sirtans had no fixity or tenure until the passing of the Kumaon Agricultural (Miscellaneous Provisions) Act, 1954, which provided them protection from ejectment.

Revenue Officials

The State constituted 2,456 villages and only one town Tehri and later Narendra Nagar.

The Sub-Divisional Magistrate was the senior most revenue official who was assisted by Tehsildars, Kanungos and Patwaris. Tehsildar was an important officer in the revenue administration. He was authorized to give adequate publicity at a public gathering to the proclamation issued by the Government, to obtain authentic information regarding land revenue, to fix revenue in consideration of the records of the previous years etc. Tehsildar was also an officer of the police.[18]

Kanungo helped the Tehsildar in performing his duties.[19] They were appointed for the proper supervision, maintenance and correction of Patwari records. The office of the Kanungo was hereditary. It was however compulsory for his heir, who was designated to succeed him that he should be sent to school and educated there.[20]

The last link in the above chain was the Patwari.[21] His duty was collection of revenue, maintenance of land records, measurement of land, execution of revenue decrees, repairing of roads and to find supplies for travellers. The Patwari used to maintain a Khasra or field statement which illustrated the number of fields during the settlement.

Besides this Government machinery, there were certain other officials such as Padhans, Thokdars, etc. who were also associated with the revenue administration, Padhan was responsible for the collection of revenue in his village which he made over to the Patwari, while he was also in his position as headman entrusted with certain minor public duties. The office of the Padhan was hereditary.[22] Where the Padhan was a non-resident he had to appoint a Mukhtiyar or deputy.[23]

The fiscal officers intermediate between the Padhan and the State were known, as Atkinson has observed, as Thokdars or Sayanas in different places by different names, and they played an important role in the administration. They had no rights in the soil over which they exercised authority. Their duty was to collect a fixed amount from the villages. The Padhans worked under them. They were invariably chosen from the principal Padhans.[24]

Forest Management

History of forests in Tehri Garhwal State, prior to the year 1840 is shrouded in oblivion.[25] In 1840 for the first time forests were leased out to some, Wilson who acquired the right of exploiting forest produce such as musk (Moschus chrysogoster), munal (Catrus wallichi), hides of wild animals, fuel timber etc. from the then Raja of Tehri Garhwal State on a paltry 'nazrana' or gift.[26] The first lease of Wilson ended in 1850, but it was renewed the same year for a very small amount of Rs. 400 per annum to use the forest produce of the Bhagirathi valley beyond Harsil. He felled deodar (Cedrus deodara) and chir (Pinus roxburghii) trees and converted them into sleepers which he sold to the Railway Department. He introduced a unique method of transporting timber by floating it through rivers, down to the plains[27], and in this respect his mode of exploiting forest wealth is a landmark in the history of forestry. Wilson's lease expired in 1864 and in 1865, Raja Bhawani Shah leased his forest for Rs. 10,000 a year to the Government for a period of 20 years with effect from 1st May 1864.[28] The lease of the Gangotri Valley Forest (later the Uttarkashi Forest Division) and the Shivpuri forests terminated in 1885. The same year, the Tehri Garhwal State established its own Forest Department and started working and utilizing their own forests, which were released by the Government. The lease of the Tons Division terminated in 1925 and the State took the management of the Tons Divison also in its hands.

In 1897, the State secured the services of Pandit Kashva Nand from the British Government and since that year, systematic forestry was started in Tehri State. In the initial stage he took in hand the demarcation of Shivpuri forests. This task was continued by his successor Pandit Sadanand and finally completed by Pandit Ram Dutt who joined the State services in 1907.[29]

Pandit Ram Dutt in 1908 prepared a scheme for the demarcation and settlement of the forests in the State, according to which the forests were divided into 3 categories, viz. first class reserved forests, second class protected forests and third class village forests which comprised all waste land not under the control of the Forest Department.[30]

In 1928-29, Tehri Durbar engaged the services of Dr. F. Heske of Trandt, Germany as Forest Advisor to the State. He inspected the State Forests for about a year and left behind detailed reports of the forests for their future management.[31] The settlement work that followed was to a great extent based on his reports. Heske in his report has mentioned that "against each attempt at regulation by the Forest Department, there is a tradition of hundreds of years of unrestricted use and also the stiff resistance by the inhabitants to this regulation." "The idea of the inhabitants", he has further said, "was only about the present day. They considered the forests as free and only meant for their use without effort. They did not think of the future generation."[32] Modifications in the demarcation in some parts of these forests was affected in 1927-28 and finally in 1933-35.

By 1940, the State forests were categorized into 4 divisions: Jamuna, Tons, Tehri and Uttarkashi, which were further subdivided into ranges. These ranges were Barahat, Dharasu, Taknore, Tehri, Shivpuri, Mukhem, Bhilangana, Alaknanda, Jaunpur, Purola, Deota, Kotigad, Singtur, Mugarsanti and Rawain.[33]

Forests were further classed into 2 types, Reserved and Open forests. Reserved forest meant forests demarcated as such and marked in the forest maps. Open forest was the unmeasured land outside demarcated reserved forest.[34] The Forest Department was headed by a conservator.

Objects of Management

The primary object of the management of State forests was preservation and improving of the existing forests, to obtain the highest possible sustained yield and revenue by a properly regulated system of exploitation of timber and other resources after full consideration of the primary aim, and to satisfy as far as possible the legitimate requirement of the local population for fodder, timber and other forest produce. Together with the above considerations, the State Forest Department undertook the work of fire protection and preservation of wild and acquatic life.

Conservation of Forests

From time immemorial the villagers had been felling timber for their dwellings and fuel from the adjacent forests. The result of such promiscuous fellings was that near the villages, the bigger trees were removed and those that remained were either in the pole stage or their stocking was very poor.

Further, revenue exploitation which had started during Wilson's lease from 1850 to 1864, resulted into ruthless, uncontrolled and destructive fellings in the Chir (Pinus roxburghii) and deodar (Cedrus deodara) forests. Unregulated fellings continued during Government lease also from 1864 to 1865. However when some ranges reverted to State control, the fellings were controlled and carried out on a very moderate scale.

Forest conservancy in the strict sense was commenced from January 1, 1897 when the services of Pandit Keshva Nand were obtained from the British Government. He prohibited cleanings of forests for cultivation and restricted lopping and grazing. Further the work of demarcation of the best forests was started by him in 1898. By 1899, the demarcation of all deodar, sal (Shorea robusta) and papri (Buxus wallichiana) forests, a large area of chir and a few small patches of banj (Quercus leucotrichophora) was completed. This work was however hampered by the opposition from the villagers. The cause of opposition was not only demarcation but also prohibition against the felling of trees like kukat (miscellaneous broad leaf species) and banj and the introduction of fire protection in all the forests.

Pandit Keshva Nand was followed by Pandit Sada Nand on deputation from Government services as Conservator of Forests on November 5, 1904. His proposals on forest management were three-fold.

a) Removal or modification of irksome restrictions on villager's forest requirements.

b) Demarcation of forests from waste land, and

c) Fellings to be reduced to an extent to meet the cost of management until demarcation, as above, and working plans of the forests were completed.

The first of these proposals was embodied in the Durbar Circular No. 11, dated March 31, 1905. This permitted villagers to fell all kinds of trees in their cultivation, to extend cultivation upto 20 chains in treeless waste land, to burn forests not felled recently and to fell trees other than deodar (Cedrus deodara), chir (Pinus roxburghii), kail (Pinus wallichiana), thuner (Taxus baccata), rai (Picea smithiana), tun (Cedrela tuna), shisham (Dalbergia sissoo), sal (Shorea robusta), sain (Terminalia tomentosa) and papri (Buxus wallichiana) which were classed as reserved species; with regard to the second proposal, demarcation and forest settlement of the least burdened forests in Shivpuri Range and deodar patches of Jaunpur were carried out in 1905 and 1906. Further revenue fellings were reduced to 2,000 chir per annum. Pandit Sada Nand's work was terminated by opposition and his deputation expired on March 30, 1907.

A new era in forest conservancy began with the advent of Rai Bahadur, Ram Dutt Raturi on July 22, 1907 as Conservator of Tehri Garhwal State forests. He demarcated the forests and the waste lands classifying them further into 3 categories, viz. the first class reserve forests, the second class protected forests (both under the Forest Department and interchangeable) and the third class village forests comprising all waste land. These forests of the third class were not under the control of the Forest Department. The main objective behind this classification was to have the incidence of the usual forest concessions confined to the second class forest. Third class forests were assigned to the villagers for their bonafied use but in the event of gross misuse they were liable to be taken within the forest demarcation.

In the first class reserves use of all the existing paths and canals were permitted while grazing, fuel, litter and free grant trees were allowed in special cases only. In the second class forests almost all the forest requirements were permitted against insurance of no injury to the crop, e.g. grazing and grass cutting were allowed in areas not under regeneration. Felling of green kukat and oaks (Quercus species) was permitted for huts and agricultural implements. Permits were however, required for deodar, thuner, firs (Abies pindrow), kail, chir, tun, shisham, sal, papri, sain, bakhli (Anogeissus latifolia), haldu (Adina cordifolia), khair (Acacia catechu), akhrot (Juglans regia), darli (Cedrela serrata) and oaks. Lopping of kukat was allowed excluding the upper quarter of a tree, branches above 4″ girth, recklessly lopped trees and the same tree every year. Thorny shrubs for fencing and grass for thatching was allowed. Dry and fallen wood for fuel or building and litter could be removed if the forests were not directly harmed. Areas not close to fire could be burnt annually in or before March with necessary precautions. Edible roots, fruits, medicinal roots, herbs and ringals (bamboos) could also be removed and even sold, provided no contract for them had been given. For temporary and permanent cultivation permission was however necessary and shooting was restricted.

The third class forests which were meant entirely for villagers use but where they were dense enough, and after satisfying the villager's requirements there was a surplus of forest product, it could then be disposed off by the Durbar in any manner thought fit. In treeless areas cultivation could be extended, for other tracts however permission had to be obtained from the Durbar. In third class forests, trees could be felled without permit excepting those along roads, in 'paraos', encampments or on stream banks upto 100 feet and also chir (pinus roxburghii), tun (Cedrella tuna), shisham (Dalbergia sissoo), deodar (Cedrus deodara) which were required to be marked by State officials. Burning of forest area was permitted provided it did not endanger the neighbouring forests. Shooting of all birds except kastura (Moschus chrysogoster) and munal (Catrus wallichi) was allowed. These forests could however be annexed to demarcated forests if misused. Forest roads and timber depots could also be constructed on them, but for any loss to land or crop the department was to pay compensation.

Pandit Ram Dutt's proposals were carried out in the teeth of opposition but by the end of the year 1910, he however succeeded in demarcating certain areas as reserved and protected forests.[35] In order to exclude the assessed land which by mistake was included within the demarcated area, a second revision was done in 1927-29. Although Pandit Ram Dutt's policy was directed towards conservation, it was felt that the forests were not receiving the attention and care they deserved. In 1937, the State Forest Advisor, E.A. Benskin brought matters to a head and initiated the preparation of a new working plan. This plan was prepared for 1939-40 to 1969-70 by Conservator Prem Nath Khosla for Tehri Division only. To attain the objective of preservation, the forests of Tehri Division were classified into the following circles.

1. *The Chir Regular Working Circle*

This comprised all the chir areas for commercial exploitation, extending over a vast tract between 2000' and 7500' altitudes. Most of them contained pure chir crops, while others had an admixture of oak and its associates towards the top parts or in shady ravines and low level kukat species including some sal (Shorea robusta) in their lower portion.

2. *The Unregulated Working Circle*

In this circle were grouped together the residual chir areas and the poor type of kukat forests which owing to their inferior quality were of no commercial value then, but were useful for the prevention of denudation and for meeting the demands of the local population.

3. *Mixed Kukat Working Circle*

This contained all the low level kukat and sal areas which lay within an easy access of the motor roads and were of commercial value for timber, fuel and other forest products.

4. Box Wood Circle

This species was found in small isolated areas. However, owing to its high commercial value, its very slow rate of growth and uncertainty about the correct method of treatment required, it was considered advisable to place them under a sounder system of working by constituting them into a separate working circle.

5. Ban Oak Working Circle

This constituted of the ban oak areas which were of no commerial importance, but were used or likely to be subjected to lopping by the villagers for leaf fodder. The aim of management would be to preserve the areas and to prevent their destruction.

6. The Protection Working Circle

This constituted of all the other high level forests of kharsu and other oaks, fir (Abies pindrow) and associated species, with the exception of the box wood areas.

7. Bamboo Working Circle

It consisted of all those compartments in the Protection Working Circle which provided summer grazing and also those of the mixed kukat working circle.

This plan would have been implemented to other divisions also but in the meantime the Second World War broke out and during that period timber was supplied to the British Government to aid them against the Axis powers. According to the Annual Administration Report of Tehri Garhwal State for the year 1943-44, "The Forest Department did not lag behind in coordinating their war effort. They tried to supply as much timber from the State forests as they could possibly do for supplementing the requirements of the Government of India through the State Department agency and its contractors. Over two crore cubic feet of all sorts of timber has been supplied."[36]

However with the working plan of Tehri Division, deodar (Cedrus deodara), kail (Pinus wallichiana), chir (Pinus roxburghii), rai (Picea smithiana), murinda (Abies pindrow), thuner (Taxus baccata), tun (Cedrela tuna), sheesham (Dalbergia sissoo), sal (Shorea robusta), papri (Buxus wallichiana), sain (Terminalia tomentosa), bakhli (Anogeissus latifolia), haldu (Adina cordifolia), khair (Acacia catechu), baurola (Cordia vestita), and mulberry (Morus alba) were classed as valuable speices, but deodar, kail, chir, rai, murinda, sal, papri and walnut could be exploited for commercial use.[37]

Fire Protection

Since forests were prone to fire, preventive measures were taken against it as early as 1880 when they were on lease with the Government. That year however, fire protection was implemented in deodar forests only but since 1885, it was extended to chir forests also. In order to protect these forests from fire, some fire tracts were made which were burnt annually. The result of this sort of protection was very satisfactory and so towards the close of the last century, it was extended to other forests of the State also like fir and broad leaved forests. By 1938, however, all the forests included within the demarcated area by the Forest Department were fire protected.

Next year when the plan for the Tehri Forest Division was being prepared for the years 1939-40 to 1969-70 by Prem Nath Khosla it was realized that although annual burning as against intermittent burning was probably the best protection, it was not recommended except for especially exposed forests for the following reasons.

a) Erosion of the soil surface would be intensified by annual fires.

b) It was essential to make provisions for the grazing requirements of the villagers, and this would not have been secured if all the grass was burnt annually. Cattle required fresh grass in summer, which came upon the burnt areas in spring, and also grazing during the winter and early spring before the grass grew.

Khosla gave certain suggestions in his plan for the protection of incendiary fires.

1. Fire protection of all patches of seedling crops. Removal of any old and rotten wood lying in such patches.

2. Thinning out saplings to an average distance of 4 ft. Removal and burn slashing in open places along with the cut stems and then running a controlled fire down hill a few days after the winter rainfall.

Further all fire cases, he said, should be reported twice, first to a preliminary report immediately on the occurrence of the fire and then in the final report after careful inspection of the affected areas.

All burnt areas of over 5 acres in extent, he further suggested, should be shown on a special set of 2″ scale maps and personally visited by the Divisional Officer. His note of inspection together with the report of the Range Officer should be preserved with the fire record tracing as a permanent record.

Preservation of Animal and Acquatic Life

The laws for protection of wild and acquatic life were enacted in 1929. The important areas were as follows:[38]

1) "No person is entitled to shoot animals or birds within the limits of a reserved forest without obtaining a shooting license. This lincense shall be issued by the Durbar.

Although shooting licenses are issued to farmers for protection of their fields from wild animals, for hunting they will have to obtain separate licenses from the Durbar. For retainers of gun licenses other than farmers, they will also have to seek the Durbar's permission and obtain a license for hunting. In the license, the area of forests in which the hunter has been permitted to shoot will be clearly indicated.

2) There is a ban and strict action will be taken against:

a) Killing of animals and birds during snow, especially those animals and birds who have taken refuge in dwelling houses owing to the cold during the winter season.

b) Smearing poison on the dead bodies of animals so that other animals may fall a prey to this trap.

c) Shooting animals from vehicles except for tigers and bears before dawn and after dusk.

d) Chasing deers with hounds and killing them.

e) Hunting animals from 'machans' except for bears, boers and tigers with the aid of artificial light.

f) Trapping animals and killing them.

g) Killing animals in wild life sanctuaries.

3. It is the foremost duty of the Forest Department to protect animals and birds found above 7000 ft, e.g. munal, kastura, white

and red bear etc. There is also a ban against the killing of birds which are recognized for dancing and singing.

4) Due precautions will be taken by the Forest Department against destruction of eggs and nests of birds.

5) Unless the hunter cannot clearly distinguish a male from a female, he will not shoot at that animal during mating season.

6) From 1st April to 14th October, no licenses shall be issued for hunting animals and birds.

7) The following rivers and rivulets, Hinval, Varun, Assi, Gular Gad and Ganga inside the Uttarkashi area are prohibited.

8) The use of dynamite in killing fishes is not permitted."

Thus the authorities in Tehri State adopted a scientific approach towards forestry and forest management. They realized the importance of forests and tried to preserve them. Even in open forests where the villagers had full rights of exploiting timber and other forest products, ". . . . they were shouldered with the responsibility of planting trees in open forests under the direction of the Forest Department. They were also required to keep a portion of the open forest closed to grazing in order to permit regeneration."[39]

The statistics available of the revenue taken from the forests before 1947 and by comparing it with the revenue taken by the Forest Department after 1947, it can be assumed that the motive behind forest management in Tehri Garhwal State was not exploitation and deforestation but preservation. The available data of revenue taken from the forests in Tehri State between the years 1931 to 1937 is as follows:

Year	Revenue in Rs.
1931-32	34,812
1932-33	33,874
1933-34	81,693
1934-35	1,14,002
1935-36	1,41,880
1936-37	78.154

During the war years there was some indiscriminate felling of trees, and the Raja of Tehri Garhwal State to help the British, supplied timber to the Government. The total amount of wood supplied to the British Government was 1,43,66,831 c. ft during 1939-42.[40]

Data available of the revenue taken after 1950 from the Tehri forests is as follows:[41]

Year	Revenue in Rs.
1957-58	80,88,328
1958-59	1,11,72,176
1959-60	99,47,122

In 1963-64, the revenue taken from the forests of Tehri soared upto Rs. 1,40,00,250 and to Rs. 1,86,55,651 in 1965-66[42] which is a clear indication of the rapid increase in promiscuous felling of trees after 1947. This has led to soil erosion and ecological hazards.

Although the State Forest Department was working in consonance with the policy of preservation of forests on the one hand, on the other no efforts were made to impress upon the people, the utility and value of forests. If the people were not fully cognisant of the value of forests, it was the duty of the administration to appeal to their reason and remove their misapprehension. The local people felt that their rights were being encroached upon and their resentment was first manifested in 1906 and later in 1930[43] in the form of forest uprisings.*

Further the authorities in Tehri Garhwal State did not concentrate on planting broad leaved trees which prevent soil erosion and are congenial for the growth of ground vegetation. As regards preservation of wild and acquatic life, it can be said that the rules framed by Tehri State were strict and humane. According to the Annual Administration Report for the year 1943-44 of Tehri Garhwal State, "indiscriminate distruction of natural fauna is strictly forbidden and for the protection of wild life, shooting permits are given in very special and rare cases. Besides there are several sanctuaries all over the State where shooting and fishing are prohibited."[44] An interesting example which has been cited already is that there was a ban on killing those birds and animals which had taken refuge in dwelling houses owing to the cold during winter season. Similarly it was the duty of the Forest Department to take due precautions against destruction of nests and birds. Further, it is a common practice in the hills to kill

*These uprisings have been discussed in the next chapter.

fishes in the rivers by dynamiting, and the Forest Department
in the neighbouring regions ruled by the British overlooked this
practice. But in Tehri, there was a strict ban on this mode of killing. Similary in the neighbouring hilly tracts no measures were
taken to plant shrubs and trees like mulberry, walnut, and wild
rose which are compatible for the propagation of wild life, since
they are fruit bearing. In the present times also this aspect is
neglected. But in Tehri Garhwal State as is evidenced by the Annual Administrative Report of 1918-19, mulberry and other
fruit bearing bushes and trees were planted since 1919.[45]

Judicial Administration

In the beginning, since 1815 there was no set constitution of
courts in the State. The Raja had all the powers, criminal, civil
and revenue invested in him and he used to dispense justice himself and sometimes through officials appointed by him who were
known as 'Ditha' or 'Hakim Ilaka' in different parts of his domain. He also appointed a 'kamdar' in each patti/pargana who
besides collecting the revenue, decided civil and criminal cases
and was replaced every year. Since the Raja was the sole authority in the State, the only court was situated at the capital. The
people being ignorant were afraid to face the Raja, therefore,
petty cases were hushed up by the village community.[46] However, if the people were not satisfied with the decision of the village community, then they resorted to 'Bunda'. In it the plaintiff
and defendant both would proceed to a selected deity and after
propitiation, one of the party which agreed upon to give up the
cause of the dispute would with folded hands repeat the text thus,
"O God my opponent pledges himself to be right in this dispute,
but the facts of it are known to thee, so that I give up my cause
with a view that thou would do me justice," and thus the case
would come to an end.[47]

Raja Pratap Shah who was coronated in 1870 tried to reform
this system. He felt that justice was not being dispensed properly.[48] Thus, since 1870, the court of the Raja was named as the
Chief Court. The courts under the Chief Court were known as
the Magistrate Court, Deputy Collector's Court and the 'Dithas'
Court. The presiding officers of these courts administered justice
in all the branches of criminal, revenue and civil cases. Under the

Deputy Collector's there were the courts of the Tehsildar whose main function was to dispense petty revenue appeals and magisterial cases.[49]

The appeal of Deputy Collectors was heard by the Magistrate who was just like the District Magistrate of British India and exercised similarp owers, that of a first class magistrate in criminal, revenue and civil cases. In practice, the collector was however occupied with revenue and executive work and the judicial work was left to the concerned deputy collectors with their headquarters at Tehri, Pratap Nagar, Narendra Nagar, Kirti Nagar and Rajgarhi. They possessed 1st class magisterial powers in criminal matters and exercised powers of a civil judge, to entertain suits upto Rs. 3000 valuation.[50]

During the rule of Raja Kirti Shah, the procedure followed in British Garhwal was adopted for dispensing justice by the various above courts in the State. The Raja however remained supreme and gave decision in murder cases and other heinous crimes, complicated revenue matters and the highest civil cases. Death sentence could be passed by him alone. He also heard the appeals of the lower courts.

In 1920, Raja Narendra Shah established the Hazoor Court. Its chief function was then that of an appellate court. A Chief Justice was appointed in the Hazoor Court who heard appeals from the subordinate courts, and also certified appeals to the Raja. The court of the civil and sessions judges were also formed.

On his birthday, 4th August 1938, Raja Narendra Shah, by a Charter constituted the Tehri Garhwal State High Court and abolished the Chief Court. By the same Charter, His Highness constituted also a judicial committee to advise him in judicial matters, to dispose off appeals submitted to His Highness against the decisions of the High Court. The Charter also reserved to His Highness the power to entertain appeals against the judgements of the High Court, even without the certificate of the High Court. With the formation of the High Court, only such cases as were certified by the High Court were entertained by the judicial committee and were heard in further appeal by the Hazoor Court. Besides the appellate work, the miscellaneous applications connected with the land and administrative matters were submitted to the Hazoor Court directly.[51]

Apart from the above mentioned courts there were the Saklana Muafi Courts. The two Saklana Muafi Courts were: (a) the Senior Muafi Court, and (b) the Junior Muafi Court, both exercised 2nd class magisterial powers in criminal matters, and in civil and revenue matters, they had jurisdiction over all cases within the Muafi villages. All appeals of criminal, as well as revenue and civil cases, against the decisions of the Muafi Courts, were heard by the appellate courts of the State.

During the rule of Raja Narendra Shah, there were two Jagir courts, the court of Her Highness the Maharani Saheba, and of Birendra Singh Saheb, who were empowered to exercise the same criminal and civil powers and jurisdiction in their Jagirs as the sub-divisional officers in their sub-divisions.[52]

According to the Tehri Revenue Settlement Report of 1924, it seems that some time before 1924, Panchayat Raj was established in towns as well as the villages of Tehri State. There were Nagar Pur Pachayats as well as Gram Panchayats for the rural areas. These Panchayats were given the power to decide minor cases.[53] There were also three Panchayat Courts at Chowras, Bhardar and Taknor. They exercised 3rd class magisterial powers and entertained civil suits upto the value of Rs. 50.

There were three Honorary Courts also. They were the 2-Bench Courts at Uttarkashi and Deoprayag and the Honorary Magistrate's Court at Tehri. These three honorary courts excercised 2nd class powers in criminal matters and also entertained civil suits upto the value of Rs. 200.[54]

There being no specific laws in the beginning, cases were decided on the basis of usage and customs. It was during the rule of Raja Kirti Shah that some laws were constituted regarding criminal matters. Later, under Raja Narendra Shah definite laws were framed for civil and criminal cases. The Tehri Garhwal State Penal Code (Act 1 of Samvat 1982, i.e., 1925 A.D.) with an appendix relating to local offences was enacted in his regime. Earlier, Narendra Hindu Law had been compiled in 1917. In the Penal Code, Magistrates—classes 1 and 2, bench Magistrates, members of village Panchayats, Jagirdars and Judges have been termed as Nyayadhisa. In the judicial hierarchy, the highest court was the Raja himself who usually transferred the appeals to the Wazir.

As regards Narendra Hindu Law, it was based on local customs and usages which were more or less common to the Kumaon Customary Law, compiled by Sir Panna Lal. However, the most interesting and peculiar features were the safeguards given for the 'Yajmani', i.e. profession of those Brahmins who performed religious rites and were given alms for it. The following clauses were enacted for this profession.[55]

Clause 460: Religious donations were of three types: first which were given to the Brahmins or their relations, second which were given to temples and monasteries, and the third which was given in the form of Sadāvrata,* popularly known as Sadāvarat.

Clause 461: Religious donations could be given to the Brahmins only and it was the foremost duty of different castes and communities to give alms to the Brahmins.

Brahmins who received these alms could be classed into three categories, first the family Brahmin or 'Purohit' who performed the religious rites, second, Brahmins who were priests of temples, and the third, those who performed religious rites during pilgrimage.

Clause 464: In Garhwal there are four main pilgrimage centres, Gangotri, Jumnotri, Badrinath, and Kedarnath. The 'Pandas' or priests of these religious shrines and their claims were hereditary. No 'Panda' was permitted to make an encroachment upon the territory of other 'Pandas'.

Clause 465: A 'Panda' who didn't have a male heir could bequeath his rights to a 'Ghar Jawain', i.e. son in law who stayed with him or to a legally adopted heir who should be of Brahmin descent or from the family of 'Pandas'.

Clause 466: To settle personal disputes, Pandas sought the help of law courts in the following cases:

i) If a 'Panda' performed religious rites of a family during pilgrimage with whom he did not have inherent connections by bluffing the family concerned that there was no Panda available of that family or beguiling the pilgrims by

---

Sadāvrata was the term applied to an endowment provided by land revenue of assigned villages for providing food to indigent pilgrims visiting the shrines of Badrinath and Kedarnath. (Walton, H.G.: op cit., p. 104).

posing as a legal heir of their family 'Panda' and to support his imposture by presenting a false family description
of the pilgrim's ancestry, whereas the genuine records were
available with the real 'Panda', or if he in any other way
harmed the real Panda through his notorious activities.

ii) When any individual who was not of a Panda lineage but
masqueraded as one and even practised the rites.

iii) When a 'Panda' performed the religious rites of a Sudra.

iv) When a 'Panda' accepted alms from a family for which he
was not entitled or for which he had no innate rights.

Clause 469: The family 'purohit' or priests were to be hereditary.

Clause 470: The priests of important temples in the State were
to be nominated by the temples trust, however quite a sizeable
number had inherited this position. The priests could be terminated on the following grounds:

i) If they resigned on their own account.

ii) If they were not knowledgeable and did not deserve to be
in that position.

iii) If they were found to be morally degenerate.

When there was a controversy regarding the legal heir of the
priest, then the trust was authorized to give decisions.

In the criminal side, the Indian Penal Code was in vogue with
a few additions or amendments to certain clauses, and was known
as the Tehri Garhwal State Penal Code. The clauses in which
there were some changes from the Indian Penal Code were as
follows:[56]

Clause 1: If a peasant disposed or mortagaged the land he
tilled or owned without prior permission of the Durbar, then
the parties involved were to be penalized and were given pecuniary punishments which could amount to Rs. 1000. The money
involved in the deal was confiscated, and as regards the disposed
or mortgaged land, orders for its release were issued from the
Durbar.

Clause 2: Any peasant who sold his land to an outsider without the Durbar's permission, could be held guilty and was

fined an amount which could be upto Rs. 1000. Cases of naturalization* were however excluded.

Clause 3: An individual who did not possess proprietary rights over an unmeasured piece of land but tried to enclose it with a fence or occupied and cultivated it without obtaining prior permission from the Durbar, he was considered guilty and could be fined upto Rs. 1000. Further that piece of land was also confiscated from him.

Clause 4: One who cultivated escheated land without obtaining permission from the Durbar would be given pecuniary punishment upto Rs. 500, and that land would also be confiscated. But if he was cultivating the land of a Maurusidar, who had left or died and who did not have a legal heir would not be regarded as guilty. However, he would have to tender information to the Durbar in that connection. If the Padhan of the village tried to hide facts he would be held guilty and could be fined upto Rs. 500.

Clause 5: Any person who divorced his wife or permitted divorce to a lady under his guardianship without going to the court and gave her in marriage, would be given a pecuniary punishment upto Rs. 2000. Further, that individual, who knowingly established nuptial relationship with the woman concerned who had not been divorced legally, would be subjected to a similar punishment.

Clause 5 ka: Any individual who divorced his wife or widow

*Naturalization: "The Tehri Garhwal State Naturalization Act came into force with retrospective effect from January 1, 1934. According to the Act, the Durbar could grant a certificate of naturalization to any person who is not already a state subject and who made an application on this behalf and satisfied the Durbar: (a) that he is a minor, (b) that he is of good character, (c) that he has an adequate knowledge of Garhwali or of Hindi language, (d) that he has during a period stated below for each case immediately preceding the date of application resided in Tehri Garhwal State, as a servant of the State for atleast 10 years, or carried any business or trade within the State for atleast 15 years, or cultivated land in the State as a Maurusidar for atleast 11 years or he possessed a house or property of the value of not less than Rs. 2,000 for 10 years, (e) that he intends, if the application is granted, to reside in Tehri Garhwal State or to enter or continue in the services of the State." (The Tehri Garhwal State Naturalization Act of 1934, pp. 1-2).

who was under his marital guardianship non-officially and did not pay the court fee, the party involved would be held guilty and could be fined upto Rs. 1000. If the divorcee claimed more money than actually spent, that extra amount would be confiscated.

Clause 6 ka addendum: (i) If a person without prior permission from the Durbar married his daughter or any girl under his guardianship to two or more than two persons or any individual who permitted his spouse to establish nuptial relationship with other men also, even if he was his real brother, the persons involved would be held guilty and could be subjected to pecuniary punishment, the limit of which could be upto Rs. 500.

(ii) This rule was implemented from October 1939. However, the polyandrous* marriages before that date were legalized.

(iii) It was the duty of the Padhan to tender information to the Patwari immediately about any polyandrous connections in his village, failing which he would be penalized and subjected to a fine whose limit could exceed upto Rs. 500.

Clause 6 kha: In those marital connections where nuptial expenses were to be defrayed by the groom; but before marriage if the engagement was broken and conjugal relations were established with a third party without obtaining permission from the court, then in that case the parties who were involved in giving and taking money for the girl's marriage would be fined, the limit of which could be upto Rs. 500.

Clause 6: One who married a woman about whom he knew that she had been discarded by her parents or husband, but had inherited money for her marriage and accepted the amount, the parties involved were given pecuniary punishment, the limit of which could be upto Rs. 500.

Amendment to Clause 6: Any person who took money in kind or cash on marrying an unmarried girl, widow or a legally divorced women would be sujected to pecuniary punishment, the limit of which could be upto Rs. 100.

However, there were following exceptions where financial assistance could be sought:

*Polyandry was prevalent only in the Jumna valley and the Ganga valley adjoining the Jumna region in Tehri Garhwal State.

i) For purchasing clothes and jewellery for the bride and groom which were accepted in the form of dowry.

ii) Money given to the priest for performing the conjugal rites.

iii) Rs. 100 as foodgrains of equal value for entertaining the marriage party.

iv) Money spent in the court in those cases where the bride was legally divorced from her first husband.

Clause 7: He who gave in marriage a girl or woman under his guardianship to someone:

a) who was not a citizen of the State or who had not taken a citizenship certificate under the Naturalization Act of Tehri State,

b) or who was a follower of different religion, without prior permission from the Durbar, then in that case both the parties were held guilty and could be subjected to either two years of imprisonment or a pecuniary punishment, or both.

The Padhan of the village or the Police Officer of the town who was aware of the situation but did not tender information to the Durbar, would also be held guilty and could be given one year's imprisonment or a fine of Rs. 500, or both.

Exception: (i) Nuptial relationship could be established outside the State only in the following places, British Garhwal, Jaunsar Babar, Rai Garh, Kyunthal, Rai, Bushar, and Jubbal, after observing complete rites and rituals.

ii) People from the plains or Kumaon who were in the services of the State or who were residing there as businessmen could marry outside the State but would perform all conjugal rites.

Clause 8: Any individual who tried to separate the calf of a buffalo or any other animal from its mother, or if he threw it with the intention of killing it, he would be held guilty and could be fined any amount upto Rs. 500.

Clause 9: He who did not comply with the rules of the Durbar and did not give 'Begar'* to the courtiers could be fined any amount upto Rs. 500.

*Coolie Begar: Under this system, the hill people had to work for the British officials on tour without payment. According to the Regulations of the Govt. of Fort Williams, Coolie Begar was the practice of pressing cer-

Clause 10: One who did not give 'Burdayash'** to the officials concerned or prevented other people from giving it, he could be fined or sentenced to two years imprisonment or could be subjected to both punishments.

Clause 11: Contrary to the prevalent custom any person who hit the first strike on the sacrificial male buffalo when not authorized for the same would be regarded as a criminal and could be fined an amount upto Rs. 500.

According to the custom the king struck the sacrificial animal first.

Clause 12: Against the customary precedence, the person who irrigated their land first from the irrigational feeder channel when not authorized for the same would be penalized and could be subjected to pecuniary punishment as well as imprisonment.

According to the custom, the water from the channel irrigated the fields of the Padhan first and then of the villagers.

Clause 120 ka: If two or more than two persons indulged in (i) any unlawful act, (ii) an act not unlawful but performed through unlawful means or caused other people's indulgence, it would be termed as a 'punishable conspiracy', but with the condition that until one or more such persons causing indulgence did not indulge in any other act, then the indulgence under clause (ii) of the order would not be termed as punishable conspiracy.

Clause 120 kha: If a person was an accomplice in a punishable conspiracy hatched to commit such an offence which was punishable with death, externment or rigorous imprisonment for two years and more, and if there was no specific punishment in the provisions for such a conspiracy, then the concerned persons would be sentenced to a punishment equivalent to persons for abetting the crime.

Clause 481 gha: If any individual who possessed a gadget or tried to sell or buy one with which currency notes could be coun-

---

tain classes of the inhabitants of the towns and villages under the denomination of begarees or coolies for the purpose of carrying baggage or other loads from stage or village to village. (The Regulations of the Government of Fort Williams, Volume II, Regulation III, p. 605).

**Coolie Burdayash*: According to this practice, free ration had to be supplied to the officials on tour, and the people were penalized if they failed to do so. (Stowell, V.A.: A Manual of the Land Tenures in Kumaon Division, p. 137).

terfeited, he would be sentenced to life imprisonment or 10 years imprisonment and could also be fined.

Clause 497: A man who had sexual intercourse with a married woman (whom he knew or on whom the woman could have had faith upon) without the permission of her husband, and the inter-course may not have reached to the limit of a rape, he would be held guilty of adultery and would be sentenced to imprisonment whose limit could be upto five years or he could be awarded a pecuniary punishment.

Clause 497 ka: One who had sexual intercourse with a widow or an unmarried girl without the permission of the guardian or the legal heir and the intercourse may not have reached to the limit of rape, would be charged of adultery and would be award-ed the punishment as mentioned in clause 497.

Clause 502 ka: If a person who had been assigned by custom the duty of playing the 'naubat', in villages on auspicious occa-sions, and if he did not do so as per custom with the intention that such a slip would amount to humiliation of that person in whose house the celebrations were taking place, he would be given either of the punishments, one month's imprisonment/penalty.

As regards the judicial set up in Tehri Garhwal State, it can be assumed that according to modern law and jurisprudence, it was faulty and inexhaustive. In the beginning, the king wielded all powers, civil, revenue, and criminal besides his administrative power. He had prerogative among the customary law and uses. Whatever he pronounced in his judgement became law and was unchallengeable. There was no procedural law as such.

It was during the reign of Kirti Shah that some changes were made by him. But still the king remained the Chief Justice of his State, wielding all powers of law within him which was against the norms of justice. The residents of Tehri Garhwal State were thus wholly at the mercy of the king; since every power was vested upon the Raja, one could not expect justice from him.

During the rule of Narendra Shah, laws were codified, especi-ally the Narendra Hindu Law, which was to an extent like the Kumaon Customary Law prevalent in British Garhwal. But that was also not a complete law because the supreme power was still vested in the king. Moreover, while language of the statutes remains unchanged from the date of enactment, the law grows through judicial process which was lacking in the State.

Further the laws were discriminating. To maintain his superiority the Raja gave importance to the priestly class and the Padhans. According to the Narendra Hindu Law, clause 461 which has been cited already, it was the foremost duty of different castes and communities to give alms to the Brahmins. Similarly in clause 12 of the Tehri Garhwal State Penal Code, it has been mentioned that according to customary precedence, the water from the irrigational channel irrigated first the fields of the Padhan and then of the villagers. One who did not adhere to this precedence was subjected to pecuniary punishment as well as imprisonment.

Police

Until the merger of the State with the Indian Union, the maintenance of law and order was the Raja's responsibility. However in Tehri Garhwal, people were by and large simple and honest, and even today there is a general absence of heinous crimes. Thus as in British Garhwal, the concept of police in Tehri State was that of revenue police, e.g., a Patwari had within his circle, the powers of the Police Officer incharge of a police station.[57] The village Padhan had also police powers. Pauw is of the view that the Padhan had the power to arrest those persons without any warrant who had committed serious crimes.[58]

The State Police Department functioned in its two divisions, the urban and the rural. According to the Administration Report of 1940-41, "The Rural Police consists of Patwaris as officers in charge of Police Stations in their respective Pattis."[59]

The concept of urban police came with the rule of Raja Pratap Shah. A regular Police Department was constituted for the first time in 1873 by Raja Pratap Shah and a police station was set up in Tehri. During the reign of Kirti Shah, to assure safety to the pilgrims, police sub-stations were established in different parts of the State.[60] The Police Department was divided into two branches, viz. the civil and armed police. The civil police* was posted

---

*By 1943, there were 5 police stations and 14 outposts all over the State. (The Annual Administration Report of Tehri Garhwal State for the year 1943-44, p. 6).

at Tehri, Pratap Nagar, Kirti Nagar, Muni ki Reti and Deo-prayag. The duty of the latter was to keep guard over the Jail, Treasury, and the Palace and was stationed at Tehri.[61]

Although theft was very rare, whenever a case occurred, police officials were not permitted to torture the accused. The administrative report of the State for the year 1918-19 vividly refers to it. According to the report,[62] "the working of the Police Department for the year is not satisfactory, recovery of stolen property is less and further there has been a case of torture by the police."

Jail Administration

There was only one jail in the State where prisoners were taught crafts like tailoring, blacksmithy, masonry, carpentry, etc. A few prisoners were also sent to the State forces as labourers.[63] The jail had its own printing press as well. The Annual Administration Report of 1940-41 has given an interesting detail of the prisoners in the jail for that year.[64]

Jail Population: "At the beginning of the year there were 56 prisoners in the jail. 113 prisoners came in the jail during the year. 169 is the highest number of prisoners who were in the jail, whereas in the previous years there were 194 prisoners. The daily average of prisoners in the year was 48 as against 52 of the last year. Out of that 169 prisoners who were the inmates of the jail, in the year, 109 were convicted for criminal offences, 46 were under trials, and 46 were civil prisoners who had been sent to jail in default of money decrees. During the year 114 prisoners were released from the jail at the expiration of their terms. At the end of the year there were 55 prisoners in the jail."

General Health: "The general health of the prisoners throughout the year was good. There is an indoor dispensary in the central jail, under the charge of the Medical Officer, Civil Hospital, Tehri, who daily visits the jail. No epidemic broke out in the jail. There were no deaths by any diseases or accident in the jail."

Jail Industries: "Long term prisoners are employed in indoor industries, such as manufacture of Pahari (hill) paper from Satphura which is very durable and is used for Land Record Documents, printing press and the making of ropes and mats, and tailoring and smithy works. The short term prisoners do the gardening work within the jail compound, in the jail gardens and the State gardens at Tehri."

Education

Before the rule of Bhawani Shah, there were no educational institutions in the State. During his rule Sanskrit 'Pathshalas', (schools) were opened to educate the people.[65] English education was introduced into the State by Raja Pratap Shah when in 1883 he established the Anglo Vernacular Middle School in Tehri. In 1891, it grew into a High School. On 31st March 1908, the total number of students in Pratap High School was 253. In 1940, this school was raised to an Intermediate College,[66] and in the year 1943-44, there were 248 boys on rolls of the college as against 241 in the previous year. The college sent up 21 students for the High School examinations and 11 boys for the Intermediate examinations. The percentage of pass was 95.2 and 27.3 respectively. The college staff consisted of 17 teachers including eight M.A.'s of whom six were B.T.'s.

The system of education was akin to that in British India. All Sanskrit, Hindi and English institutions in the State were affiliated to Boards of different examinations in U.P. and the same standard of efficiency was maintained as was laid down by the above educational bodies.[67]

Upto 1901 only 2.2% of the population was able to read and write. That year there were five primary schools with 303 pupils. The number however was steadily increasing. In 1880-81, there were only three schools with 203 students.[68] By 1935 the number of primary schools had increased to 260.

According to the Annual Administration Report of Tehri Garhwal State for the year 1943-44, it is evident that the Durbar was making constant endeavours to eradicate illiteracy and in order to achieve this end, free education was imparted in the State's, lower, upper and middle classes. A number of scholarships were given to poor students at the primary and middle level and the Durbar also awarded stipends to promising students for higher education as well as for industrial training in foreign countries. In addition to the above, to espouse the cause of education, aid was given to other educational and vocational institutions in and outside the State.

There was a fine network of primary schools both State owned and aided, spread over the whole State. Even in parganas Rawain and Jaunpur, the polyandrous belt, where the people had natural apathy towards education previously, there were 26 State owned schools besides a large number of private schools. The total number of primary schools both State owned and private was 270 in 1944 as against 268 in the previous year, and the number of teachers was 277. The total number of students on rolls during the year in primary schools above was 8,501. The number of students who appeared in the primary examinations was 727 out of which 623 were declared successful.

Besides the Pratap Anglo Middle School which formed part of the Pratap Intermediate College and the above mentioned primary schools, there were 6 Hindi Middle Schools, 2 Sanskrit Colleges, 1 Carpentry School, 1 Weaving School for boys, and 1 Lower Middle School for girls. There was a Teachers' Training School at Tehri which trained primary school teachers in teaching methods.

There were altogether 9,518 students in all the institutions over the State during the year 1944 as against 8,387 in the previous year. Of these 248 were on the rolls of the Pratap Intermediate College. In the middle section there were 769 students and 43 teachers. The number which these schools sent for vernacular final examination was 106 out of which 59 came out successful.

The Sanskrit institutions of Shri Kirti Pathshala, Uttarkashi and Hewett Pathshala, Tehri sent 16 students for the Prathama and Madhyama Examinations of the Benares University out of which 6 passed in Prathama and 5 in Madhyama Examinations.

For the education of girls, the Maharani Kanya Pathshala was started. It imparted education including needle work and sewing upto lower middle standard. It had 69 girls on its rolls as in 1944 against 83 of the previous year and it sent 9 girls for the final examination of whom 6 passed and 4 secured first division.

General health of the students in all the institutions was reported to be satisfactory and good discipline was maintained.

During the year 1943-44, the expenditure on education was Rs. 90,327 as compared to Rs. 1,05,256 of the previous year. This amount included Rs. 29,235 on the scholarships awarded by the Durbar and excluded several stipends that were given from the Privy Purse.

Medical

In the beginning only ayurvedic medicines were prescribed. The first allopathic hospital was opened in the State in 1866. By 1901 there were two hospitals. The most common endemic which infested the people was small pox. Plague was not heard of. During the reign of Kirti Shah, to put a check on small pox, he appointed vaccinators throughout the State and dispensaries were opened on pilgrim routes.[69] Statistics is available of the people vaccinated from 1906 to 1910. In 1906-1907, 10,315 people were vaccinated and 13,319 in 1907-1908. In 1908-1909, the total number vaccinated was 13,869 which rose upto 14,274 in 1909-1910.[70]

When Narendra Shah came to the helm of affairs, the Tehri Garhwal Rajya Teeka Vidhan was passed in 1943, with the intention of eradicating small pox completely. According to the Act, it was essential for the parents to get their infants vaccinated when they were eight months old. Then upto the age of 14, it was regarded as the duty of the parents to take their children to the vaccinators personally and get them vaccinated after every two years, failing which they were fined an amount which varied from Rs. 50 to Rs. 100.[71]

During his rule, several other important measures were undertaken. By 1925, hospitals had been established in Tehri, Deoprayag and Uttarkashi. In 1925 Hailey Hospital was opened at Narendra Nagar by him and fresh dispensaries were started in different parts of the State. The Red Cross Society was instituted at Narendra Nagar in 1934 and Narendra Shah became its first director. It had two branches, one looked after the welfare of the expectant mothers and the other cared for the poor and destitute.[72] In 1939, the Tehri Garhwal Rajya Kusth Vidhan was passed according to which a leper had to be certified that he was suffering from leprosy by a qualified doctor and then he was admitted to the Srinagar Leprosy Centre which was aided by the State.[73]

According to the Annual Progress Report of the year 1941-42, the total number of medical institutions run by the Durbar was 22. In 1943, the number had increased to 23. Out of these there were 4 hospitals, 3 dispensaries and 16 rural Ayurvedic Aushadhalayas. All these were staffed by trained and qualified doctors and 'vaids'. The 'vaids' were given first aid training and were trained to give injections, inoculations etc.

Clinical work of all hospitals and dispensaries was done at the Headquarter Clinical Laboratory, Narendra Nagar. The whole staff consisted of the Chief Medical Officer, one Lady Assistant Surgeon, 3 Sub Assistant Surgeons, 3 hospital Assistants, 1 Inspector of Vaccination and Aushdhalayas and 16 'vaids', besides a number of 'dais' and compounders.

The following table will show the work done on the allopathic side.

Particulars	1943-44	1942-43
Total number of patients treated	45,063	48,453
Total number of indoor patients	760	760
Total number of major operations	70	56
Total number of minor operations	1,739	1,410

This report of 1943-44 has given other details also which gives us a vivid picture of the working of this department.

There were 10 deaths amongst the indoor patients as compared to 18 of the preceding year and the medico-legal post mortems performed by medical officers were 25 as against 10 of the previous year.

The daily average attendance of patients in the allopathic institutions was 123.47 whereas it was 140.9 during the preceding year.

On the Ayurvedic side the work is shown below:

Particulars	1943-44	1942-43
Total number of patients treated	19,329	22,658
Total number of minor surgical operations	305	579

The daily average attendance of patients in the Ayurvedic dispensaries was 11.6.

There were 10,196 births in 1943-44 as against 11,547 registered during the preceding year. The total deaths were 6,250 as against 7,254 recorded during the previous year. The rates of births and deaths per thousand were 25.8 and 15.6 respectively as against 21.5 and 13.5 of the preceding year.

There was an outbreak of plague in 1943-44 in the villages Sar and Leutari in pargana Rawain. There were 16 seizures and all of them ended in deaths. Medical aid was promptly sent; 601 anti-plague inoculations were given and 148 houses were disinfected. There was no other serious outbreak of epidemics.

The total number of people vaccinated during the year under report were 10,846 as against 9,196 of the previous year. The percentage of successful vaccinations to total vaccinations and re-vaccinations given were 95.35 and 72.6 respectively. The number of chidren under one year and 1 to 6 years who underwent successful primary vaccination was 3,510 and 4,727 respectively as compared to 3,310 and 4,334 of the previous year.

The total expenditure incurred during the year was Rs. 34,197 as against Rs. 23,767 in the previous year.

Communication

It was during the rule of Sudarshan Shah that the Haridwar Gangotri road was constructed.[74] In 1905-1906 a Public Works Department was established in the State for the construction and renovation of roads.[75] Later the village and town Panchayats were also entrusted with this duty. During the rule of Kirti Shah, the Imperial Service Sappers was constituted, it was manned by 170 people and its chief function was bridge and road construction.

In 1921, Rishikesh was linked by a motor road with Narendra Nagar. Later this motor road was connected with Tehri. In 1937, the Rishikesh-Deoprayag and in 1938, the Deoprayag-Kirti Nagar Motor roads were constructed. By 1940, the important motor roads in the State were, Rishikesh-Narendra Nagar, 53 miles and Rishikesh-Deoprayag-Kirti Nagar, 63 miles.

There were forest roads also. According to the Administrative Report of 1939-40, the total length of forest roads in the State were 809 miles.

Post and Telegraph

Postal service was started as early as 1873 when the first post office was opened in Tehri. Runners were appointed those days who carried the post rapidly.[76] A cess called the Dak cess was levied with which the postal service was gradually extended to different parts. According to the Annual Progress Report of the year 1943-44, by that year, there were 10 British Indian post Offices in the State to serve an inhabited area of about 4,000 square miles and a population of over 5,00,000 people. So according to this, on an average, a post office in the State served about 400 square miles and 50,000 people. This clearly shows that the postal service in the State was not at all adequate. The report further says that.

"It is hoped that the postal authorities will soon consider the question of opening more post offices. This need has been felt very keenly by the relations of people on active service. News takes a long time to reach and in order to receive money orders they have to travel long distances. The Durbar has got its own system of local dak between various administrative headquarters of their main offices, in the headquarters and in different parts of the State. Though this system is open to public it does not afford full facilities owing to its limitations as it is not linked with the British post offices."

There were 2 telegraph offices at Narendra Nagar and Tehri. The Narendra Nagar telegraph office was State owned. The State had a local telephone system also which connected important and central places for the facility of official business only.[77]

Local Self Government

Municipalities: There were no big towns in the State but at important places, viz., Tehri, Narendra Nagar, Deoprayag, Kirti Nagar, Muni ki Reti and Uttarkashi local bodies had been constituted under the State Municipal and Town Areas Act No. 3 of Samvat 1981, i.e., 1924 A.D. Most of these places lay on the pilgrim routes to the holy shrines of Uttarakhand where thousands of pilgrims thronged during the pilgrim season every year. These local bodies looked after sanitation.

Patti Panchayats: Panchayat Raj had been introduced in the

State quite early and to ensure better working of these local bodies in the towns and villages, a number of laws were framed by the rulers of Tehri Garhwal State based on ancient customs and traditions. Some of the important laws relating to the local bodies were the Village Panchayat Act No. 1 of 1922. Nagar Panchayat Vidhan of 1924, Prant Panchayat Vidhan 1930, Nagar Tatha Pur Panchayat Vidhan 1932, and Prant Panchayat Vidhan 1938.

There were Nagar Panchayats for the towns of Tehri, Narendra Nagar and Deoprayag, Pur Panchayats for smaller townships of Kirti Nagar and Muni ki Reti and Gram Panchayats for rural areas. There used to be a president and a number of elected and nominated members for each of these Panchayats. The Panchayats were entrusted with the management of works of local interests like sanitation, construction and renovation of buildings,[78] street lighting, provisions of drinking water, supervision of village schools, distribution of the pay of teachers[79] and to check deforestation. The Soyam Jungle or the III Class Forests were in the hands of the Patti or Prant Panchayats. They were also given minor judicial powers. The entire expenditure of the Panchayats was met by the State revenue and the income was deposited in the State treasury.

Management of the Sources of Living

In Tehri Garhwal State agriculture supported a vast majority of the population, approximately 92%. A few people were however associated with the making of baskets, woollen blankets, carpentry and masonry.[80] Other sources of income were pilgrim traffic, trade with Tibet, cattle breeding, labour in the reserved forests of Bhabhar] and domestic services in hill stations. Pauw is of the view that, "Tibetan trade offered employment to thousands in the most sterile parts of Garhwal and provided a market for produce in the same region thus encouraging agriculture."[81] Through Garhwal, the easiest road to Tibet was secured by the British which opened for the merchants all prospects for developing trade.[82] Imports as early as 1876-77 were horses, cattle, borax, salt, wool and gold. Exports included woollen cloth, gram, spices and sugar.[83] Internal trade as well as trade with the plains of British India was also important. Chief exports to British occupied territory were ghee, potato, fruit, timber, medicinal herbs, lime, limestone, gypsum and other forest produce. Chief imports included sugar, gur, salt, tobacco, kerosene oil, metals and cloth.[84]

Pilgrim trade was an important source of income and with the opening of the Najibabad Railway the number of pilgrims increased enormously. As early as 1896, the total earning from pilgrims was Rs. 5 lakhs. The main income on the pilgrim routes those days was from 'Chattis' (halting and resting places which were maintained at intervals of 2 to 8 miles. A chatti was like a verandah with arrangements for cooking and a shop which supplied provisions at reasonable prices. The pilgrims welcomed the security of the 'chattis' where they rested before commencing the onward journey.

Forest labour which was also an important mode of earning was plentiful during the winter season when most of the work was carried out. During the rains and harvest time a certain amount of difficulty was met with, and the wages went upto 12 annas per day as compared to 8 annas a day, the usual rates per individual.[85] A small number took to forest contracts.

The most considerable cash income of the population was derived from services in the plains and hill stations, recruitment in the army, police and para forces. However with the opening of the cantonment at Lansdowne in 1887, a sizeable number was diverted to the forces though the recruitment of the Garhwalis in the army had started even earlier. Sir Frederick Roberts who took over command in India in November 1885 had long held a very high opinion of the soldierly qualities of the hill men in Garhwal of which there were some in every Gurkha unit by then. He added that he had been looking the matter up and found that out of the rank and file of the Gurkha Regiments decorated with the Indian Order of Merit, a very large proportion of men were Garhwalis. Thus in April 1871, the first, and in December 1890, the second battalion of the Garhwal Rifles were raised.[86] The payment to Garhwali officers and men aggregated over a lakh of rupees yearly those days and the amount which steadily poured in materially affected the wealth of the people, and the material standards of the people went up. Gradually with the passage of time other battalions of the Garhwalis were raised owing to which the monetary status of the military families was further elevated. It is interesting to note that in the food distress of 1917 which hit Garhwal, the Garhwali troops from both British Garhwal and Tehri Garhwal State, contributed over Rs. 10,000.[87]

Miscellaneous

Representative Assembly: The administration of the State was carried out by the king with the help of the Executive Council, the Secretaries and the Representative Assembly. The Wazir of the State used to be the Chief Executive Officer. The advice of the executive members in important subjects and matters of policy was taken by the king individually or collectively. The budget was passed by the Executive Council. There was a Chief Secreaty in the State and during the time of Raja Narendra Shah a Chief Justice was appointed in the High Court. Ganga Prasad Rastogi who was working as the Chief Judge of the Chief Court, was appointed the first Chief Justice of the High Court in Tehri Garhwal State.

The Representative Assembly constituted of 35 members, 20 of whom were elected, 15 from the rural areas and 5 from the urban, 4 non officials were nominated by the king to represent the minorities and 11 were nominated officials. Until 1938, the President of the Representative Assembly used to be an official nominated by the king but since that year during the Holi session, the king nominated one of the elected members as its President. The king also appointed an elected member to the Council of Ministers.

The State Forces: During the rule of Kirti Shah a miners and sappers force was established by reorganizing the State military. This force was used in peaceful times for the construction of roads and bridges. The State Sappers and Miners did meritorious services in the First Great War in France and Mesopotamia and later in the 3rd Afghan War. On both occasions they earned laurels and were highly praised by the Commander-in-Chief of the Indian Army. During the Second World War, the Tehri Garhwal State's Sappers and Miners, Field Service Coy. and No. 1209 Tehri Indian Auxillary Pioneer Company were deployed in Burma and Europe on active duty and their work was highly appreciated.[88]

Store Purchase Department: There was a departmental agency for sale and purchase of Durbar stores. The State's requirements of controlled articles were purchased and entrusted to this department for distribution and sale to different parts according to the quota sanctioned by the Durbar. The services rendered by this department were of immense help to the inhabitants. This department also worked as a purchase agency for certain foodgrains such as wheat, rice, barley grain etc. for the public.

Garden and Horticulture Department: This department was established to promote horticulture. The Superintendent of the Garden and Horticulture Department and his staff members looked after the State gardens, toured the State and advised people to layout fruit gardens, and supplied seeds of vegetables and fruits to the villagers.

Trout Fish: The Ganga Bhilangana Forest Division ran two hatcheries at Kaldiyani and Kaudiya and the breeding in these hatcheries met with considerable success. In the Jamuna Tons Forest Division the only stock in the Gangar tank was planted in the river.

Exploitation of Minor Forest Produce: The items of minor forest produce which were sources of revenue consisted of the following contracts:[89] charcoal, fuel, lime, grass, drift and waff wood, fishing, and bamboos.

REFERENCES

1. The Annual Administration Report of Tehri Garhwal State, for the year 1945-46, p. 2.
2. Tehri Garhwal State Records, File No. 220/1905, p. 3.
3. The Annual Administration Report of Tehri Garhwal State, for the year 1943-44, p. 24.
4. The Annual Administration Report of Tehri Garhwal State, for the year 1938-39, p. 2.
5. The Annual Administration Report of Tehri Garhwal State, for the year 1945-46, p. 2.
6. Rizvi, Saiyid Ali Akhtar: Uttar Pradesh District Gazetteers (Tehri Garhwal), pp. 78-79.
7. Doval, Ram Prasad: Revenue Settlement Report, Tehri Garhwal Rajya Babat, Samvat 1980, pp. 105-106.

8. Raturi, H.K.: Garhwal Varnan, pp. 150-51.
9. *Garhwali*, November 1913, p. 276.
10. Pargana Pratap Nagar, Jila Tehri Garhwal ki Assessment Report, 1924, p. 3.
11. *Garhwali*, November 1913, pp. 269-70.
12. Uniyal. Bhairav Dutt: The Annual Administrative Report of the Tehri Garhwal State for the year 1918-19, p. 2.
13. Burh, R.: Census of India, 1901, Volume XVI, Part I, N.W. P. and Oudh, p. 42.
14. The Annual Administration Report of Tehri Garhwal State, for the year 1938-39, p. 1.
15. The Annual Administration Report of Tehri Garhwal State, for the year 1945-46, p. 3.
16. The Annual Administration Report of Tehri Garhwal State, for the years 1943-44 and 1945-46, p. 3 and p. 2.
17. Tehri Garhwal Rajya ke Bhumi Sambandhi Adhikar Niyam Tatha Vidhan, pp. 2-3.
18. Settlement Letters Issued 1839 to 1842, Volume II, Letter No. 56, dated 7th September 1839, State Archives, Lucknow.
19. Settlement Letters Issued 1837 to 1839, Vol. 1, Letter No. 3, State Archives, Lucknow.
20. Powell, B.H. Baden: The Land System of British India, Vol. II, p. 273.
21. Moreland, W.H.: The Revenue Administration of the United Provinces, p. 736.
22. Beckett, J.O.B.: Report on the Settlement of Kumaon, p. 10.
23. Stowell, V.A.: A Manual of the Land Tenures of Kumaon Division, p. 118.
24. Atkinson, E.T.: Himalayan Gazetteer, Vol. III, pp. 498-99.
25. Varma, V.P.S.: Working Plan for Tehri Forest Division, 1973-74 to 1982-83, p. 61.
26. Report of the Kumaon Forest Fact Finding Committee, p. 22.
27. The Annual Administration Report of Tehri Garhwal State, for the year 1939-40, pp. 24-25.
28. Tehri Garhwal State Records (Political Agent for Tehri State) No. G-30-8/Tehri, Letter No. C. 59, dated 12th February, 1927.

29. Khosla, Prem Nath: Working Plan for the Tehri Forest Division, 1939-40 to 1969-70, p. 29.
30. Pant, K.P.: Working Plan for the Tons Forest Division, 1945-46 to 1964-65, p. 16.
31. Raturi, Padma Dutt: Working Plan for the Uttarkashi Forest Division, 1938, p. 40.
32. Heske, Franz: Problem Der Walderhaltung in Himalaya, Tharandter Forestlichen Jahrbuch, 1931, Volume 82, No. 8, p. 553.
33. The Annual Administration Report of Tehri Garhwal State, for the year 1938-39, p. 2.
34. Saklani, Indra Dutt: Tehri Garhwal Rajya Forest Manual, p. 31.
35. Raturi, H.K.: Annual Report of the Tehri Garhwal State, for the year 1909-10, p. 6.
36. The Annual Administration Report of Tehri Garhwal State, for the year 1943-44, p. 11.
37. Tehri Garhwal Rajya Forest Manual, p. 31.
38. Typed copy of 'Niyam Babat Marne Shikar va Machhli', dynastic collection of Tehri Durbar, pp. 1-10.
39. Tehri Garhwal Rajya Forest Manual, p. 39.
40. *Indian Forester*, December 1942, pp. 631-33.
41. Annual Progress Report of Forest Administration in U.P. for the years 1957-58, 1958-59, and 1959-60, p. 24, p. 21 and p. 32.
42. Annual Progress Report of Forest Administration in U.P. for the years 1963-64, 1965-66, p. 53 and p. 33.
43. Tehri Garhwal State Records, F.No. 42/1907, Letter No. 46, and F.No. 247/1930, Letter No. 2513.
44. The Annual Administration Report of Tehri Garhwal State, for the year 1943-44, p. 11.
45. The Annual Administration Report of Tehri Garhwal State, for the year 1918-19, p. 10.
46. Personal communication, Thakur Shoor Beer Singh, former Home Secretary, Tehri Garhwal State.
47. Parmar, Pati Ram: Garhwal Ancient and Modern, pp. 221-222.
48. *Garhwali*, January 1912, p. 160, and November 1913, p. 270.
49. Personal communication, Jai Krishna Raturi, former Peshkar in the State.

50. The Annual Administration Report of Tehri Garhwal State, for the year 1940-41, p. 6.
51. The Annual Administration Report of Tehri Garhwal State, for the years 1938-39, and 1940-41, p. 7 and p. 5.
52. The Annual Administration Report of Tehri Garhwal State, for the year 1940-41, p. 7.
53. Tehri Garhwal Rajya Nagar tatha Pur Panchayat Vidhan, 1932, p. 25.
54. The Annual Administration Report of Tehri Garhwal State, for the year 1940-41, p. 7.
55. Narendra Hindu Law, pp, 784-802.
56. Tehri Garhwal State Penal Code, pp. 169-92.
57. Rules and Orders relating to Kumaon Division, p. 161.
58. Pauw, E.K.: Report on the Tenth Settlement of Garhwal District, p. 34.
59. The Annual Administration Report of Tehri Garhwal State, for the year 1940-41, p. 9.
60. *Garhwali*, January 1912, p. 165, and November 1913, p. 265.
61. Raturi, H.K.: Annual Administrative Report of Tehri Garhwal State 1909-10, p. 4.
62. Uniyal, B.D.: Annual Administrative Report of Tehri Garhwal State, 1918-19, p. 6.
63. H.K. Raturi: op. cit., 1909-10, p. 5.
64. The Annual Administration Report of Tehri Garhwal State, 1940-41, p. 11.
65. *Garhwali*, November 1913, p. 252.
66. Raja Narendra Shah's Biography (Dynastic collection, Tehri), p. 2.
67. The Annual Administration Report of Tehri Garhwal State, for the year 1943-44, pp. 18-19.
68. Burh, R.: Census of India, 1901, Volume XVI, N.W.P. and Oudh, Part 1, p. 272.
69. Shastri, H.D.: Tehri Garhwal Tirth Varnan, p. 79.
70. Raturi, H.K.: Annual Administrative Report of Tehri Garhwal State, 1907-1908, p. 9, and 1909-10, p. 10.
71. Tehri Garhwal Rajya ka Teeka Vidhan, pp. 3-4.
72. Raja Narendra Shah's Biography (Dynastic collection, Tehri), p. 2.

73. Tehri Garhwal Rajya Kusth Vidhan, p. 1.
74. *Garhwali*, November 1913, p. 265.
75. Sinha, Hari: Annual Administrative Report for Tehri Garhwal State, 1905-1906, p. 6.
76. *Garhwali*, November 1913, p. 273.
77. The Annual Administration Report of Tehri Garhwal State, for the year 1943-44, pp. 13-14.
78. Tehri Garhwal Rajya Nagar tatha Pur Panchayat Vidhan, 1932, pp. 11-25.
79. Tehri Garhwal Rajya Prant Panchayat Manual, pp. 15-17.
80. Jila Tehri Garhwal ka Audyogik Drishtikon, Prativedan, 1956, p. 49.
81. Pauw, E.K.: Report on the Tenth Settlement of Garhwal District, p. 107.
82. Ramakant: Indo Nepalese Relations, 1816 to 1877, p. 37.
83. Report on the Administration of N.W. Provinces for the year 1876-77, p. 109.
84. The Annual Administration Report of Tehri Garhwal State, for the year 1945-46, p. ii.
85. Brahmawar, R.N.: Working Plan for the Garhwal Forest Division, 1928-29 to 1937-38, p. 10.
86. Woodyatt, Major General Nigel G. (ed.): The Regimental History of the Third Queen Alexandra's Own Gurkha Rifles 1815-1927, pp. 53-54.
87. (1) The Report of the Working of the Garhwal Central Scarcity Committee, p. 1.
    (2) The Annual Administration Report of Tehri Garhwal State, for the year 1938-39, pp. 2-5.
88. The Annual Administration Report of Tehri Garhwal State, for the years 1940-41, and 1943-44, p. 10 and p. 5.
89. The Annual Administration Report of Tehri Garhwal State, for the year 1935-36, p. 19.

7

Political Movements in Tehri Garhwal State

As regards the British motive of annexing Garhwal, most of the authors on border studies have highlighted the prospects of Indo-Tibetan trade through this terrain. "Prospects of trade with Tibet through the passes of Kumaon and Garhwal led the British to annex this area."[1] Ramakant[2] and Sewak[3] have supported this view. As is well known, Mana and Niti passes in Garhwal were the traditional routes to Tibet, and interestingly enough Indo-Tibetan trade was an important source of income of the Garhwalis even during the Parmar rulers of unified Garhwal.

Ram Rahul has advocated a different view. He observes, ". . . the need to check the growth of Russian influence in Central Asia and the isolationist nature of the policies of Tibet largely moulded the British policy in the Himalayas."[4] The attitude of the British Government towards Tibet, he has further remarked, was that, it had no desire to annex the country or control its administration. Its sole interest was that Russia should not bring Tibet within its sphere of influence, since that could have involved a slight, though by no means a serious threat to India's security. India's policy towards Tibet was determined by the view that wider the barrier of mountainous and roadless country between Russia and the Indian frontiers, the better. This strategic requirement was satisfied by Younghusband's* mission to Tibet.[5] The explorations of Pandit Nain Singh and Kishan Singh also

*Younghusband was posted in the King's Dragon Guards Regiment. He was a great explorer and had been the President of the Royal Geographical Society of England (Younghusband, Francis: Wonders of the Himalayas, p. 1).

allude to the British design over Tibet. Nain Singh's first famous journey was from Kathmandu to Lhasa and thence to Mansarovar Lake and back to India in 1865-66. His last journey to Lhasa was conducted in the years 1873-75. Kishan Singh's first important journey to Lhasa was performed in 1872 and the last during 1878 and 1882.[6]

In the 19th century, Assam border was of little use for Tibet. Geographically Western Tibet was nearest to the Russian territory and its position gave it a great political importance.[7]

The route to Tibet through Garhwal was known to the Europeans as early as 1624 A.D. C' Wessels is of the view that the same year, Father Antonio de Andrade, a Jesuit missionary visited Tsaprang in Tibet via Garhwal. The aim of the Jesuit's visit was to spread Christianity, as is evident from Andrade's travel account. He laid the foundation of a Church at Tsaprang on 11th April, 1626 A.D.[8] Andrade's journey to Tsaprang through Garhwal is confirmed by another author, Sir Edward Maclagan.[9] It's possible that even before 1624 A.D., the Garhwalis had access to Tibet, because Moorcraft has mentioned that the Rajas of Garhwal claimed tribute from some parts in Tibet.[10] Moorcraft had visited Tehri Garhwal State on 6th February, 1820.[11]

It seems that in the initial stages, it was the Indo-Tibetan trade which inspired the British to annex Kumaon and Garhwal. In the later phase owing to its geo-political advantages, this terrain assumed a new importance for the alien rulers. The British commercial motive is vividly realized by a letter dated 16th September, 1802, in which the British had resolved to hold a trade fair from 9th November 1802 to 8th December 1802 in Kashipur.[12]

On the basis of the above authors, the strategic importance of Garhwal can be well visualized. Through Garhwal, the British had occupied one of the most important tracts of the N.W. Frontier line, and thus while administering this terrain the strategic importance of Garhwal was kept in view. To maintain a friendly area in the North, the British administered in consonance with this view and to win over the people in British Garhwal, they did not tamper with the local traditions and emotions whenever possible.

The attitude of British administration towards British Garhwal was reflected in Tehri Garhwal State as well. Keeping in view its strategic importance, the British it seems wanted to have a strong hold over this pocket by a shrewd admixture of respect for the king and the threat of taking over control. Hence the status quo of the king was maintained but he was hinted discreetly at the British capabilities of take over. The Sunud of 10th December, 1824 investitured to the then king, Raja Sudarshan Shah of Tehri Garhwal State is a clear testimony to the British motive. According to it, ".... as long as the Raja of Tehri Garhwal is faithful, the Governor General is pleased to bestow upon him, the territory known as Tehri Garhwal State."[13] Raja Sudarshan Shah whose father had lost his kingdom to the Gurkhas, had been reinstalled in Tehri Garhwal State by the British and was at their mercy; though the help extended to him was a shrewd move by the British. They were well aware of the fact that his ancestors, the Parmars had been ruling the whole of Garhwal since the 14th century and were regarded as the reincarnation of Badrinath by their subjects. Thus through the divine halo of the king it was easier to win over the loyalty of his subjects.

Further to cement this loyalty indirect methods were adopted, e.g., Raja Sudarshan Shah who did not have a son was being threatened since 1824 that his territory would lapse after his death.[14] In 1848 the king was further terrorised regarding the succession issue.[15] However, he was later permitted to adopt a successor.

Similarly, Rawain was made a disturbed zone by the British. The British knew that the people of this area had cultural affinities with Jaunsar region. In 1815 with the British annexation, Rawain was with Dehradun and Jaunsar. But in 1824, it was ceded to Tehri Garhwal State.[16] The people were interested to be reverted to British rule and the Superintendent of Dehradun also recommended their case which is vividly evidenced from his letter of 22nd August 1833, to the Government.[17] But the recommendation was condoned and resentment prevailed over that area[18] which reached its acme in the 20th century in the form of Rawain Incident.

The administration of Tehri Garhwal State was essentially a prototype of British Garhwal in theory and practice. The kings adopted similar revenue and other administrative policies and thus indirectly implemented the policy of divide and rule. In fact through Padhans, Thokdars and Kanungos, posts which were inherent, they encouraged the perpetuation of traditional hegemony in order to form a group loyal to them and isolated from the rural folk. Appointment of a son in place of his retiring or deceased father transmitted the doubtful benefit of skills at the family level, the obvious result of which was concentration of power the most important asset of rural population, the land, and to groups, closely identifiable with and evidently loyal to the establishment. Mention worthy is that though they definitely introduced certain reformatory measures like establishing an agriculture bank to help the peasants, abolition of the practice of keeping Harijan slaves in 1878,[19] sale of poor and low caste women in the plains,[20] tendering help during famines, opening a house for the poor and destitute etc., to solve contemporary problems, but not unlike their counterparts, the administrators of British Garhwal, the kings too were a fiasco with the problems of forestry and Coolie Begar, and these two issues ultimately fomented political dissent. The Tehri Garhwal State's policy of forest preservation was widely misunderstood and the first shock against this policy was felt on 26th December 1906, when the villagers of Bangarh, just adjacent to Tehri town singed the conservator of forest, though their intention was to burn him alive.[21]

Like Kumaon Commissionery the practice of Coolie Begar, Coolie Utar etc. prevailed in Tehri Garhwal State also.

Coolie Begar: Under this system the hill people had to work for the officials on tour without payment.[22]

Coolie Utar: When the officials toured the hills it was regarded as the duty of the local people to provide Coolie Utar. Coolie Utar was compulsory, and the status and condition of the individual concerned who was subjected to the system was not kept in view.[23] In the State, Coolie Utar was of two types, 'Choti Burdayash' and 'Bade Burdayash'.

According to Choti Burdayash, the people had to manage coolies for carrying the luggage of the courtiers and the State guests; everyone except for a few people from the higher class and caste had to pay Choti Burdayash and it was fixed according to the revenue assessed. In certain cases people were exempted from Choti Burdayash by paying money.[24]

When coolies were arranged for the royal household, the royal guests, political agents and for the officials of the Political Department, then it was known as Bade Burdayash. In 1930, the name Bade Burdayash was changed and it was popularized as Prabhu Sewa. Unlike Choti Burdayash, in the initial stages there could be no exemption from Bade Burdayash on grounds of money, class or status. Only women and the impecunious were an exception. But duing the rule of the later kings, one could be exempted from Prabhu Sewa on pecuniary grounds or by giving foodgrains. Every family had to tender Prabhu Sewa four times a year. Prabhu Sewa like Choti Burdayash was free of cost.[25]

Apart from Burdayash the State officials were entitled to take foodgrains free of cost on tour, which was known as 'Bura'. For each official this quota was fixed.[26] In the neighbouring Kumaon Commissionery, the system was slightly different. There, 3 pies per rupee was levied extra with the revenue and this tax was known as 'Buniya Dubal' and the amount thereby collected was given to those merchants who provided foodgrains free in the Government camps and to Government officials on tour.[27] Then there was the custom of 'Dasturi'. Under this head came all those taxes which were unrecorded.[28]

However there were certain other factors together with the forest policy and the social maladies of Coolie Begar etc. which aggravated the feeling of resentment amongst the hill people.

Politically, Tehri Garhwal State was backward as compared to the neighbouring Kumaon region. Whatever occurred in the two districts of Almora and Naini Tal, its echoes were sounded in British Garhwal and then they resonated in Tehri Garhwal State.

In Kumaon Commissionery the first uprising was in 1857. After that there was a political vacuum. In 1912[29] with the opening of a branch of the Congress Party in Kumaon, the people tried to associate themselves with the national stream of consciousness. In 1914, a branch of the Home Rule League was started in Almora.[30] Later in 1916, the Kumaon Parishad was established in Naini Tal. Its main objective was to discuss political, economic and social problems in the hills. In 1914, Prem Sabha was established in Kashipur (District Naini Tal). It was a branch of the Nagari Pracharani Sabha. Before that in 1913, Swami Satyadeva had started the Shuddha Sahitya Samiti in Almora. In 1935, Bal

Sabha was established in Tehri Garhwal and in 1939 the Tehri Rajya Praja Mandal in Dehradun. In 1940's the Deoprayag Library, Saraswati Vidyalaya and the Himalaya Vidyapeeth were established in Garhwal. The main objective of all these organizations was to infuse the spirit of nationalism.

Press was an important media which struck at the roots of the establishment. In 1871, the Debating Club of Almora started the publication of Almora Akhbar.[31] Before 1913, it gave local news mainly but that year when Pandit Badri Dutt Pande became its editor, he gave it a political colour owing to which the circulation increased 30 times. The Government reacted to this policy immediately and as a sequel in 1918 a security of Rs. 1000 was demanded. Since the amount could not be paid, the publication had to be stopped.[32]

The void created by discontinuing Almora Akhbar was however filled up with publication of Shakti Saptahik in 1913. Badri Dutt Pande was its first editor.[33] In 1942 its publication was also stopped owing to the policies of the Government but in 1946 with the efforts of Pandit Govind Ballabh Pant, it was started again. The paper is still being published from Almora.

Another paper which was published from Almora those days was the *Swadhin Praja*. It was a weekly and in 1930 its publication was started by Victor Mohan Joshi.[34]

Those days in 1905 the Garhwal Union in Dehradun also started the publication of the newspaper Garhwali. In the beginning it was a fortnightly, but in 1913 it was converted into a weekly. The newspaper advocated political and social awareness both in British and Tehri Garhwal.

In 1939, the publication of Karm Bhumi Saptahik also commenced from Lansdowne. Sri Deo Suman, a leader of the political movements in Tehri Garhwal State was in the editorial board and he wrote articles on the social and economic condition in Garhwal. In the present times, this newspaper is being published from Kotdwara in Garhwal.

Apart from the above mentioned newspapers, a few others with a lesser circulation were published from Kumaon and Garhwal. They were the *Jagrit Janta, Garhwal Samachar, Tarun Kumaon Vishal Kirti, Purusharth, Kumaon Kumud* and *Kshatriya Beer*.

In the 19th and 20th centuries, there were some literary talents in Kumaon and Garhwal,[35] who preached about the social evils and infused a spirit of nationalism. Amidst these literatis, Gumani, Mola Ram, Gaur Da, Hem Chandra Joshi, Dr. Bhagwati Prasad Panthri, Barrister Mukandi Lal, and Badri Lal Sah etc. are most illustrious.

The Arya Samaj also tried to eradicate the social maladies[36] rampant in Garhwal by laying stress on education and paved way for political uprisings against the establishment.

Finally it was the martial qualities of the Garhwalis which infused in them a spirit of dissent against the British and the rulers of Tehri Garhwal State. The military traditions of the Garhwalis are more or less undisputed. The Germans called the Garhwalis, "the storm troops of the Allies." Out of the first 5 V.C's won by Indian Corps by the Indians during the First World War, 2 were won by Garhwalis, Darban Singh and Gabar Singh. Out of the 10 M.C's awarded to Indians, 4 went to Garhwalis, and out of the 8 recipients of the Order of British India, 2 were Garhwalis.[37] The British recognized the military talent of the Garhwalis and raised the Royal Garhwal Rifles. Their recruitment in the Armed Forces added to the mobility of the Garhwalis. Undeniably, the brave soldiers of the Royal Garhwal Rifles performed their duties loyally, but gradually they came closer to the realities of life. The exposure of these troops to the outside world and particularly the great sweeps of national movement broadened their horizons. In the initial stages it was a period of reluctance, characterized by the refusal of Chandra Singh Garhwali to fire on the Pathans and disobey British orders. Eventually the natural martial instinct of Garhwalis found expression in the Second World War, when 2 battalions of the Garhwalis joined the I.N.A.

In 1930, during the Salt Satyagraha, Chandra Singh's parental battalion, 2/18 Royal Garhwal Rifles was posted in Peshawar.[38] When Chandra Singh Garhwali and his companions were ordered to fire on the followers of Khan Abdul Gaffar Khan in Peshawar on 23rd April 1930, they refused and were arrested immediately. At the court martial proceedings, the Garhwalis said, "We will not shoot our unarmed brethren. . . . you may blow us from the guns if you like."[39] Frank Moraes, the author of 'Witness to an Era', is of the view that the incident shook the British.[40] Sparks of this incident flew far and wide throughout Kumaon and Tehri Garhwal State and thereafter efforts were made to tamper with Garhwali troops stationed at Lansdowne by the Congressmen. In a letter, dated 14th June 1930, General J.S.M. Shea, General Officer Commanding in Chief, Eastern Command had tendered information to the Chief of the General Staff, Army Headquarters, Simla, in this connection. He wrote, ". . . . efforts are being made to tamper with the Garhwali troops at Lansdowne and Congressmen are now in Lansdowne with that object."[41]

General Mohan Singh of the I.N.A. fame has observed that the heroic example of Chandra Singh Garhwali inspired the Garhwalis to join the I.N.A.[42] In September 1942, 2 battalions of the Royal Garhwal Rifles, 2/18 and 5/18 joined the I.N.A. There were 2,500 Garhwalis in these 2 battalions out of which 600 were killed in action. The Garhwalis held some very important positions in the I.N.A. Lt. Colonel Chandra Singh Negi was appointed as Commander of the Officers Training School in Singapore, Major Dev Singh Danu was deployed as Commander of the personal guards battalion of Subash Chandra Bose. Lt. Colonel Budhi Singh Rawat held the esteemed position as personal adjutant of Subash Chandra Bose. Major Padam Singh was commanding the 3rd battalion and Lt. Colonel P.S. Raturi the 1st battalion of Subash Regiment. For his gallantry and outstanding qualities of leadership, Raturi was decorated with Sardar-e-Jung by Netaji himself.[43]

During the Burma campaign in 1944, Raturi's battalion saw action in the Arakan front. The troops under his command occupied Mowdok and the various posts around it. The attack on Mowdok was launched at night with a lightening speed. It came as a complete surprise to the enemy who fled leaving behind large quantities of ration and ammunition.[44] As regards the Garhwalis joining the I.N.A., Philip Mason has remarked, ". . . . the behaviour of this battalion was I believe typical of many. It did contain an element of nationalism."[45] The intrepidity of the brave soldiers exhibited in the I.N.A. encouraged the Garhwalis at home and outside.

POLITICAL MOVEMENTS

It was from the early part of the 20th century that the people of Tehri Garhwal State started manifesting their resentment against the feudalistic set up. Later the resentment was directed towards a higher goal, nationalism, and the people of Tehri Garhwal State demanded the integration of the State with the Indian Union.

1857 and Tehri Garhwal State

The then ruling king Raja Sudarshan Shah felt that both Tehri State and British Garhwal could be endangered by the uprisings of 1857 so he rendered help to the British. He ordered voluntary recruitment of his subjects in the British forces and also advanced them financial assistance. During those critical days, a few British families had taken refuge in Mussoorie and it was feared that insurgents from the plains would infiltrate and kill those refugees. Hence Sudarshan Shah deployed 200 armed guards between Dehradun and Mussoorie for their protection.[46]

The timely assistance tendered by Raja Sudarshan Shah was immediately rewarded. Mian Prem Singh[47] is of the opinion that the British wanted to bestow upon him a fief in Bijnor district, but the king demanded Dehradun and Srinagar, his ancestral capital. Correspondence ensued in this connection between Sudarshan Shah and the British authorities, but he suddenly expired in 1859 and the matter was dropped. Pandit Hari Krishna Raturi has corroborated the view of Mian Prem Singh.[48]

Raja Sudarshan Shah was wise enough and far-sighted to extend help to the British. His was a newly established State and it was only with the aid of the British that he was able to retrieve a part of his ancestors' lost territory. Moreover he did not have a male heir to succeed him and on the slightest pretext the British could have lapsed his kingdom. As such the British had already expressed their doubts about Bhawani Shah, the successor of Sudrshan Shah stating that he was an illegitimate son of Raja Sudarshan Shah. Walton has mentioned that,

"During the Mutiny Sudarshan Shah rendered valuable assistance to Government. He died in 1859 without a direct male

issue and the State lapsed to the Government, but in considera-
ration of the service of Sudarshan Shah, a near male relative
Bhawani Shah, was allowed to succeed and he subsequently
received a sunud giving him the right of adoption."[49]

Actually Bhawani Shah was neither an adopted heir nor an
illegitimate child of Raja Sudarshan Shah but a legal son from a
Kshatriya wife. The British in January 1927 had asked the State
authorities to send a narrative of the ancestory of the rulers of
Tehri Garhwal State[50] and in the letter they had also sounded
the doubtful legacy of Raja Bhawani Shah. The then Wazir of
Tehri State, sent a letter of protest in compliance with this letter.

"Perhaps the ambiguity resulting from the expression that
Bhawani Singh was Raja Sudarshan Shah's illegitimate son
requires to be cleared. Raja Bhawani Shah had no title to succeed his father's territory according to the agreement executed
by the late Raja but the implication that Raja Bhawani Shah
was not born from a Kshatriya girl and a lawful wife is altogether false. The Tehri Durbar strongly resents this. If this had
been true then relationships of the present ruler and his father
with Kshatriyas of the purest origin, in the family of Maharaja
Jang Bahadur of Nepal and in the family of Maharana of Udaipur and Jodhpur would not have been possible. In the treaty
itself the word illegitimate does not occur."

Together with this letter an account of the rulers is attached and
the ambiguity has been cleared.[51] According to this narrative,

"During the period 1803-1815, when Raja Sudarshan Shah
remained dispossessed of his territory he had lawfully married
a pure Kshatriya girl, though not descended from a ruling
chiefs family. On the restoration of a portion of his territory
to Raja Sudarshan Shah in 1815, in his anxiety to marry himself in the families of ruling chiefs and to facilitate such marriages, he took an undertaking from his pious and faithful
wife agreeing to the succession of the eldest son of any of the
wives he may marry from a ruling chiefs family. In consequence
he had several wives from the houses of the ruling chiefs
of Khanot, Keonthal and others. A son named Surjan was
born to the Khanot Ranee and was according to the terms of

agreement appointed heir apparent to the Gaddi. The young prince, however, died at an early age; and Raja Sudarshan Shah was persuaded to believe that the young prince's death was due to certain ceremonies detrimental to his life performed by the family priest Radha Pati, at the instigation of other wives. Raja Sudarshan Shah therefore, declined to appoint any heir apparent, or to nominate any of his surviving sons to succeed him, and decided that his whole State should lapse to the British Government after his death."

"During the mutiny of 1857, the Raja rendered valuable assistance to the Government. He died in June 1859 and in accordance with the terms of the treaty the State lapsed to the Government; but in consideration of the services of Raja Sudarshan Shah, his eldest son, Bhawani Shah (born of the wife Raja Sudarshan Shah had married before the territory was restored to him) was allowed to succeed (Sunud No. XIX). Raja Bhawani Shah, subsequently in 1862 received a Sunud No. XX, guaranteeing him the right to adoption."

It is possible that after Surjan Shah died Raja Sudarshan Shah was displeased with his queens and in a fit of depression he took the decision that the State should lapse to the British. On second thought after recovering from the shock he realized his mistake and must have decided to nominate Bhawani Shah as his successor, but at the same time he was bound by the undertaking that the eldest son born from the mother of royal descent would succeed him. In the meantime the mutiny broke out and in that critical period he advanced help to the British. Later, before he could take any decision of nominating Bhawani Shah as heir apparent, he died and the State lapsed to t he British.

Sudarshan Shah after recovering from the shock of Surjan Shah's death must have dropped the idea of lapsing the State to the British, otherwise when the British offered him a fief in Bijnor in lieu of his help he would not have demanded Dehradun and Srinagar, the ancient capital, and correspondence would not have ensued between him and the British.

As regards the help extended by Raja Sudarshan Shah, it can be further stated that it would have been a breach of faith to deceive the British. He has himself admitted that he was a true

Rajput and could not betray his saviour, the British. It is said that the Nawab of Najibabad had sent a letter to the Raja of Tehri to extend him help against the British in lieu of which he would be able to get back the whole of his kingdom. The Nawab also threatened him that if he did not pay heed to his advice and help him, the Nawab would launch an attack on his State. But Raja Sudarshan Shah replied that he was a Kshatriya in the true sense and could not betray the British. He further advised the Nawab to surrender to the British.[52]

Sudarshan Shah was succeeded by Bhawani Shah. Dabral has mentioned that the people of Rawain and Jaunpur were not happy with his rule and consequently they revolted.[53] But as has been mentioned earlier, it was not the question of Bhawani Shah's rule; Rawain had been made a disturbed zone by the British purposely. This uprising was a fiasco. The king was successful in suppressing the rebellion by fining the insurgents and asking them to write an affidavit.

During the rule of Pratap Shah as has been referred to in chapter Five, there were minor disturbances. The first was by the people of Patti Khas, the next was in Basar in 1882 and the third was that of 1886 by the villagers who lived near the township of Tehri. They were actually directed against the officials of the State and were quelled easily.

There was equanimity in Tehri Garhwal during the rule of Kirti Shah, the successor of Raja Pratap Shah. But the people were against the forest policies of the State. Although the State Forest Department was working in consonance with the policy of preservation of forests on the one hand, no efforts were being made, on the other, to impress upon the people the utility of forests. If the people were not fully cognisant of the value of forests, it was the duty of the government to appeal to their reason and remove their misapprehension. The local people thus felt that their rights were being encroached upon and their resentment was first manifested in 1906.

The Forest Uprising in Chandrabadni

On 27th December 1906, the forests surrounding the Chandrabadni temple about 14 miles from Tehri town were being inspected preparatory to having brought them under reservation.

The same day about 200 villagers armed with sticks assembled at the camping ground where the official tents were pitched and objected to the State interference in the forest over which they claimed full and extensive rights. They attacked the Conservator against whom they had a special grudge for introducing forest regulations. The villagers tore his tent and broke his gun, but somehow he managed to escape.

Next day the Raja sent his brother with an armed force to quell the disturbance and arrest the ring leaders, but the attempt failed. The people gathered from different villages over a considerable tract of country and according to a member mustered a strength of about 3000; they opposed the magistrate and started collecting arms. The Raja thereupon appealed to the British for armed assistance. His belief was that the protective measures applied by his forest policy were used as an opportunity by others and that the outbreak had been really planned and engineered by dismissed officials. But the British Government did not send any help because they thought that their interference would lower the Raja's prestige in the eyes of his subjects and encourage disorder and faction.[54] Soon the fire of discontent died down.

The people of Tehri Garhwal State voiced their resentment again in 1930 against the forest policy in the form of Rawain Incident.

The Rawain Incident

In 1927-28, it is said that when the village folk of pargana Rawain appealed to the forest authorities regarding the grazing rights, they remarked, "the State will not bear any loss owing to the animals, roll them down the hill." The peasants were infuriated by this obnoxious reply and they immediately retaliated. Hira Singh, Daya Ram and Baij Ram were the leaders of the villagers. They established an Azad Panchayat, i.e. Independent Panchayat and declared, that the people residing near the forests had full rights over them. The officers of the State present over there were flabbergasted on visualizing the situation and they vacated the place. The people then constituted a parallel Government and as in the Nepalese system, Hira Singh was designated as 'Paanch Sarkar', i.e. the king and Baij Ram was given the title of, 'Teen Sarkar', i.e. the Prime Minister. They also rejected the new forest limits and on 20th May 1930 put fire to a part of the forest.

Gradually the movement and the organization of the villagers in Jaunpur and Rawain started gaining popularity. Regular meetings were held, and a place known as Chandadojri in Tilari was selected as the venue for the meetings of the Azad Panchayat. On witnessing the activities of the villagers, the ex-Wazir, Pandit Hari Krishna Raturi was sent on behalf of the State to establish peace. The people demanded a repeal of the forest laws. Pandit Hari Krishna Raturi gave them due assurances and returned to Tehri. In the meanwhile, the D.F.O. of Tehri Garhwal State filed a case against the leaders of the movement, Daya Ram, Rudra Singh, Ram Prasad and Jaman Singh. The S.D.M. Surendra Dutt Sharma and D.F.O. Padma Dutt Raturi arrested the leaders in Rawain. On the 26th of May 1930, when they were proceeding from Raj Garhi towards Tehri, the villagers attacked them with the intention of releasing their leaders. Raturi fired at the assailants to scare them, but in the firing three people died and some were severely wounded. As a sequel the people retaliated, they caught hold of Surendra Dutt Sharma and injured him badly, whereas the D.F.O. and the police men fled the site. When news of this incident reached Tehri, Dewan Chakra Dhar Jayal approached the Governor of the United Provinces and he was granted permission to use arms against the so-called rebels during emergency. Raja Narendra Shah was on a tour of Europe those days. The Diwan thus issued orders to Colonel Surendra Singh to suppress the recalcitrants by force, but he refused. His services were immediately terminated and Nathu Singh Sajwan was posted in his place and sent there to deal with the people of Rawain.[55]

On 29th May 1930, the State army arrived at Raj Garhi. When the people came to hear about this, they felled trees and placed them on the roads to hamper further progress of the army. But all went in vain. It is said that the army ravaged and plundered the harmless villagers.

Next day, 30th May, a meeting of the Azad Panchayat was being held in Tilari. Discussions were in full swing about the arrival of the State militia, when the army suddenly surrounded the innocent people from three sides and opened fire. Diwan Chakra Dhar Jayal was issuing the orders. The people were so terrorised that a few of them lay on the ground, a few climbed the trees and some of them jumped into the Yamuna to save their lives. Afte the bloodshed, the leaders were arrested. Two of the arrested leaders tried to escape and the Diwan shot them with his own pistol. Thereafter a platoon was especially deployed to hide the corpses. The soldiers tied stones to the dead bodies and threw them into the Yamuna. Ram Prasad's shop, who was responsible for disseminating consciousness amongst the masses, was gutted. People under suspicion were also arrested and the troops returning to the capital plundered the people further.[56]

As cited in the book,[57] published by the Information Deparment of U.P., more than 200 people were killed in Rawain. Sundar Lal Bahuguna, has been a freedom fighter himself, as such his view is more authentic. According to him 17 died and many were severely wounded.

After the brutalities in Rawain, the people tendered an application to the Viceroy to make a probe into the incident and penalize Diwan Chakra Dhar Jayal and the D.F.O. Padma Dutt Raturi who were responsible for these atrocities.[58] Concomitantly, it was also requested to extend pecuniary assistance to the widows and children of the people who died in Rawain. But the British Government did not comply with the demands of the people.[59]

Later, law suits were filed against those who were arrested in Rawain and a condition was laid that they would not consult lawyers outside Tehri State. Finally, all of them were found guilty and sentenced to rigorous imprisonment varying from one year to 20 years. Out of the convicted, 15 died in the prison whose bodies were thrown into the Ganges.[60]

The repression did not limit to this only. When the people reproached and wrote articles against the culprits in the newspaper *Garhwali*, Diwan Chakra Dhar Jayal got annoyed and ordered its editor, Vishamber Dutt Chandola to apologise for the article written by him. But Chandola refused. The Diwan then sought the help of the law court and got Chandola convicted. He appealed to the High Court but his appeal was rejected and he was sentenced to one year's imprisonment.[61]

The Rawain massacre had a deep effect on the people of British Garhwal. A meeting was organized there as a protest against the incident. The public semblance of the Diwan was denigrated and he was nicknamed as 'Khuni', i.e. the murderer.[62] The incident shocked the people so much that even today songs are sung in Garhwal to commemorate this tragedy.

The Rawain incident was the second wave of forest unrest in Tehri Garhwal State which coincided with the Civil Disobedience upsurge of 1930-31. Those days, Gandhi and the Congress leaders urged local organizers again to initiate non-violent resistance against arbitrary laws. Again there were protest fires in the Siwaliks and throughout the 1930's, Forest Department employees had to face physical violence or the threat of it from the villagers in the hills. In the neighbouring Kumaon region, F.C. Ford Robertson is of the view that, "until 1931, Kumaon was the centre of self destructive incendiarism, the reserved forests being fired 157 times."[63]

It seems that after 1930, the fervour and struggle for independence that was going on in British India affected the people of this State who were gradually becoming conscious. But the divine status of the king, who was regarded as the living embodiment of God Badrinath, was impedimental in the path of those people who were trying to advocate consciousness amongst the masses. To motivate the people against feudalism and to associate them with the freedom struggle was a formidable task. In the beginning whenever there was a disturbance in the State, it was directed against the officials, their corrupt practices and nepotism, but never against the king. Gradually the people became aware of their civic rights and of the mode of exploitation and they became vociferous against the king also. But their resentment was restricted to verbal and written protests only, there was no uprising against the king, nor any attempt was made by the people to associate themselves with the national stream of consciousness. A copy of the confidential note on the Annual Administration Report of 1922-23 bears testimony to the nonchalant attitude of the people. The Diwan of Tehri Garhwal State has mentioned in that note,

"During the year under report, a non cooperator from Saharanpur visited Juapatti and just when he began to give a speech abusing the British Government and your Highnesses' Government, he was beaten by the village people and turned out."

In the same report it has been stated further that,

"The Mohattam Police reports that some Gandhi caps were burnt. The people simple as they are wore them as the fashion of the day, although they are quite ignorant of the political movements. Most of the people are those who take the Ganges water for sale in the plains."[64]

In the National Archives, New Delhi, there is a letter dated 11th July 1934 written by Bhakt Darshan, a Congress worker, to Pandit Govind Ballabh Pant, the great nationalist leader that, in Garhwal no Congress work has been done hitherto.

It was for the first time in 1913 that an article was published in the newspaper *Garhwali* which was aimed against the king. In the article a comparison has been made between the condition of the State and its officials during the rule of Kirti Shah and Pratap Shah. The article is a day to day account of the time when Raja Pratap Shah was in his death bed. The translation of the article titled, 'The King on his Death Bed', is preserved in the National Archives, New Delhi. The article has praised Raja Kirti Shah and severely criticised the personal life of Raja Pratap Shah. It states that his life was given to debauchery to an extreme degree and at the time of his death his treasury was robbed by his officials. Pandit Shanker Dutt Deodi was the chief of those evil spirits who robbed the treasury.[65]

Similarly in 1925 an article was published against the important officials of the State, especially the Diwan, Bhawani Dutt Uniyal and his caucus who had made Raja Narendra Shah a puppet in their hands. In the article published in *Kshatriya Beer* on 15th July 1925, it is mentioned that owing to the influence of Diwan Bhawani Dutt Uniyal, his son-in-law, Ram Prasad Dobal was made a judge through wrong means. Ram Prasad Dobal was an ordinary man and was working as a writer with the Saklana Muafidar. With the kindness of Rai Bahadur Jodh Singh Negi, he was made an 'amin' in the settlement operations. Later he was raised to the position of the settlement officer and aferwards was made an officer of the law court.[66]

This paper had levelled charges of nepotism and parochialism against Bhawani Dutt Uniyal previously also. In the article published in 1922, it has been stated that the Durbar was against

Kshatriyas and only Brahmins got employment in the State.[67] This view was also expressed by the District Magistrate of British Garhwal stationed at Pauri. In a letter dated 3rd November 1923, addressed to Wyndham, the Commissioner of Kumaon at Naini Tal, he has written, "It is notorious that in Tehri State, under a Rajput Raja, there is not a single Rajput official."[68]

Bhawani Dutt Uniyal, it seems was a very powerful but treacherous person. On the one hand he was posing to be a loyal official of the king and under that camouflage he was appointing his relations and the members of his caucus in important positions, and on the other he was supporting Mukandi Lal for election to the U.P. Council.[69] His main motive behind supporting Mukandi Lal was caste politics as is evident from the letter of the District Magistrate of British Garhwal to the Commissioner of Kumaon. He has written,

"The Brahmins, of course, are fighting to keep their power which is threatened by the new election system and the numerical superiority of the Rajputs, and one cannot blame them, but Bhawani Dutt as Wazir of Tehri, has no business to employ a man like Ansuya Prasad, or to use his undesirably wide influence in this district in favour of a professed non-cooperator with a C.I.D. record such as Mukandi Lal."

In the same letter it has also been mentioned that Bhawani Dutt was extending financial assistance to Mukandi Lal.[70]

Raja Narendra Shah, it seems was completely under the spell of Bhawani Dutt, and in a letter dated 20th December 1923, which he wrote to the political agent, he has stated that Bhawani Dutt was holding a responsible position in the State and could not be involved in such seditious activities.[71] Similarly in 1925 when the article appeared in *Kshatriya Beer* against Bhawani Dutt, he tried with all his might to defend him.[72]

Later Bhawani Dutt was removed from the post of Diwan and the people of Tehri Garhwal State were extremely happy about it and they thanked the British Government for its good deed.[73]

In 1939, the Praja Mandal which was founded at Dehradun started a regular movement for liberating the people from the shackles of the despotic rule of the Raja. The most prominent of the leaders of this movement was Srideo Suman, a journalist

who was born on 20th May 1915 in the village Jaul of pargana
Narendra Nagar. In order to coordinate the activities of the
people of the State who were residing outside, branches of the
Praja Mandal were established at Mussoorie, Lahore and Delhi.
Srideo Suman was also associated with the Indian National Congress and had contacts with its leaders, particularly Jawahar Lal
Nehru. On visualizing the activities of the Praja Mandal and the
situation of a rebellion, Raja Narendra Shah reciprocated with a
progressive gesture. A State Constituent Assembly was formed
and the students of the Pratap Intermediate College were permitted to organize a debating society where they could voice their
grievances. Consequently, the students started organizing and
soon they raised the demand for a student's union. The State
officials rejected their demand, and so they went on strike in
September 1940. Before the agitation could gain any momentum,
the authorities adopted every method fair or foul to suppress it
and eventually within three days, the students called off their
strike. Seven students were fined and the leaders Daya Ram Uniyal and Prem Dutt Sobhal were rusticated.[74]

The State authorities mistook the students agitation for a mass
movement and they resorted to repressive measures. As a sequel
the students formed secret organizations, the guiding force behind them being Srideo Suman. On his advice the student leaders
from Tehri, Prem Dutt and Daya Nand attended the 'Deshi Rajya
Vidyarthi Sammelan', a conference of the students of various
feudal states held in Benares in 1940. Through this conference
the students of Tehri came in touch with leaders from different
parts of the country. This contact enabled them in channelizing
their energies in a right direction. In the beginning they started a
poster campaign against those teachers who were the henchmen
of the State. One of these posters was also aimed at the Principal of Pratap Intermediate College. The students had thrown a
challenge that they would murder him at any moment. This
caused a great sensation and in 1941, one of the student leaders,
Ram Chandra Uniyal was arrested. After him a number of other
students were interned and owing to the stern measures adopted
by the State, the student movement started dwindling.[75]

But in 1942, the Quit India Movement gave a new impetus to
all political activities in Garhwal. In 1942, under the influence

of this Movement, the Praja Mandal demanded that the Raja must sever relations with the British. But as soon as the agitation started, Srideo Suman with 31 others was arrested at Deoprayag and interned in Tehri Jail. Suman vehemently protested against the inhuman treatment of the jail authorities and at last on May 3, 1944, he had to go on hunger strike. In the jail Suman caught pneumonia and his frail health could not withstand this illness and he died.

The martyrdom of Srideo Suman gave an unprecedented impetus to the movement for independence and all the branches of the Praja Mandal outside the State became vocal in their attack against the Raja. On July 25, 1945, despite the Raja's police and prohibitory orders, 'Suman Balidan Divas' was celebrated in Tehri Garhwal and G.B. Pant was invited.[76]

The Tehri Movement (1946)

In July 1946, people from different parts of Tehri State under the leadership of Daulat Ram and Nagendra Saklani went to Narendra Nagar to place their demands in the presence of the king. But he failed to meet their demands of preventing his officials from taking bribe, improving the condition of the schools, hospitals and roads within the State, changing forest laws and lifting the ban over meetings. On the contrary he issued orders to arrest the leaders. The detention of these leaders roused the people against the king.

Rahul Sankrityayan is of the view that the British were adopting a dual policy as regards the activities in Tehri Garhwal State. On the one hand they were feigning indifference about the happenings there and on the other they were instigating the king to quell the uprisings by force.[77]

On 15th August, 1947, when the people of Tehri Garhwal State were celebrating Independence Day, Paripurna Nand, a leader of the Praja Mandal was arrested. His detention was followed by strikes all over the State.[78]

The Saklana Uprising

When India achieved Independence the people of the fief of Saklana were inspired to rise against feudalism. In the beginning they demanded maintenance of roads, hospitals and schools and decided not to pay the land tax until their demands were met with. The authorities on witnessing the state of affairs deployed troops and sent a special Magistrate to collect the revenue. These officials terrorised the people by plundering them, auctioning their property and interning the poorest. The members of the Praja Mandal opposed the oppressive policies of the State authorities, and to redeem the people from the fetters of feudalism, they started recruiting Satyagrahis and a Satyagrah camp was established outside the State. When the Satyagrahis started infiltrating, the State police arrested and deported them to the forests where they would get lost. On 16th December 1947, the Muafidars of Saklana surrendered their rights to the Praja Mandal and declared themselves independent. This resulted in setting up of the Azad Panchayat by the Praja Mandal in Saklana. Other places also followed the example of Saklana and established Azad Panchayats. Even in Kirti Nagar, the most important pargana centre, a wing of the Azad Panchayat was started and the State officials there scurried to Narendra Nagar.[79]

Kirti Nagar Movement (1948)

On 16th January 1948, a group of people rallied in Kirti Nagar with the intention of disintegrating it from the State. A few armed guards were present in Kirti Nagar, but their number was negligible as compared to the strength of the mob. The soldiers on witnessing the crowd surrendered their arms, and their guns were thrown into the Alaknanda. At that moment a youth leader, Nagendra Saklani arrived at Kirti Nagar and a meeting was organized immediately. A committee was also formed which was entrusted with the duty of taking over the court of Kirti Nagar. Concomitantly the members of the committee hoisted the tricolour over the Kirti Nagar Court. The next day some officers of the State accompanied by troops arrived at Kirti Nagar. These officials and troops tried to seize the court but they were resisted by the people. Ultimately the troops burst tear gas shells but that too went futile. The agitated mob in the meantime set the court on fire and the soldiers there were helpless in preventing the arsonage.[80] According to the information gathered from Tehri the names of the officers who were sent to Kirti Nagar were Baldeo Singh, Major Jagdish Prasad and Lalita Prasad Pande.

The Azad Panchayat of Kirti Nagar then issued warrants against the officers of the State for their arrest. A few of the Satyagrahis who were entrusted with this task apprehended the soldiers, whilst the officers escaped to the jungle. Rahul has stated that Narendra Saklani and Molu Ram pursued these officers, but before they could arrest them, they were shot by them. According to the information gathered from the inhabitants of Tehri, people involved in the Kirti Nagar Movement and freedom fighters like Chandra Singh Garhwali, it appears that on visualizing the violent attitude of the agitated crowd, the three officers tried to escape from the scene. Nagendra Saklani and Deo Dutt Tewari followed them. Saklani somehow managed to ground the Special Magistrate Baldeo Singh and mounted on his chest. When he was trying to strangle him, Havildar Hari Singh on the orders of Major Jagdish Prasad fired at Saklani and killed him. It is said that earlier when Nagendra Saklani had reached Kirti Nagar, he had announced that either he would kill the king or his brother. Since Baldeo Singh, the special magistrate happened to be the king's cousin, he tried to kill him.

Rahul has cited the name of Narendra Saklani's companion as Molu Singh. He was actually Molu Ram as is evidenced by the edifice erected at Kirti Nagar to commemorate the martyrs of the aforesaid uprising. About Molu Ram's death it is said that when the infuriated crowd was trying to arrest the officials, Molu Ram went berserk. He was prancing around with a dagger in his hand when he was shot dead by one of the officials.

After the death of Nagendra Saklani, the leadership of Tehri movement came into the hands of Chandra Singh Garhwali, the hero of the famous Peshawar case. On 12th of January, 1948, the funeral procession of Nagendra Saklani and Molu Ram started from Kirti Nagar. When it reached Deoprayag, a wing of the Azad Panchayat was established there also. The number of State troops in Deoprayag was at that moment about 25 and when they witnessed the huge crowd, they immediately surrendered. The procession then moved ahead. Enroute the people came out of their houses to venerate the martyrs and laid wreaths upon their dead bodies. A few of them also joined the procession. On 15th January, the procession arrived at Tehri. Raja Narendra Shah, the then ruling king had already left for Narendra Nagar on foreseeing the predicament that he would have to face. The State officials who were left behind became jittery and the agitated crowd seized their weapons. After the obsequies of the martyrs were performed, the people took a solemn oath to struggle against feudalism.

In the evening a meeting was held outside the State office. People were divided into two groups. One voted for a responsible form of a Government under the king while the other was interested in integrating the State with the Indian Union. Finally the second emerged as a stronger group. At that moment it was announced that Raja Narendra Shah was advancing with his army towards Tehri town. To prevent him from entering the town, the bridge which was the only entrance to Tehri, was locked and 50 volunteers were put on guard. The king did come, but was without his bodyguards or army, and on seeing the lock returned to Narendra Nagar.[81]

After the meeting of 15th January, 1948, a wing of the Azad Panchayat was established in Tehri and soon its flags could be seen fluttering over the Police Station, the Court, the State Office and the State Treasury. When the Indian Government came to know about these incidents, the Sub-Divisional Officer and the Superintendent of Police, Dehradun, accompanied by a hundred soldiers from the Military Police were sent to Tehri. On 16th January they took over the reins of the Government on the pretext of establishing peace in the State. The same day, Mahavir Tyagi, Bhakt Darshan and other leaders came to Tehri and a meeting was organized. Daulat Ram was elected to preside over, and in the meeting it was decided that the political detenus would be released, the State property would be transferred to Indian Government and the people would be exempted from the State debt.[82]

In February 1948, an interim Government was set up in the State, and in the ministry, four members were nominated by the Praja Mandal and one by the State Government. The interim Government which functioned for more than a year underwent some developments, but on August 1, 1949, a proclamation was made by the Indian Government to integrate Tehri Garhwal State with Uttar Pradesh.[83]

REFERENCES

1. Sen, S.P. (ed.): The Sino-Indian Border Dispute, a Historical Review, p. 70.
2. Ramakant: Indo Nepalese Relations, 1816-1877, p. 37.
3. Sewak: Fascinating Uttrakhand, p. 12.
4. Rahul, Ram: The Himalayan Borderland, p. 45.
5. Husain, Asad: British India's Relations with the Kingdom of Nepal, p. 282.
6. Rawat, I.S.: Indian Explorers of the Nineteenth Century, pp. xvi-xvii.
7. Sherring, Charles A.: Western Tibet and the British Borderland, p. 1.
8. Wessels, C': Early Jesuit Travellers in Central Asia, p. 97.
9. Maclagan, Edward: The Jesuits and the Great Moguls, p. 342.
10. Foreign Secret Department, File No. 28, Letter dated August 3, 1842, para 3.
11. Moorcraft and Trebeck: Travels in the Himalayan Provinces of Hindustan and Punjab (1819-1825), Volume 1, pp. 12-13.
12. Home Public Department, File No. 9, Letter dated 16th September 1802.
13. Foreign Department, Political, Box No. 57, Sunud of 10th December, 1824, para 5.
14. Ibid., para 5.
15. Foreign Department, Political, 1848, File No. 62, Letter No. 611, and File No. 63, Letter No. 612.
16. Darshan, Bhakt: Garhwal ki Divangat Vibhutian, p. 139.
17. Foreign Department, Political Proceedings 16-20, August 1833, File No. 86, Letter dated 22nd August 1833.
18. Foreign Department, Political Proceedings, 19-27 September 1833, Letter Nos. 7 and 8.
19. *Garhwali*, November 1913, p. 270.
20. Sir Kirti Shah ka Sunkshipt Jeevan Charit, p. 7.
21. *Garhwali*, January 1907, p. 3.
22. Joshi, Sudha: Kurmachal Kesari, p. 20.
23. *Almora Akhbar*, 4th August 1913.
24. Niyam Prabhu Sewa va Coolie Utar, pp. 4-6.

25. Ibid., pp. 1-3.
26. Niyam Vasooli Bura, p. 1.
27. Joshi, Sudha: op. cit., pp. 17-18.
28. Sankrityayan, Rahul: Veer Chandra Singh Garhwali, pp. 11-12.
29. Sankrityayan, Rahul: Kumaon, p. 128.
30. Pande, B.D.: Kumaon ka Itihas, pp. 500-501.
31. Nayal, Indra Singh: Swatantrata Sangram mein Kumaon ka Yogdan, p. 15.
32. Joshi, Sudha: op.cit., p. 9.
33. Sah, Shambhu Prasad: Govind Ballabh Pant ek Jeevani, p. 44.
34. Pant evam Trevedi: Tyagmurti Mohan Joshi, p. 65.
35. Chatak, Govind: Garhwali Lok Geet: Ek Sanskritik Adhyayan, pp. 197-99.
36. Dayalu, Shiv (ed.): Itihas Arya Samaj Pratinidhi Sabha, Uttar Pradesh, Volume 1, pp. 93-94.
37. Evatt, Captain J.: Hand Book on Garhwalis, pp. 37-38.
38. Home Department, Political, Government of India, File No. 393/30, p. 30.
39. Tendulkar, D.G.: Abdul Gaffar Khan, p. 70.
40. Moraes, Frank: Witness to an Era, p. 7.
41. Home Department 1930, Political, File No. 174, Letter No. 57915/28/G, 14th June 1930.
42. Sankrityayan, Rahul: Veer Chandra Singh Garhwali, p. 37.
43. Personal Communication, Lt. Colonel Budhi Singh Rawat, Personal Adjutant of Subash Chandra Bose.
44. Khan, Shah Nawaz; My memoirs of Netaji and its I.N.A., pp. 79-82.
45. Toye, Hughe: The Springing Tiger, p. vii.
46. Raturi, H.K.: Garhwal ka Itihas, p. 465-66.
47. Prem Singh, Mian: Guldust Tawarikh Kot Tehri Garhwal, p. 174.
48. Raturi, H.K.: op. cit., p. 467.
49. Walton, H.G.: op. cit., p. 210.
50. Letter of Political Agent Tehri Garhwal State, Letter No. 2/125 C-IV-A, dated 5th January, 1927.
51. Tehri Garhwal State Records (Political Agent for Tehri State) No. G-30-8/Tehri, Letter No. C.59, dated 12th February 1927.

52. Raturi, H.K.: op. cit., p. 468.
53. Dabral, Shiv Prasad: op. cit., Vol. VI, pp. 223-26.
54. Tehri Garhwal State Records, File No. 42/1907, Letter No. 46.
55. Personal Communication, Barrister Mukandi Lal.
56. Personal Communication, Sundar Lal Bahuguna.
57. Information Department (U.P.): Swatantrata Sangram ke Sainik, Garhwal Division, p. 'jha'.
58. Tehri Garhwal State Records, F. No. 247/1930, Letter No. 2513.
59. Information Department (U.P.): Swatrantrata Sangram ke Sainik, Garhwal Division, pp. 'cha-ja'.
60. Lal, Mukandi: Personal Communication.
61. Dabral, Shiv Prasad: op. cit., Volume VI, p. 318.
62. Jayal, Vidya Dhar: Diwan Chakra Dhar Jayal and the Traditions of His Family, p. 150.
63. Robertson, F.C. Ford: Our Forests, p. 31.
64. Copy of the confidential note on the Annual Administration Report for 1922-23, dated 15th July 1923.
65. Tehri Garhwal State Records, File No. 281/1913, pp. 2-5.
66. *Kshatriya Beer*, 15th July 1925.
67. Copy of the confidential note for the Annual Administration Report of 1922-23, pp. 16-20.
68. Tehri Garhwal State Records, File No. 55/1923, Letter dated 3rd November 1923, p. 4.
69. D.O. No. 2542, dated 12th November 1923, Allahabad.
70. Tehri Garhwal State Records, File No. 55/1923, Letter dated 3rd November 1923, pp. 3-5.
71. Tehri Garhwal State Records, File No. 55/1923, Letter dated 20th December 1923.
72. Letter dated 8th August 1925, of Raja Narendra Shah to the Political Agent, Tehri Garhwal State.
73. Letter dated 8th August 1925 from the subjects of Tehri Garhwal State to P. Wyndham, Commissioner of Kumaon.
74. Chandra Singh Garhwali: Personal communication.
75. Rawat, Ajay Singh: Garhwal Himalayas: A Historical Survey, pp. 200-201.
76. G.B. Pant Papers, File No. 4/3, Item No. 22, Letter dated 17th July 1945.

77. Sankrityayan, Rahul: Veer Chandra Singh Garhwali, p. 344.
78. Rawat, Ajay Singh: op. cit., p. 202.
79. Ibid., p. 202.
80. Sankrityayan, Rahul: Veer Chandra Singh Garhwali, p. 344.
81. Rawat, Ajay Singh: op. cit., pp. 203-205.
82. Bhagwati Prasad Panthri: Personal communication.
83. Bhakt Darshan: Personal communication.

8

An Overview

Garhwal at present comprises the Chamoli, Dehradun, Pauri, Tehri and Uttarkashi districts. Hitherto very less has been written about this tract, and Garhwal Himalayas to this day remain a relatively unexplored area. The rugged topography and an inaccessible terrain, at least in the past, has been largely responsible for insulating this indigenous political history. Hence Garhwal Himalayas, even though they belong to the mainstream of Indian history have a distinctive quality about them which persists even to this day.

The earliest reference regarding Garhwal and its pride spots are cited in the Skanda Purana (Kedar Khand) and the Mahabharata in the Van Parva. Skanda Purana (Kedar Khand) defines the boundaries and extent of this holy land. In the Van Parva (Mahabharata), where Dhaumya is narrating to Yudhisthira, the pilgrimage centres of India, the name Gangadwara, i.e. Haridwar and Kankhala, the sacred spot in its proximity have been referred. As regards the name of the region in those days, it is possible that it must have been famous as Himvat. According to Van Parva, when the Pandavas started off on their pilgrimage to Badrinath, Yudhisthira told Bhim to sojourn with Draupadi and others in Gangadwara until he returned from his journey to Badrinath, Gandhmadan, Kailash etc. But later it was decided that all of them should go. In the description of their sacred wanderings, the name of Himvat has often been cited. On the basis of the above description and taking into account the places which are familiar like Badrinath, Gangadwara etc., it can be assumed that the hilly tract of Garhwal those days was known as Himvat.

The earliest ruling dynasty of Garhwal known to authentic history is of the Katyuris. The Katyuri Raja of Uttrakhand (Kumaon and Garhwal) was styled, Sri Basdeo Giriraj Chakra Churamani, and the earliest traditions record that the possessions of the Joshimath Katyuris in Garhwal extended from the Sutlej as far as Gandaki and from the snow to the plains, including the whole of Rohilkhand. Tradition gives the origin of their Raj at Joshimath in the north near Badrinath and a subsequent migration to Katyur valley in Almora district, where a city called Karthi-Keyapura was founded.

The Katyuris ruled Uttrakhand upto the 11th century and in certain pockets even after their decline. In Garhwal their disruption brought into existence many independent chiefs, fifty-two in number. One of the important principalities in that period was that of the Parmars, who held their sway over Chandpur Garhi or fortress. Kanak Pal was the progenitor of this dynasty. Raja Ajay Pal, a scion of the Parmars in the 14th century is credited with having brought 52 of these chiefs under his rule. After his conquest Ajay Pal's domain was recognised as Garhwal owing to the exuberance of forts. It is possible that after annexing all the principalities, Raja Ajay Pal must have become famous as 'Garhwala', i.e. the owner of forts and with the passage of time his kingdom came to be known as Garhwal.

Dr. Shiv Prasad Dabral with other historians of Garhwal history, supports the tradition of nomenclaturing Garhwal, but at the same time he states that the word 'Garhwal' has been refered to for the first time by Mola Ram, the protagonist of Garhwali School of Painting, somewhere around 1815. But there is a copper plate inscription of Raja Man Shah of the year 1610 A.D. in the temple of Raghunath Ji at Deoprayag in which the word Garhwal has been referred to. Then there is a copper plate inscription of Maharaja Fateh Shah of the year 1667 A.D. in which the word Garhwal has been mentioned again. The inscription is a land grant endowed to some Balak Nath by Maharaja Fateh Shah. The great poet Bhushan has also referred the name Garhwal in a panegyrical poem eulogizing Maharaja Fateh Shah.

Ajay Pal ruled Garhwal in the 14th century, but upto the 17th century we have no mention of the word 'Garhwal'. Owing to paucity of source material, one cannot arrive at a conclusion.

However, it can be hypothesized that in coining the word 'Garhwal', the pretext must have been the same, i.e. Ajay Pal's consolidation of the 52 principalities, but the legend must have been metamorphosised in a later period. Since the progeny on the throne of Garhwal was of the Parmars even in the 17th century, it is possible that the then ruling king, to glorify his ancestor's victory of the 14th century, took it as a pride cause for naming his kingdom as Garhwal.

What was the name of this terrain before the reign of Ajay Pal, is shrouded in oblivion. There are only allusions like the one by Atkinson. He is of the view that the ancient name of Kumaon and Garhwal was Khas-Des, i.e., the country of the Khasas. Dr. D.C. Sirkar states that the Stri Rajya was located in Kumaon and Garhwal of the Himalayas. But they have given no historical proofs to corroborate their views.

About Stri Rajya, it was Hiuen Tsang who wrote that, "to the north of the country in the great snow mountains was the Suvarngotra country. The superior gold which it produced gave the country its name. This was the Eastern Women Country so-called because it was reigned by a successor of woman. The husband of the queen was the king, but he did not administer the Government." It is interesting to note that gold washing was a source of revenue during the rule of Parmar dynasty in Garhwal. Further the progenitor of the Parmar dynasty, Kanak Pal was given the kingdom of Chandpur Garhi in dowry by some Raja Son Pal. Kanak Pal had come to Garhwal on a pilgrimage, but after conjugal felicity, he settled down in Chandpur Garhi as a 'ghar jawain'. However on the basis of stray references no hypothesis can be developed. Dr. A.B.L. Awashi is of the view that, "Brahmapura is identified with Garhwal and Kumaon". But he too has not corroborated his view. About Brahmapura and also Govisana, it was the Chinese traveller Hiuen Tsang who has cited them in his accounts. Cunningham identifies Brahmapura with Lakhanpur in Kumaon, while Atkinson thinks it refers to Barahat in Garhwal. However both agree that the reference is in connection with the Katyuri kingdom of the Himalayas. Govisana is placed near Kashipur in Naini Tal district.

Medieval Garhwal which was ruled by the Parmars, is now distributed into seven districts of Dehradun, a part of Saharanpur, Tehri, Uttarkashi, Pauri, Chamoli and a part of Bijnor.

There are four lists of the Parmar rulers of Garhwal. One of the earliest is that prepared by Captain Hardwick in 1796 A.D. The second list is taken from an official report of 1849 and is the same as that accepted by Beckett. A third list is given by William and differs in some respects from Beckett's list. The fourth was obtained through an Almora Pundit and may be called the Almora list.

Among these lists, the one prepared by Beckett is the most authentic since it tallies fully with Raja Sudarshan Shah's genealogy of his ancestors in his writing 'Sabhasar'. The original manuscript of this work is in the dynastic collection of Thakur Shoor Beer Singh of Purana Durbar, Tehri, one of the scions of the royal family of Garhwal. Interestingly enough, the chronology of the Parmar kings which was sung by the bards also tallies to a great extent with Beckett's list. There are two more lists in the form of stone inscriptions in the temple of Parshuram and Vishwanath at Uttarkashi. These are of the later rulers of the Parmar dynasty, from Pradip Shah upto Sudarshan Shah.

The ancient history of this dynasty up to the reign of Raja Ajay Pal lacks in archaeological and other evidential details. Ajay Pal is the 37th in the list of the Parmar kings and the date of his demise as given in the list by Beckett is Samvat 1446, i.e. 1389 A.D. He ruled for 31 years, which means that he came to the throne somewhere around 1358 A.D. The same year he transferred his capital from Chandpur Garhi to Srinagar after consolidating the 52 principalities.

There are several original sources which corroborate that Raja Ajay Pal was ruling Garhwal. In Devalgarh, right in front of the temple of Vishnu, there is a relief showing Raja Ajay Pal with a male figure. Ajay Pal is seated in a lotus posture and is donning a turban and ear rings.

Devalgarh is on a hillock at a distance of about 8 to 9 miles from Srinagar. It is a 'pith', i.e. the seat of saint Satnath of the Gorakhnath Panth. Incidentally Raja Ajay Pal was also a disciple of this sect. George W. Briggs, the author of 'Gorkhnath Panth and the Kanphata Yogis', suggests that Ajay Pal was the founder of one of the 10 sects of Gorakhnath panthis. His name also appears in the list of the 84 'siddhas', the elevated ones. There is a very ancient manuscript in the dynastic collection of

Thakur Shoor Beer Singh. In this manuscript Raja Ajay Pal has been addressed as 'Adi Nath', which clearly indicates the position of esteem held by him amongst the Gorkhpanthis. Apart from this manuscript there are several other 'tantrik' manuscripts in the dynastic collection of Thakur Shoor Beer Singh in which the name of Raja Ajay Pal has been mentioned. He has been invoked as the first initiator of some of the 'mantras' compiled in the manuscripts.

Ajay Pal was succeeded by Kalyan Shah. From Kalyan Shah to Bijay Pal, the 41st ruler of the Parmar dynasty we do not have any information about their rule, except that their names are mentioned in the list given by Beckett and the one provided by 'Sabhasar'. After Bijay Pal comes Sahaj Pal, the 42nd ruler of the dynasty about whom we have sufficient inscriptional evidence as detailed below:

a) An inscription of 1605 Vikrami, i.e. 1548 A.D. on the stone door of the temple of Kshetra Pal at Deo prayag.
b) An inscription of 1608 Vikrami, i.e. 1551 A.D. in a bell at the temple of Raghunath Ji at Deoprayag. This bell is supposed to be dedicated to the temple by Sahaj Pal.

Sahaj Pal ruled from 1548 to 1575 A.D. The poet Bharat has highly eulogised Sahaj Pal and says that Garhwal was in a prosperous state during his reign. Sahaj Pal was Akbar's contemporary; although the whole of Northern India was approximately under Akbar's sway, Garhwal retained its independence.

After Sahaj Pal, Balbhadra Shah came to the helm of affairs. He was the first ruler to have adopted the title of Shah. This title is also used by Kalyan Shah, the 38th ruler of Beckett's list and the immediate successor of Raja Ajay Pal, but it was only after Balbhadra Shah that this surname was popularized by the rulers of Garhwal. According to Bhakt Darshan, when Aurangzeb defeated his brother Dara Shikoh, the latter is said to have taken refuge in Srinagar Garhwal, but he was treacherously sent to Delhi and for this act of prodition the Raja was investitured with the title of Shah. But this view is sceptical since Aurangzeb ascended the Imperial throne in 1658 A.D., whereas both Kalyan Shah and Balbhadra Shah reigned during the later half of the 16th century.

Dr. Pati Ram Parmar is of the view that, a Bartwal from village Satera in Talla Nagpur is said to have been sent to Delhi on state affairs. During his stay there one of the female members of the royal seraglio fell seriously ill. The messenger of Garhwal implored to be allowed to diagnose her suffering through a thread tied to the wrist of the patient. On his success he asked for the title of Shah for his Raja instead of the reward intended for him.

Walton has referred that, a royal prince of the Delhi house came to Garhwal for change of climate. On his return his account of the reception given to him pleased the Emperor so much that he bestowed the title of Shah upon the Raja. This visit he said was made in 1483 A.D.

How far the traditions as revealed by the aforesaid authors are correct, cannot be said because, the contemporary chronicles are silent about the incident. However it can be concluded that after conquering the 52 principalities and establishing the vast kingdom of Garhwal, which extended upto Sambhal in Morada-bad district, and which was not under the sway of the Delhi Sultanate, Raja Ajay Pal must have been recognized as Shah, the Imperial Majesty. This also leads us to the conclusion that his immediate successor Kalyan Shah must have adopted this title on the above pretext. Ajay Pal did not change the cognomen of Pal to that of Shah though he had established his independent hegemony, because, he was already famous as Ajay Pal, and moreover being a follower of the Gorakhnath sect, the title of Shah must not have appealed to his saintly ego. After Kalyan Shah, the 38th ruler of Beckett's list, the subsequent rulers upto Balbhadra Shah, the 43rd ruler, must have also adopted this cognomen, but it took some time to come into vogue, since it was an alien name and, therefore, the surname Pal with their first name is more popular.

Balbhadra Shah, the successor of Sahaj Pal ruled Garhwal from 1575 to 1591 A.D. There are no primary sources available of the reign of Balbhadra Shah. Walton has mentioned that in 1581 A.D., Balbhadra Shah fought a battle against the neighbour-ing kingdom of Kumaon at Gwaldum. During those days Rudra Chand (1565 to 1597 A.D.), a scion of the Chand dynasty was ruling Kumaon. Dr. Shiv Prasad Dabral is of the view that this battle was waged somewhere around 1590 and 1591 A.D. The year of the battle cannot be fixed but it certainly means that Balbhadra Shah was ruling Garhwal during that period.

According to Beckett's list Balbhadra Shah was succeeded by Man Shah. There are sufficient inscriptional evidences of his reign which are as follows:

a) An inscription on the door of the temple of Kshetra Pal at Deoprayag, dated 1665 Vikrami, i.e. 1608 A.D.
b) Another inscription in the temple of Raghunath Ji at Deoprayag. It is of Samvat 1667, i.e. 1610 A.D.

Both the inscriptions are land grants conferred on the temple. Apart from these inscriptions there is another source of information about Man Shah's reign. In the book, 'The Early Travels in India, 1589 A.D. to 1619 A.D.' by Foster, one European traveller, Finch has given lucid details of his tour in India from 1608 to 1611 A.D. He mentions the country of Garhwal and the name of the ruler Raja Man Shah. He says that the very rich and all powerful king Man Shah's kingdom lies in between the rivers Jumna and the Ganges. It is said that he takes his meals in big golden utensils. The length of his domain is 300 kos and the breadth about 150 kos. One of the borders of his kingdom is 200 kos from Agra.

From the account of William Finch, it can be assumed that Raja Man Shah must have been on the throne of Garhwal upto 1611 A.D. and he must have ruled approximately from 1591 to 1611 A.D.

Man Shah was succeeded by Shyam Shah, the 44th ruler of this dynasty. He was a famous king and his name is also referred to in the 'Tuzuk-i-Jahangiri' or the memoirs of Jahangir. It is an account of the presentation of a horse and an elephant to Raja Shyam Singh, alias Shyam Shah of the kingdom of Srinagar (Garhwal) by the Mughal Emperor. There is also a copper plate inscription of Shyam Shah of Samvat 1672, i.e., 1615 A.D., which corroborates that Shyam Shah ruled Garhwal during the reign of the Mughal Emperor Jahangir. This copper plate inscription is in connection with the endowment of land to some Shivnath Jogi of the village Silasari.

As regards the fixation of dates of Raja Shyam Shah's rule in

Garhwal, Shiv Prasad Dabral has stated that he was on the throne from 1611 to 1630 A.D. Shyam Shah's predecessor was ruling Garhwal until 1611 A.D. which indicates that he must have come to the helm of affairs around 1612 A.D. The presentation of the horse and elephant by Jahangir was made in April 1621 A.D. after which there are no evidential details to indicate that Shyam Shah ruled after this period. Thus it can be assumed that Shyam Shah ruled Garhwal approximately from 1612 to 1622 A.D. Raturi states that Shyam Shah died without any issue, so his uncle Mahipat Shah succeeded him. Raturi has not given a definite date of Shyam Shah's demise. Walton and other authors are also silent about the death of Shyam Shah. Thus it can be assumed that Mahipat Shah must have been crowned somewhere around 1622 A.D.

Mahipat Shah was famous in Garhwal as 'Garva Bhanjan', i.e. one who destroyed the pride of his enemies in the battle field. It is said that there were frequent tiffs between Garhwal and the neighbouring Kumaon region during his reign and he was successful in defeating his enemies. Andrade, a Jesuit missionary has mentioned his invasion of Tibet in 1624 A.D.

Dabral is of the view that Mahipat Shah reigned from 1631 to 1635 A.D. Rahul Sankrityayan and others have given no particular dates. It is said that Mahipat Shah died while fighting against the Raja of Kumaon. As tradition goes, he was determined to end his life in this campaign since he had killed a few innocent Nagas (serpent Gods), and then he had gouged out the eyes from the statue of Bharat in the temple of Bharat at Rishikesh. He was so contrite about his misdeeds that he wanted to finish his life on a battle field. However there is no account of the last battle fought by Mahipat Shah in the history of Kumaon, written by Badri Dutt Pande or Rahul Sankrityayan. It seems that Mahipat Shah ruled from 1622 to 1631 A.D. From the aforesaid account of Andrade, it is evident that Mahipat Shah was ruling Garhwal in 1624 A.D. There is another information which supports the view about Mahipat Shah's rule in that period. Atkinson has referred to an inscription of Mahipat Shah of the year 1625 A.D. at Keshav Rai ka Math, i.e. monastery of Keshav Rai at Srinagar in Garhwal. But when I visited the monastery in 1976, the inscription had been obliterated by then. The inmates of the monastery told me that it was decipherable until September 1972, after which it was effaced by vandals.

Apart from C' Wessels, the author of 'Early Jesuit Travellers in Central Asia, 1603-1721 A.D.', Andrade's journey to Tibet, via Srinagar Garhwal has also been confirmed by another author, Sir Edward Maclagan in his book, 'The Jesuits and the Great Mogul'. He states that, ". . . . on March 30, 1624, Father Antonio de Andrade left Agra with a lay brother, Manual Marques, to follow the king, Jahangir, on his journey to Kashmir. On reaching Delhi, however, he learnt of the projected departure of a band of Hindu pilgrims to Badrinath in the Himalayas, and with characteristic prompitude he decided to join them with a view to penetrate beyond the mountains." Maclagan has mentioned that Andrade was accompanied by Manual Marques; C' Wessels has also given the name of Andrade's companion as Marques.

From the account of Azevedo, another Jesuit missionary, who visited Tsaprang, it is evidenced that Mahipat Shah died in 1631 A.D. Francis de Azevedo was appointed in 1627 A.D. to the Mogor Mission by the Society of Jesuits at Agra. On June 28th, he started from Agra to Tsaprang, via Srinagar Garhwal. He was at Srinagar in July 1631 A.D. Thus it can be construed that Mahipat Shah ruled from 1622 to 1631 A.D. and not 1631 to 1635 A.D.

The aim of the Jesuits to visit Tsaprang was to spread Christianity. From their accounts it can be concluded that Mahipat Shah was an independent ruler and could challenge the might of the Mughals. Andrade has mentioned that no regard was paid to Jahangir's decrees by the Garhwalis when Andrade was passing through Garhwal to visit Tsaprang.

Mahipat Shah was succeeded by Prithvi Pat Shah. From the accounts of the Jesuit missionary Azevedo, it is known that Prithvi Pat Shah was only seven years old when he became heir apparent. The local historians are also of a similar view, they state that his mother had taken the reins of the State in her hands to look after his welfare and rule the kingdom on his behalf. But these authors and the British historians like Atkinson, Walton and G.R.C. Williams, have not mentioned the real name of the queen. They have stated that she was known by the name of, 'Nak-kati-Rani,' i.e. a queen who chops off the noses. Her name was actually Rani Karnawati as is evident from the copper plate inscription of 1640 A.D. issued by her on behalf of her son Maharaja Prithvi Pat Shah, confirming a land grant to the Hatwal Brahmins of the village Haat in Chamoli district of Garhwal. Maharani Karnawati's name is also mentioned in an old manuscript, 'Sanwari Granth'. This manuscript deals with 'tantra', and her name has been cited in a similar manner as in the copper plate inscription of 1640 A.D. She has been addressed as 'Maharani Mata Karnawati', i.e. queen mother Karnawati. The manuscript is in the dynastic collection of Thakur Shoor Beer Singh of Purana Durbar, Tehri.

In this connection, I may clarify an old misunderstanding and rectify the mistake committed by G.R.C. Williams and also by Atkinson. They have stated that Karnawati was the wife of Ajboo Kuwar or Kuwar Ajab Shah. Actually Maharani Karnawati was the consort of Maharaja Mahipat Shah, whereas Ajboo Kuwar was one of the nine sons of Prithvi Pat Shah. This means that Ajboo Kuwar was the grandson of Maharani Karnavati and not her husband as has been pointed out by the foreign authors.

There is an interesting incident which speaks of Rani Karna-vati's bravey, and the reason she was nicknamed as, 'Nak-kati Rani'. Niccolao Manucci, the author of 'Storia Do Mogor', has mentioned that Shah Jahan deployed an army to invade Garh-wal. In the battle that ensued, the Mughal forces were defeated very badly and the noses of the survivors were chopped off.

'Mughal Durbar ya Maasirul Umra', which is a translation from the original text has also related this incident. Manucci has not given the name of the general, but 'Mughal Durbar ya Maasi-rul Umra', has mentioned the name of the general also. He was known as Najabat Khan. Travernier has also recounted this inci-dent, but he has mixed it with the period when Suleiman Shikoh took refuge in Garhwal.

The date and year of the battle have not been accounted for by the above authors and it is not possible to fix the exact date owing to the paucity of source material. However on the basis of the copper plate inscription of Rani Karnawati of the year 1640 A.D., it can be assumed that the Mughals must have invaded Garhwal before or around 1640 A.D. and also Rani Karnawati was ruling on behalf of Prithvi Pat Shah upto that period. From the accounts of Manucci and others, as cited above, the Mughals were defeated by Rani Karnawati alias 'Nak-kati-Rani', the ruler of Garhwal and not Prithvi Pat Shah. Thus the battle between the Garhwalis and the Mughals must have been fought during that period when Karnawati was ruling as his guardian. Prithvi Pat Shah ascended the throne in 1631 A.D. at the age of seven years. In 1640 A.D. he was only sixteen years and thus was not in a position to fight the Mughals on his own before or during that period.

This period which can easily be termed as a glorious era of the history of Garhwal, is also distinguished by another landmark. According to 'Muntakhabu-l-Lubab', in 1659 A.D., after the defeat of Dara Shikoh in the battle of Samugarh on 29th May 1658 A.D., his son Suleiman Shikoh took refuge in Garhwal. Travernier, Bernier, Manucci and the modern his torian Dr. K.R. Qanungo have also referred to Suleiman Shikoh's escape to Garhwal.

Aurangzeb sent messages to Prithvi Pat Shah to surrender the prince, but his persuasion and threats were met with contempt. Bernier has cited that the Raja wrote to Aurangzeb that stones would be enough to stop the forces of 'four Hindustan' so that he was constrained to turn back. Manucci has also mentioned the defiant attitude of the Raja of Garhwal. He wrote to Raja Jai Singh that on no account he could harm his reputation by making over to Aurangzeb anyone who had sought his protection. He was however thankful for Raja Jai Singh's friendship, as for Aurangzeb he heeded neither his promises nor his menaces. In the end he has commented, ". . . . let him know that he who could cut off noses could equally cut off heads." Aurangzeb then took recourse to ruse. Dr. Qanungo is of the view that when Jai Singh could not convince the king of Garhwal to surrender Suleiman Shikoh, he instigated a powerful Brahmin minister against him who tried to give him poison in the form of medicine. But the vigilant prince tested the adulterated medicine on a cat and was saved. When the king came to know about his minister's treachery, he got him beheaded. Afterwards Jai Singh inspired the Garhwali prince Medni Shah to emulate Aurangzeb and revolt against his father.

Later Suleiman Shikoh was surrendered to Aurangzeb somewhere around December 1660 A.D. because according to Dr.

Qanungo, he was brought before Aurangzeb on 5th January 1661 A.D. Manucci has stated, the aged Raja of Srinagar felt so greatly the vileness of the deed carried out by his son and so great was his sorrow that in short space he ended his days in disgrace, saying he would have lost his territory and all his wealth rather than that his son should be guilty of such an act of infamy. It seems that Medni Shah was banished from Garhwal to Delhi where he died in 1662 A.D. for his treachery. His death in Delhi is corroborated by the Farman which Aurangzeb sent to Prithvi Pat Shah in 1662 A.D. It is important to note in this connection that the authors of Garhwal's history like Dr. Shiv Prasad Dabral and others have stated that Medni Shah ruled Garhwal from 1660 to 1684 A.D. whereas he had died in 1662 A.D.

Local historians, Dabral, Raturi and others who have relied upon British historians like Atkinson, Walton and others have stated that Prithvi Pat Shah ruled upto 1660 A.D. This view is not correct because the Farman that Aurangzed sent to Prithvi Pat Shah about his son Medni Shah's death is of the year 1662 A.D. Then there is another Farman of Aurangzeb of the year 1665 A.D. which he sent to Fateh Shah on his grandfather Prithvi Pat Shah's death. It appears that Prithvi Pat Shah was alive upto 1667 A.D. The Government of India had invited the Chinese attention to a copper plate inscription of that year which bears the seal of Raja Prithvi Pat Shah of Garhwal, in support of their case regarding the boundary dispute about Nilang. Both Ram Gopal and Shanta Kumar have cited this inscription. Then there is another copper plate inscription of Maharaja Fateh Shah, the grandson of Prithvi Pat Shah, which bears the seal of Prithvi Pat Shah. This inscription is also of the year 1667 A.D. and is a land grant.

From the inscriptions cited above, it is obvious that Prithvi Pat Shah was alive upto 1667 A.D. It seems that he had abdicated the throne in 1665 A.D. in favour of his grandson Fateh Shah since he had banished his son Medni Shah from Garhwal. When the Mughal court received the information that Fateh Shah has been crowned as king of Garhwal, Aurangzeb must have conceived that Prithvi Pat Shah is dead because Aurangzeb who had himself seized power by interning his father could never have imagined that one can abdicate in favour of his grandson.

The Farmans issued by the Mughal Emperor to the Rajas of Garhwal, Prithvi Pat Shah and Fateh Shah, are couched in the phraseology as if the kings of Garhwal had accepted the suzerainty of the Mughal Emperor. It is not substantiated by realities; Garhwal was absolutely independent during the medieval period as has been brought out earlier. Moreover the defeat of the Mughal army during the rule of Shah Jahan and the very fact that Suleiman Shikoh took refuge in Garhwal shows that the king of Garhwal was not under the Mughal Emperor and that the fugitive prince thought him capable to withstand the threats of the Mughal court. These Farmans are just a ruse to illustrate the suzerainty of the Mughal Emperor in the hills and particularly in the latter case to brow beat and allure the young king to his subjugation. What he could not achieve on the battle field during the rule of Prithvi Pat Shah, he tried to attain it in the reign of Fateh Shah with the help of this Farman. The Farman of 1665 A.D. was aimed also at resuscitating the influence of Aurangzeb in Kumaon with the help of the Garhwali king.

Prithvi Pat Shah was not only a brave and independent ruler but he was liberal and religiously tolerant also. Maclagan is of the view that he permitted Father Ceschi to build a Church at Srinagar and also allotted him some land for an orchard.

There are several primary sources of the reign of Prithvi Pat Shah. Apart from the two Farmans of Aurangzeb and two inscriptions of Raja Prithvi Pat Shah cited already, the following other sources are available:

a) Nishan of Dara Shikoh sent to Prithvi Pat Shah, dated 15th May 1647, as has been quoted in the book, 'Mughal Farmans 1540 A.D. to 1706 A.D.', Volume I, edited by Dr. K.P. Srivastava.

b) Inscription in the monastery of Madho Dass in Laxmi Narayan temple of the year 1642 A.D. at the village Bhaktiana, just adjacent to Srinagar. The inscription is in the outer portion of the main temple wall.

c) Inscription of the year 1664 A.D. on the southern door of the temple of Raghunath Ji at Deoprayag.

d) An inscription on the western doorway of the temple of Raghunath Ji in Deoprayag. This inscription is also of 1664 A.D.

Prithvi Pat Shah was succeeded by Fateh Shah at the age of 33, which is evident from his portrait in the dynastic collection of Thakur Shoor Beer Singh. The age of Fateh Shah at the time of accession has been mentioned by the artist of the portrait. In the painting Fateh Shah is mounted on a horse and is giving a very stately look. So the belief that his mother was ruling as his guardian as advanced by Pandit Hari Krishna Raturi, and Dabral's view that Fateh Shah came to the throne at the age of seven years is not correct. Prithvi Pat Shah had abdicated in his favour in 1665 A.D. and Fateh Shah must have been installed as the ruler of Garhwal only when he had attained adulthood.

According to 'Vichitra Natak', the autobiography of Guru Gobind Singh, the famous battle between Fateh Shah and Guru Gobind Singh was fought at Bhangani, a village six miles from Paonta, the residence of Guru Gobind Singh. Dr. Fauja Singh is of the view that the battle of Bhangani was the first of the many battles fought by Guru Gobind Singh.

The following ancient and panegyrical works of his period are available today:

a) 'Fateh Shah Karna Granth', by Jatadhar or Jatashankar. The original manuscript is preserved in the Ved Shala Library of Pandit Chakradhar Shastri at Deoprayag.

b) 'Fateh Prakash' by Ratan Kavi or Kshem Ram. The original munuscript is in the dynastic collection of Thakur Shoor Beer Singh and he has edited and published it from Bharat Prakashan Mandir, Aligarh in 1961. Both authors were the court poets of Fateh Shah.

c) 'Vrit Vichar' by Kavi Raj Sukhdev Misra. This manuscript is in the dynastic collection of Thakur Shoor Beer Singh.

d) 'Vrit Kaumudi' or 'Chhandsar Pingal' by Mati Ram. The original manuscript is also in the dynastic collection of Thakur Shoor Beer Singh. A few pages of the manuscript are also available in the 'Nagari Pracharani Sabha', Varanasi.

Ratan Kavi has eulogised the glory of Fateh Shah and also the splendour of his kingdom Garhwal. The famous poet Bhushan has also eulogised Fateh Shah. Mati Ram's famous work, 'Vrit Kaumudi', is replete with the praise of Fateh Shah. He has compared

1. a) Raja Ajay Pal after whom Garhwal was named

1. b) Raja Shyam Shah. Mukandi Lal has mistook this king for the painter Mola Ram.

1. c) Upendra Shah.

1. d) Raja Pradip Shah.

1. e) Raja Lalit Shah.

1. f) Raja Jai Krit Shah.

1. g) Raja Pradyumna Shah.

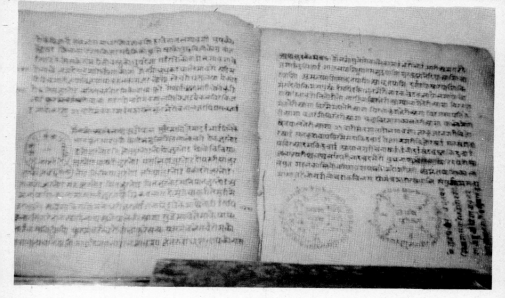

2. 'Tantrik' manuscript in which Ajay Pal has been referred to as a saint.

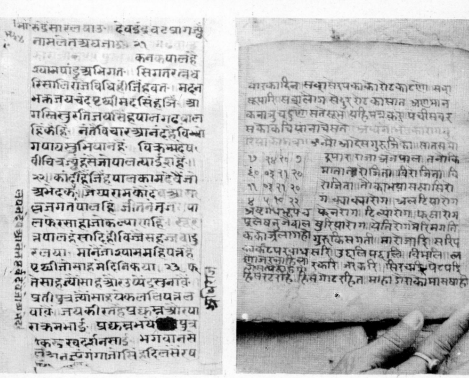

1. h) 'Sabhasar' by Raja Sudarshan Shāh in which the genealogy of the Parmar rulers has been traced.

3. Page of ancient manuscript 'Sanwari Granth' in which the name of Raja Ajay Pal has been mentioned.

4. Inscription on the stone slab on the main door of 'Keshav Rai ka Math'.
   The inscription is of Raja Mahipat Shah of the year 1625 A.D.

5. A stone inscription in the Laxmi Narayan temple of Srinagar.
   It is of the year 1642 A.D. of Raja Prithvi Pat Shah.

6. Inscription of Prithvi Pat Shah of the year 1657 A.D.

'Kholi ka Ganesh'. The trunk of Lord Ganesh is turned towards the right hand side.

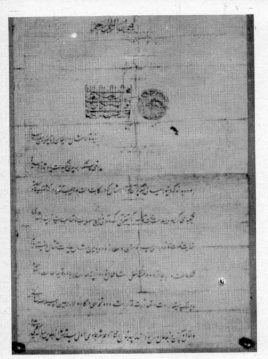

8. Farman of Aurangzeb to Raja Prithvi Pat Shah of the year 1662 A.D.

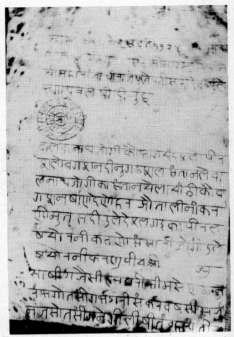

9. Copper plate inscription of Raja Fateh Shah of the year 1667 A.D.

10. Farman of Aurangzeb to Raja Fateh Shah of the year 1665 A.D.

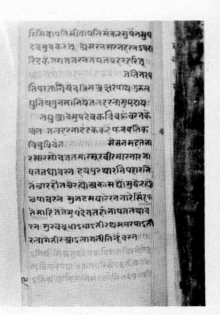

11. A page from ancient manuscript 'Vrit Vichar'. The poet has eulogised Raja Fateh Shah.

12. A page from 'Vrit Kaumudi' by Mati Ram in which the date of composition of the manuscript has been mentioned as 1701 A.D.

13. A page from 'Vrit Kaumudi' in which Mati Ram has praised Fateh Shah.

14. 'Fateh Prakash' by Ratan Kavi. The poet has eulogised Fateh Shah.

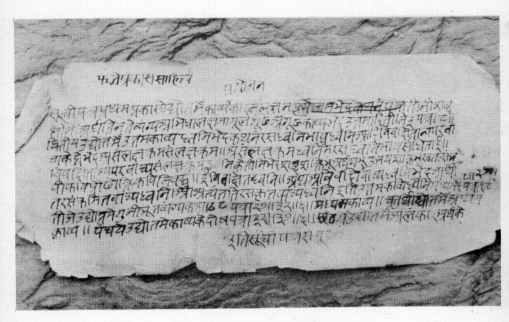

15. Title page of 'Fateh Prakash'.

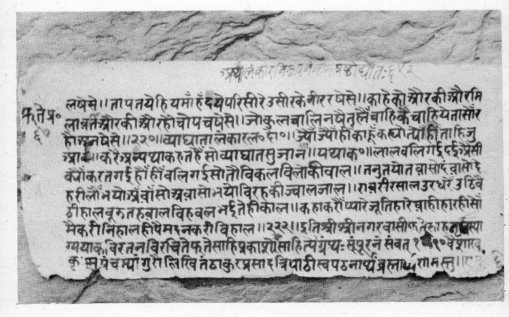

16. Last page of 'Fateh Prakash'.

17. Coin of Raja Pradip Shah.

Obverse side.   Reverse side.

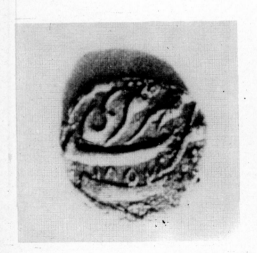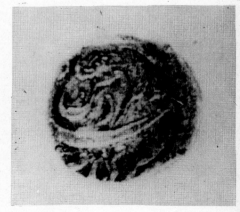

18. Coin of Raja Pradyumna Shah.

Obverse side.   Reverse side.

श्रीमहागणपतयेनमः॥संवत्अष्टादहिसेसतारूनकेसालाजाविरहम
वरचाकरीकुंर्रपरत्रमनालाम॥९॥सेतुमसौरुहनतेहेंसुनोपंचमनम
याकौपादकेसंतानकीजीमनमहिगराय॥२॥वारिसीकौकीनरुकेरीलीआद
निकासंनूरमेरीआनहैसवदासनकौतासं॥३॥नवपरायपयहुंरूरमेंस्वेत
वरीकीनासरवकुकीन्हेहरुनमगुनिकालीनीदीनव॥४॥यरुगरदीगदमेंवृत
गोपंचरेंदगान॥बेरुरीष्टीषामेंसभीवाकेरूरतरुवंवन॥५॥वैयापांहरूरमभ्रहि
सावकितावरवरहीअवगुमनकरी॥परदवेकोलुरनहेंवहवहींपरनारविहारहि
कोमरदी॥जानिकांनकेदंडउवारुनहेंवववेवतहेंवरतवरदी॥कविमेलाग्राभिविचार
करी॥रेसीगदमेंहिपुंगरदीदुःए॥रेसीगरदीसहरमेंवउडेंनरहक्षांनकौग
नुकेबानूंकौभ्याम्हाकलकान॥सुंदररारिहरीकेजेतहेंकुररादीनाथादंवं
वरौगांनोहेंमेंसासपदहुनुवाफूनवर॥माधोहोंदुमासलोनाहरुकेरमेंराग्राग्रूऊऊऊ
दूदाराइंइदेतवकाांगोहरवारा्न॥गीनीगूवमर्तीमेंमुनोपंचवमनलाप॥सहस

Tehri Garhwal State Records F.No.42/1907

...

No.46.

To

Sir L.W. Dane K.C.I.E.C.S.I.
Secretary to the Government of India,

For. Deptt.

Sir,

I am directed to submit for the information of the Government of India a report on a disturbance which recently broke out in the native State of Tehri the accounts of the affair which so far have reached the Government are incomplete and the real object of the out break is somewhat obscure. The greater part of the revenue of H.H. the Raja are derived from his forests and for some years he has been steadily introducing a policy of stricter forest conservancy modelled on the system in force no British territory. It has been the practice of this Government to lend the services of an officer belonging to the provincial forest service to act as conservator of the State. The Officer now holding the appointment is P. Sadanand Sarola who has been in the State since Nov.04. It appears for one the information available that forest settlement operations are at present being carried out in Patti Khas - the sent divisions in which the capital town of Tehri situated. A settlement officer the unded Raja is in charge and is assisted generally by the conservator on Dec.27th 1906 the forest surrounding the Chandrabadni temple about 14 miles from Tehri town were being inspected preparatory to having them this being by ought under-reservation. It is reported

21. Information about the first forest uprising in Tehri Garhwal State in 1907. This was the first forest uprising in the Himalayan region.

Nanda Datt   Clerk   "   "
Narain Datt   Office Superintendent " "
Girdhari Lal   Treasury Head Clerk " "
Rajendra Datt   Kanungo, Barashyun

    It is obvious that he can exert considerable influence
in the district.

    It is notorious that in the Tehri State, under a
Rajput Raja, there is not a single Rajput official.

    The Brahmans, of course, are fighting to keep their
power, which is threatened by the new election system and the
numerical superiority of the Rajputs, and one cannot blame
them; but Bhawani Datt, as Wazir of Tehri, has no business to
employ a man like Ansuya Prasad, or to use his undesirably
wide inflence in this district in favour of a professed non-
cooperator with a C.I.D. record such as Mukandi Lal.

                    Yours sincerely.

                        Sd/- ....

Pauri 3.11.1923
                            District Magistrate
                            Garhwal

22. Letter of District Magistrate of British Garhwal to Commissioner Kumaon
    regarding the hold of Brahman officials in Tehri Garhwal State.

Extracts from the fortnightly D.Os of Commissioner
Kumaun.

            1st half December 1923.
    *   *

    The same methods are being used on behalf of Mukandi
Lal, the Swaraj candidate in Garhwal against the local M.L.C.
Jodh Singh. Acton reports the Tehri Wazir has spent a good
deal of money on behalf of Mukandi Lal I have been to Tehri
and mentioned the matter to the Raja the Tehri Durbar
of course would admit that their Wazir has entered the field
with money- but the opportunity I had of mentioning the matter
to the Raja was too late to have any effect on the elections.
            11th January 1924.
Acton writes :- "The intervention in the elections of H.H.
the Raja of Tehri on behalf of a candidate of the type of
Mukandi Lal did very much more harm to Government prestige
than Mukandi Lal's election."
                    ...
Copy of the confidential Note on Annual Administration for 1922-23.
From. Pandit Bhawani Datt Uniyal Dewan Tehri-Garhwal State.
To   Captain H.H. Mahara a Narendra Shah Sahab Bahadur C.S.I.
        Tehri Garhwal State.

    During the year under report a non-cooperator from
Saharanpore visited Juapatti and just when he began to give
speech abusing the British Government and Your Highness Government he was beaten by the village people and turned out.
Another man who visited Bhandaruin Patti was turned out
under the order of the Durbar. I am making enquiry about
the State Forest Official who is a resident of Dehradun and
who is reported to be wearing Gandhi Cap; and if I could be

23. Information regarding financial assistance extended by the Wazir of Tehri
    Garhwal State to the Swaraj candidate Mukandi Lal.

सद्धौर जिसमें कि वह नामजदगी के लिये रजामन्द हो, साना कहिये ।

(१२) नामजदगी के हुक्म की निवरानी डिस्ट्रिक्ट मजिस्ट्रेट साहिब बहादुर के इजलास में हुक्म होने के तीन दिनके अन्दर की जा सकती है ।

(१३) किसी उम्मेदवार को यह अखियार है कि नामजदगी होने के १५ दिन अन्दर रिटर्निंग साहिब को तहरीरी नोटिस देकर वकीलद्वारी से अपना नाम खारिज करा सकता है । ऐसी हालत में उसका रुपया वापिस कर दिया जायेगा ।

(१५) अगर कोई उम्मेदवार कामयाब न हुआ हो और वह के वोटों की तादाद उन वोटों के जो कि वह पोलिंग स्टेशन में पड़ी हो = में हिस्से से ज्यादा न हो तो जो रुपया जमा किया गया हो जब्त किया जायेगा ।

दस्तखत (अंग्रेजी में)
पं० भोलादत्त पन्त साहब
प्रलेक्शन ऑफिसर पौड़ी-गढ़वाल ।
२६—६—२५

टिहरीराज्य के चन्द स्वार्थी कर्म-चारियों की करामात ।

श्री १०८ मानू केप्टेन महाराज नरेन्द्रशाह जू देव बहादुर सी० एस० आई० के पदसपंकज में सादर प्रार्थना ।

आजकल चन्द स्वार्थ-कुशल कर्मचारी टिहरी दरबार की आड़ लेकर राज्य की दया को दिनोंदिन प्रत्यन्त संकीर्ण बनाते जा रहे हैं । राज्य का कोई भी व्यक्ति अपना दुख तथा उन कुटिल कर्मचारियों की करतूतों को यदि अपने न्यायप्रिय, प्रजावत्सल आदर्श महाराजा की सेवा में निवेदन करने का प्रयत्न करता है तो उक्त स्वार्थीदल के प्रबन्ध से अभियुक्त बनाया जा कर बेचारा निरपराध क़ीकी विहार्हियों के द्वारा बिना ही राजाज्ञा के जेल में ठूंस दिया जाता है । जलएव राज्य भर में कोई भी व्यक्ति महाराजा की सेवा में पहुंचने का साहस नहीं कर पाता, न किसी में पहुंचने की शक्ति ही है । वह स्वार्थ कुशल मंडली का प्रबन्ध क्या है मानो अब चातु का बना हुइइ दुर्ग है ।

हम सुनते हैं गांव से गांव तक नामनगर का अर्थां हो चुका होगा, कौनपुर के एक नघन-मान्य व्यक्ति भटू ने वर्तमान सेटिलमेन्ट ऑफिसर की बेजा कारवाई की बाबत कुछ हित-राज महाराजा बहादुर के हुजूर में पेश किया ही था कि स्वार्थी कर्मचारियों के गिरोह ने बेचारे की दुखपूर्ण प्रार्थनाएं महाराज तक पहुंचने ही नहीं दीं । और बाहर ही बाहर पदवन्त द्वारा उन निर्दोषों को क़ौंसी सिपा-हियों के द्वारा गिरफ्तार कराकर बिना ही हुक्म महाराजा या किसी भी प्रशासलत के जेल में ठूंस दिया । महीनों तक बेचारे इमुषाक के हेतु किसी भी अदालत में पेश न किया गया, लेकिन अब सुनते हैं कि बेचारे पर मिथया दीप मढ़े जाकर पार साल के लिये जेल में रख दिया गया !

भटू की गिरफ्तारी हो जाने के कुछ दिन बाद टिहरी राज्य के कतिपय राजभक्त लोगों ने प्रजा के घोर दुखों को अपने प्रबासस्थल और न्यायप्रिय महाराजा बहादुर तक पहुं-चाने के लिये राज्य के बाहर देहरादून में एक सभा खोली । जिसका घोर विरोध उक्त स्वा-र्थी मंडली ने किया व कराया, परन्तु शुभ कार्य की सहायता सर्वशक्तिमान, न्यायकर्ता, करुणासिन्धु भगवान अवश्य करता है, जिस की सहायता वह करता है, उसका कोई बाल भी बांका नहीं कर सकता । दुष्ट स्वार्थी चुप न रहे, सभा के एक मेम्बर नारायणसिंह भंडारी को टिहरी राज्य की नकली पुलिस द्वारा अर्थात् भारी प्रपंचु द्वारा ता० १९ जन०२५ को न्यायप्रिय ब्रिटिश सरकार के प्रातिनिमय शासनाबु के भी-तर इलाके राजपुर से भी गिरफ्तार कर लेदी गये !!! टिहरी राज्य के अन्दर लेजाकर फौज के कमंडस्त पहरे में रख कर बेचारे की फासना की अत्यहुनीय कड़ दिये गये । परन्तु परमा-त्मा की कृपा से वह भीखा पाकर दुश्मनों के पंजूं से निकल भागा । कीड़के कमंडस्त पहरे पर मानो मोहनास्त्र का प्रयोग किया गया ! (फौज का प्रबन्ध भी प्रशंसनीय होगा । सं०)
नारायणसिंह राहोंराव भयङ्कर राक्षसों की वध

24. Newspaper *Kshatriya Beer* in which there is an article on the corruption of the State officials in Tehri Garhwal.

25. Article on the war efforts of Tehri Garhwal State in *Indian Forester*, dated December 1942.

26. Annual Administrative Report of Tehri Garhwal State of the year 1943-44. In this report there is some information regarding the police department.

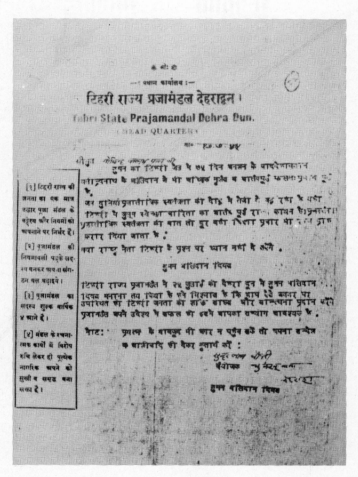

27. Invitation extended by Tehri State Praja Mandal to Pandit Govind Ballabh Pant about their celebration of 'Suman Balidan Diwas'.

28.   Raja Kirti Shah of Tehri Garhwal State.

his generosity with that of Shivaji. It is said that Fateh Shah was a great patron of painting. Ananda Coomaraswamy has mentioned that at the close of the 17th century two Hindu painters from the Mughal court, Shyam Dass and Har Dass accompanied Suleiman Shikoh to Garhwal. It is possible that these painters got patronage during the reign of Fateh Shah which might have given birth to the Garhwali School of Painting. Mola Ram, the grandson of Har Dass, who lived from 1760-1833, was a protagonist of this school of art. This art was more Rajput than Mughal.

Fateh Shah had a great reverence for the 'Nath Panth', as is evident from the copper plate inscription of 1667 A.D., issued by him in favour of Balak Nath Jogi. This Saint Balak Nath had achieved great fame amongst the 'Siddhas' (realized saints) of Northern India. He had also invited the Sikh Guru Ram Rai to his kingdom and built a Gurudwara in Dehradun. Fateh Shah made an endowment of three villages, Khurbura, Rajpur and Chamasari to Guru Ram Rai. Later, his grandson, Pradip Shah added a further grant of four villages, viz. Dhumawala, Miyanwala, Panditwari, and Dhantawala to the Gurudwara.

There are several land grants of Fateh Shah which he endowed to temples. Some of these 'tamra patras' copper plate inscriptions are still available. They are detailed as below:

a) A copper plate inscription of the year 1667 A.D. issued by him in favour of Balak Nath Jogi and which has been cited earlier.

b) A copper plate inscription of Samvat 1757, i.e. 1700 A.D., the copy of which is available in the dynastic collection of Thakur Shoor Beer Singh. This is a temple grant of the Raj Rajeshwari temple in Devalgarh 'mandal'.

c) An inscription of the year 1706 A.D. which is famous as the 'Bindakoti Tamrapatra'. It is not only a temple grant, but it also mentions that a part of the income derived from the land bestowed would be used for maintaining a 'dharamshala', where pilgrims and the poor shall get free food.

d) An inscription of the year 1715 A.D. which is a land grant endowed to the monastery of the disciples of the 'Nath Panth'. This inscription is in the dynsatic collection of

Thakur Shoor Beer Singh. Some words of the inscription cannot be deciphered.

There is also a numismatic evidence of the reign of Fateh Shah. Hari Krishna Raturi, the Wazir of the Tehri Garhwal State has given a photograph in his book of the coins issued during his reign.

The inscription of the year 1715 A.D. is quite important, since the date of Fateh Shah's demise can be calculated with its help. There are different versions furnished by various authors as regards the death of Fateh Shah. In Beckett's list, it is Samvat 1765, i.e. 1708 A.D. Dr. Pati Ram and Shiv Prasad Dabral have relied on the date given in Walton's Gazetteer, which states that Fateh Shah died in 1716 A.D. Raturi and Rahul Sankrityayan have fixed the date of his demise to a later period, i.e. 1744 A.D. Bhakt Darshan says that Fateh Shah died in 1715 A.D.

Accoding to the copper plate inscription of the year 1715 A.D. of Fateh Shah, it is obvious that he was ruling upto this year. After this copper plate inscription we do not find any evidence of his reign in the form of inscriptions, edicts etc. It is possible that Fateh Shah died in the year 1715 A.D. There is a copper plate inscription of Samvat 1773, i.e. 1716 A.D. of Pradip Shah's reign in the dynastic collection of Thakur Shoor Beer Singh. On the basis of this inscription it is obvious that by 1716 A.D., Fateh Shah was dead. The period between the issue of the two copper plate inscriptions, i.e., of Fateh Shah, 1715 A.D. and Pradip Shah 1716 A.D., is one year, one month and seven days. It is possible that Fateh Shah died after the copper plate inscription of the year 1715 A.D. was issued. Now the question arises who ruled during the time that elapsed between Fateh Shah's death and Pradip Shah's accession to the throne. It must have been a short span, about a year approximately. Bhakt Darshan is of the opinion that Fateh Shah was succeeded by his son Dilip Shah. Dabral has only cited the views of different authors. Walton states that after Fateh Shah's death his son Dilip Shah came to the throne in 1716 A.D.

Fateh Shah must have been succeeded by Upendra Shah, as is evident from Beckett's list. There is a portrait of Upendra Shah also in the dynastic collection amongst the portraits of the other

Garhwali kings, which further indicates his status as a ruler. Moreover the 'Bindakoti Tamrapatra' which has been quoted already, verifies his succession. This inscription of 1706 A.D. shows that Upendra Shah was the eldest son of Fateh Shah and Dilip Shah was his second son. Amongst the witnesses in the inscription, names of Fateh Shah's sons, Upendra Shah, Dilip Shah, Madhukar Shah and Pahar Shah have been referred. Upendra Shah's name is first in the order, which shows that he was the eldest son. Thus according to the principle of primogeniture prevalent amongst the Rajputs, Upendra Shah and not Dilip Shah must have succeeded Fateh Shah.

After Upendra Shah, Pradip Shah ascended the throne in 1716 A.D. Dabral has mentioned that three copper plate inscriptions of the years, 1725, 1734 and 1755 A.D. are available. But he has not referred to the source of their availability and the details of these inscriptions. Apart from these inscriptions another grant of Pradip Shah of the year 1716 A.D., which has been cited already, is available. Together with the aforesaid primary sources, two coins of the reign of Pradip Shah are available in the State Museum, Lucknow. Rahul has stated that inscriptions upto the year 1772 A.D. are available. But he has not given the particular years and the number of inscriptions available.

The period of Pradip Shah is notable from the view point that congenial relationship was established between Kumaon and Garhwal during his reign. Pradip Shah ruled Garhwal upto the end of the year 1772 A.D. He was succeeded by Lalit Shah who ascended the throne of Garhwal on 29th Mangsir, Samvat 1829, i.e. December 1772 A.D. There are two coins of Lalit Shah in the State Museum, Lucknow.

Lalit Shah's reign is marked with internal dissensions in the neighbouring region of Kumaon between two rival factions, the claimants to the throne and a few officials of the late king, Raja Deep Chand. In this turbulent State, some Kunwar Mohan Singh, who was also known as Mohan Singh Rautela in 1777 A.D. proclaimed himself the ruler of Kumaon. But the ministers of the late king especially Joshis, who were hostile to Mohan Singh, joined hands with Lalit Shah the ruler of Garhwal, and helped him in entering Kumaon with a big force. Mohan Singh was defeated and he left Kumaon in 1779 A.D. Lalit Shah took advantage of the situation and placed his second son Pradyumna Shah on the throne of Kumaon with the help of Harsh Deo Joshi, who was given the office of the Prime Minister of Pradyumna Shah as a reward for his services. Later Pradyumna Shah acquired the family name Chand of the Kumaoni kings and declared himself to be the adopted son of Raja Deep Chand.

Lalit Shah died immediately after his victory over Kumaon. After installing his son Pradyumna Shah he was on his way back when he died of malaria at Dulri in August 1780. Thereafter he was succeeded by his eldest son, Jai Krit Shah, a step brother of Pradyumna Shah.

The two brothers, Jai Krit Shah, the ruler of Garhwal and Pradyumna Shah, alias Pradyumna Chand were not on congenial terms. It is said that Jai Krit Shah even conspired with Mohan Singh who was in exile to oust Pradyumna Shah from Kumaon.

Jai Krit Shah ruled upto 1785 A.D. The authors of Garhwal history have given different dates of Jai Krit Shah's reign. Raturi states that he ruled from 1791 to 1797 A.D., and according to Mukandi Lal 1780 to 1785 A.D. Beckett's list gives 1780-1786 A.D. Walton has not given the date of Jai Krit Shah's demise and the other authors have quoted the view of the aforesaid authors. The dates given by Mukandi Lal and Beckett are approximately the same and are more probable. Raturi's view that he ruled from 1791 to 1797 A.D. has not been substantiated by any evidence. Moreover the letter of 1784 A.D. by Jai Krit Shah, which was quoted by the Indian Government during the boundary discussions in 1926, is a clear indication that the year of accession of Jai Krit Shah as given by Raturi is incorrect. Jai Krit Shah ascended the throne in 1780 A.D. and from 1785 A.D. onwards there is enough evidence to substantiate that Pradyumna Shah had come to the helm of affairs. Thus it can be concluded that Jai Krit Shah ruled from 1780 to 1785 A.D.

After Jai Krit Shah's demise, Pradyumna Shah left Kumaon and took over the reins of the government in Garhwal. He did not stay in peace since the time he returned from Kumaon and on 14th May 1804, he was killed in the battle of Khurbura by the Gurkhas.

Several causes can be attributed to the defeat of this gallant king. Garhwal was plagued by perpetual turmoils from the time of Raja Jai Krit Shah and this was sapping the vitality of the kingdom. Nature also wreaked havoc in the form of a famine before the Gurkha onslaught in Samvat 1851, i.e. 1794-95 A.D. This famine is still notoriously known as, 'ekawani-bawani', i.e. 51-52 in Garhwal, and 'bawani' has become a synonym for famine in Garhwal, that year. Garhwal was yet to recover from this devastation that it was struck by an earthquake. It was felt for seven days and nights continuously.

Apart from the political intrigues and natural calamities that had plagued Garhwal, the discomfiture of Pradyumna Shah as regards the instrigues of his younger brother Parakram Shah, and the treachery of Harsh Deo Joshi and Mola Ram were also responsible for the Garhwali disaster in 1804.

About the rule of Pradyumna Shah, three dates have been given. Beckett states that he ruled from 1786 to 1804 A.D. Raturi is of the view that he ruled from 1797 to 1804 A.D. and Mukandi Lal has fixed his period from 1785 to 1804 A.D. The dates given by Mukandi Lal are authentic and tally with those given by the State Museum, Lucknow. There are nine coins of Pradyumna Shah in the State Museum, Lucknow and on their basis, it has been stated that Pradyumna Shah ruled from 1785 to 1804 A.D. Thus the date of accession as given by Raturi as 1797 A.D. is obviously not correct. Moreover in the dynastic collection of Thakur Shoor Beer Singh, there is a copper plate inscription of 1788 A.D. which vividly indicates that Pradyumna Shah had ascended the throne by 1788 A.D. much before 1797 A.D. It can thus be concluded that Pradyumna Shah ruled from 1785 to 1804 A.D.

During the Parmar rule, the government consisted of a simple monarchy, but the power of the sovereign was in fact, far from absolute, being ever controlled in a greater or less degree by the will of the aristocracy. In the Kothar inscription it is mentioned that the religious head had wielded a great influence over the king and Mola Ram has referred him as 'Ojha Guru', in his works. The king was assisted by a body of ministers who looked after the various departments. The different ministers of the king were the 'Wazir', 'Duftari', 'Faujdar', 'Goldar', 'Bhandari', 'Negi' and 'Thokdar'. Wazir was the prime minister, he was also known as the 'Diwan'. Duftari, it seems was the director of the government offices and was stationed at the capital. Faujdars were the military governors who administered the parganas. Their duty was to maintain peace, collect revenue and defend the frontiers of the kingdom. Goldar was the security chief and he was responsible for the security of the royal treasury and the other offices in the capital. The revenue in the 'parganas' was collected mainly by the Thokdars who were like feudal lords and their titles were hereditary.

It appears that some individuals who were given the status of a 'Thokdar' and were assigned the revenue of certain villages for their distinguished services to the king were known as Negis. Bhandaris were the royal treasurers.

The main source of income was the land revenue, i.e. 'Sirti' and the assessment was made in accordance with the fertility of the land. One third, i.e., 'tihar' and half, i.e. 'adhela' of the total yield used to be the normal land tax. In the capital, the Duftari's office used to maintain a record of the cultivated land and the land was measured according to the amount of seed sown in a particular plot. Under the Parmar kings, the proprietary right in the land was vested in the king and was inalienable. However he could transfer his proprietary rights in the following circumstances:

a) He could donate land to the Brahmins for their erudition and this act was known as 'Sankalp' or 'Vishnupreet'.

b) The king rewarded the brave for their gallantry or to the heirs of those slain in the battle and this investiture was known as 'Raut'.

c) The king also gave land to the officers in the form of fiefs in lieu of their salaries.

Other important sources of income were, revenue from gold washing, duties on exports and imports, mining, trade and pilgrim trade. Trade was of two types, one with Tibet and the other with the plains of India. Pilgrim trade meant the income derived from the furnishing of supply to the pilgrims who annually visited the shrines of Badrinath and Kedarnath.

Judicial administration, army, education and maintenance of temples were other important aspects of administration.

The Gurkhas ruled Garhwal until 1815 A.D. when at last they

were defeated and driven away by the British forces. At the termination of the war, the portions of Garhwal situated to the west of Alaknanda except for the parganas of Rawain and Dehradun were restored to Raja Sudarshan Shah the heir apparent of Pradyumna Shah. His domain was known as Tehri Garhwal State. The territory lying to the east of the river Alaknanda was ceded to the British territory and became a part of the neighbouring Kumaon Commissionery. In common parlance it was known as Garhwal district or British Garhwal. In 1824, the pargana of Rawain was given to Tehri Garhwal State and on 26th December 1842, the political agency of Tehri Garhwal State was given to the Commissioner of Kumaon. The same day, i.e. 26th December, 1842, a resolution was also passed that Dehradun, Mussoorie and Jaunsar shall remain permanently with Saharanpur district.

Sudarshan Shah on receiving the terrain towards the west of Alaknanda, made Tehri his capital. He had a very amiable nature and soon succeeded in establishing his hold over his subjects During 1857, the Raja helped the British with men and money. It was a diplomatic move on the part of the king because his was a newly established State. In consideration of his loyalty and services the British are said to have intended to give him the Bijnor region, but he demanded instead the Doon valley and Srinagar in British Garhwal which had been the capital of his ancestors' kingdom. Negotiations in this respect had not moved far when Sudarshan Shah died in June 1859 and the matter was dropped for ever.

Raja Sudarshan Shah was succeeded by Bhawani Shah. He died in 1871 and was succeeded by his eldest son Pratap Shah. Pratap Shah ruled from 1871 to 1886. He was the first ruler who introduced English education in the State. After Pratap Shah, his son Kirti Shah succeeded him. He was a boy of only 12 years and a council of regency looked after the administration. In 1892, Kirti Shah came of age and took the reins of the kingdom in his own hands. Kirti Shah had religious leanings and on one occasion he organised a conference at Tehri of the followers of different religions. In this direction he was inspired by Swami Ram Tirth whom he not only encouraged but also extended pecuniary assistance to attend the World Religious Conference in Japan. Raja Kirti Shah died on 25th April 1913.

Kirti Shah was succeeded by Narendra Shah who was then a minor. During his minority, the administration of the State was looked after by a regency council under the presidency of his mother. On 4th October 1919, Raja Narendra Shah was coronated. He ruled for approximately 27 years and during his rule, he tried to improve the administrative set up. He started his development plan from the forest department by sending young officials for training to the Forest College, Dehradun, and inviting foreign experts to improve the forest management of the State. He got the civil laws of the State compiled in a work known as the Narendra Hindu Law. To disseminate education in the State, a number of primary schools were opened and the Pratap High School was raised to an Intermediate College. He also extended financial assistance to promising students for studying abroad. To commemorate the memory of Raja Kirti Shah, he donated one lakh rupees and announced a financial grant of six thousand rupees annually to the Benares Hindu University in 1933, owing to which, Sir Kirti Chair of Industrial Chemistry was started there.

Raja Narendra Shah tried to improve the medical facilities in his State by supplying latest equipments to the hospitals in Tehri, Uttarkashi, Deoprayag and Raj Garhi.

Narendra Shah died in a car accident on 22nd September 1950 but he had relinquished the throne in favour of his elder son, H.H. Manvendra Shah who ruled from October 1946 to 1st August 1949, when the State integrated with the Indian Union.

As regards the British motive of occupying Garhwal it can be assumed that in the initial stages, prospects of trade with Tibet, through the passes of Garhwal led the British to annex this area. Mana and Niti passes in Garhwal, as is well known were the traditional trade routes to Tibet. The route to Western Tibet through Garhwal was known to the Europeans as early as 1624 A.D. Father Antonio de Andrade, a Jesuit missionary visited Tsaprang in Tibet, via Garhwal in 1624 A.D. But later the proximity of Central Himalayas to Western Tibet largely moulded the British policies in Garhwal. The need to check the growth of Russian influence in Central Asia and the isolationist policies of Tibet in the 19th century added to the importance of Garhwal in the eyes of the British masters.

Through Garhwal, the British had occupied one of the most

important tracts of the North Western Frontier Line, and while administering British Garhwal, the geopolitical importance of this terrain was kept in view. To maintain a friendly area in the North, they did not interfere with the local traditions as far as possible.

The attitude of British administration towards British Garhwal was reflected in Tehri Garhwal State as well. Keeping in view its strategic importance, the British it seems wanted to have a strong hold over this pocket by a shrewd admixture of respect for the king and the threat of taking over control. Hence the status quo of the king was maintained but it was hinted discreetly that there were possibilities of a British take over. The Sunud of 10th December 1824 investitured to the king of Tehri Garhwal State is a clear testimony to the British motive. According to it, ". . . as long as the Raja of Tehri Garhwal is faithful, the Governor General is pleased to bestow upon him the territory known as Tehri Garhwal State". Moreover the political agency of Tehri Garhwal State was given to the Commissioner of the neighbouring region, Kumaon.

Raja Sudarshan Shah whose predecessor had lost his kingdom to the Gurkhas had been reinstated in Tehri Garhwal State by the British and was at their mercy, though the help extended to him was a shrewd move by the British. They were well aware of the fact that his ancestors, the Parmars had been ruling the whole of Garhwal since the 14th century and were regarded as the incarnation of Badrinath by their subjects. Thus through the divine status of the king, it was easier to win over the loyalty of the people.

Further to maintain a stable zone of loyalty, indirect methods were adopted, for example Raja Sudarshan Shah who did not have a son from a queen of royal descent was being threatened since 1824 that his territory would lapse after his death. In 1848, the issue was aggravated, but later his son was permitted to rule as his successor.

Similarly, Rawain was made a disturbed zone purposely by the British. They were well aware of the fact that the people of this area had cultural affinities with Jaunsar region. In 1815 with the British annexation, Rawain was with Dehradun and Jaunsar Babar. But in 1824, it was ceded to Tehri Garhwal State. The people were interested to be reverted to British rule and the Superintendent of Dehradun also recommended their case which is vividly indicated from his letter of 22nd August 1833 to the government. But the recommendation was ignored and resentment prevailed over that area, which reached its acme in the 20th century.

The administration of Tehri Garhwal State was essentially a prototype of British Garhwal in theory and practice. The kings adopted similar administrative policies, for example in the case of land revenue which was the most important source of income; the officials in Tehri Garhwal State adopted the same method of assessment as was started by the British in British Garhwal.

The first scientific land revenue settlement was made in 1916 in Tehri Garhwal State and it was completed in 1924. Prior to this, the revenue settlements from the time of Raja Sudarshan Shah upto 1916 were very sketchy. No serious attempts were made for preparing village maps and khasras on the basis of actual measurements. The settlement of 1916 which was ordered by the then ruler Narendra Shah became the basis of future settlements.

This settlement was done under the supervision of a regular settlement officer. Amins measured all the fields and prepared maps and khasra on the spot. Plots were numbered on the maps and in the khasra, classification of the soil of fields was recorded. Different categories of the land taken were, talaon, upraon, ukhar abbal, ukhar doyam and ukhar soyam.

For the first time an area unit of measurement, the land equal to 4,800 square yards or 20 nalis was adopted for assessing land revenue. A census of human beings and cattle was also conducted. In this settlement, upraon doyam land was taken to be the standard. One nali of irrigated, upraon abbal and ijran land was deemed respectively equal to 3, 1½ and 3/4 standard land. No assessment circles were formed, instead the patti was adopted as the unit of assessment. In this settlement adhoc increases were affected on the assessment made in 1903, taking into consideration factors like location of the villages, the classes of soil and extent of irrigated land in it, the rate of yield, the general economic condition of the cultivators, availability of pastures and the extent of damage caused by wild animals. After the adhoc increases in the assessment, villages were categorized into three classes. Each village came to have a different revenue rate and villages having about equal rates were classified together. Another important feature of this settlement was the abolition of the levy 'bishah' which was a sort of court due taken with the land revenue to meet the expenses of the court.

The land tenures in Tehri Garhwal State were similar to those prevalent in British Garhwal, except that in Tehri Garhwal all the proprietary rights in the land were vested in the ruler and were inalienable. There were certain exceptions however, the Saklanas of village Saklana were hissedars, proprietors, and later on, the direct relations of the king were also made hissedars in 1941. The tenures were mainly of three types, Maurusidar (possessing hereditary rights), the Khaikar and the Sirtan (tenant at will). The Khaikar held land from the Maurusidar, and the Sirtan from both the Khaikar and the Maurusidar. The Maurusidar was an agent of the Government for the collection of State revenue and other dues. He could not however, secure cultivatory possession or in any way interfere with the Khaikars or their land or cultivation. The Khaikars paid the land revenue and, in addition 10% thereon, as 'malikana' dues to the Maurusidar. The land revenue was paid to the State and the amount of 'malikana' was retained by the Maurusidar. The Sirtans, literally meaning tenants who paid 'Sirti' or Government revenue; they were divided into two categories, the descendants of old cultivators who paid a fixed rent to the Khaikars or Maurusidars, and those tenants whose rent was not settled with the Maurusidar or Khaikars. The Sirtans in the hills had no fixity of tenure until the passing of the Kumaon Agriculture (Miscellaneous Provisions) Act, 1954, which provided them protection from ejectment.

The important officials in the revenue administration were, Assistant Collector, Tahsildars, Qanungos and Patwaris. The post of Qanungos and Patwaris were hereditary. Except for the Government machinery, there were certain other officials such as the Padhans and Thokdars who were also associated with the revenue administration. Padhan was responsible for the collection of revenue in his village which he made over to the Patwari, while he was also in his position as headman entrusted with certain minor public duties. The office of the Padhan was hereditary except in special cases; where the son of the former Padhan was a minor at his father's death, a relative was appointed to perform the duty. As regards the appointment of Padhans, it was essential that he must be a shareholder in the village and as far as possible a resident. The fiscal officers intermediate between the Padhan and the State were known as Thokdars or Sayanas, in different places by different names, and they played an important role in the administration. They had no rights in the soil over which they exercised authority. Their duty was to collect a fixed amount from the villages. The Padhans worked under them. They were invariably chosen from the principal Padhans.

Next to land revenue, forest management was the most important aspect of administration. History of forests in Tehri Garhwal State, prior to the year 1840 is shrouded in oblivion. This year for the first time forests were leased out to some Wilson, who acquired the right of exploiting forest produce. During the tenure of Wilson's lease, valuable forests of deodar (Cedrus deodara) were arbitrarily felled, but his tenure is a landmark in the history of forestry. He was a pioneer in initiating transportation of wood by waterways from inaccessible places. Wilson's lease expired in 1864. Afterwards the Government of N.W. provinces took the lease for Rs. 10,000 per annum. Though the lease was for 20 years only, under an agreement of both the parties, it was extended for a year more.

After the expiry of the tenure of this lease in 1885, forests reverted to State Control on May 1, 1885. The same year the Tehri Garhwal State established its own Forest Department. In 1897, the State secured the services of Pandit Keshavanand from the British Government and since that year, systematic forestry was started in Tehri State.

Pandit Ram Dutt in 1908 prepared a scheme for the demarcation and settlement of all forests in the State according to which forests were divided into three categories, viz. First Class Reserved Forests, Second Class Protected Forests and Third Class Village Forests which comprised all waste land not under the control of the Forest Department.

In 1928-29, the Tehri Durbar engaged the services of Dr. F. Heske of Trandt, Germany, as Forest Adviser. He inspected the State Forests for about a year and left behind detailed reports of the forests and their future management. The demarcation of forest settlement work that followed his departure was to a great extent based on his reports. Modifications in the demarcation in some parts of these forests was affected in 1927-29 and finally in 1933-35.

By 1940, the State forests were categorised into four divisions, Jamuna, Tons, Tehri and Uttarkashi, which were subdivided into ranges.

The primary object of the management of State forests was preservation and improvement of the existing forests, to obtain the highest possible sustained yield and revenue by a properly regulated system of exploitation of timber and other resources after full consideration of the primary aim, and to satisfy as far as possible the legitimate requirements of the local population for fodder, timber and other forest produce. Together with the above considerations the State Forest Department undertook the work of fire protection and preservation of wild and acquatic life.

As regards the judicial set up in Tehri Garhwal State, it can be said unhesitatingly that according to modern law and jurisprudence, it was faulty and inexhaustive. In the beginning the king wielded all powers, civil, revenue and criminal, besides his administrative power. The Raja had prerogative among the customary law and uses. Whatever he pronounced in his judgement became law and was unchallengeable. There was no procedure law as such.

It was during the reign of Kirti Shah that some changes were made by him. Still the king remained the Chief Justice of his State, wielding all powers of law within him which was against the norms of justice. The residents of Tehri State were thus wholly at the mercy of the king since every power was vested upon the Raja, one could not expect justice from him. Further, the laws were discriminating. To maintain his superiority the Raja gave importance to the priestly class and the Padhans. According to the Narendra Hindu Law, Clause 461 which has been cited already, it was the foremost duty of different castes and communities to give alms to the Brahmins.

The administration of Tehri Garhwal State as has heen mentioned earlier was similar to that of British Garhwal in theory and practice. The kings adopted similar administrative policies. Noteworthy is that though they definitely introduced certain reformatory measures like establishing of an agricultural bank to help peasants, tendering financial assistance during famines, abolition of the practice of keeping Harijan slaves, sale of the poor and low caste women in the plains, opening a house for the poor and destitute etc. to win the faith of the people, but like their counterparts, the administrators of British Garhwal, the kings too failed in dealing with the problems of forestry and Coolie Begar, Coolie Utar, Coolie Burdayash etc. and these issues ultimately led to political dissent.

The forest policy both in Kumaon and Tehri Garhwal State was responsible for instigating the people against the establishment. Local inhabitants had been enjoying certain rights and concessions since ancient times in the forests. All the trees in the neighbourhood were considered to belong to the villagers within whose boundaries they were situated. When the authorities put a clamp on the indiscriminate right of felling trees, the villagers reacted to this policy violently. At this stage, the Government should have impressed upon the people the utility and value of forests. If the people were not fully cognisant of the potential value of forests, the Government ought to have appealed to their reasons through forest education and removed their misapprehension. But no such efforts were made and politicians took advantage of the situation. There was no rapport between the forest authorities and the people at the grass root level. It was thus easy for the politicians to misconstrue the State's motive of conservation and harp the tune that the Government was encroaching upon the indefeasible and innate right of promiscuous felling of trees. As a sequel, resentment against the forest policy became an important aspect of the political movement which even Independence in 1947 could not entirely cure.

However there were certain other factors which further accentuated the feeling of resentment amongst the hill people in both British Garhwal and Tehri Garhwal State. The founding of the Congress Party in the hills in 1912, the Home Rule League, development of mass media, establishing of debating societies, the opening of a few schools by political organizations, literatis, visits of great men like Swami Vivekanand, Gandhi, Swami

Dayanand Saraswati, Moti Lal Nehru, Bhagwan Dass, Annie Besant, Madan Mohan Malviya, Purshottam Dass Tandon etc. to the hills and finally martial traditions of the Garhwalis infused in them a feeling of dissent against the British and the State authorities.

Martial traditions of the Garhwalis are more or less undisputed. The Germans called the Garhwalis, the storm troops of the Allies. Undeniably the brave soldiers of the Royal Garhwal Rifles performed their duties loyally, but soon they came closer to the realities of life. The exposure of these troops to the outside world and particularly the great sweeps of national movement broadened their horizons. In the initial stages it was a period of reluctance characterized by the refusal of Chandra Singh Garhwali to fire on the Pathans and disobey British orders in 1930. Eventually the natural martial instinct of Garhwali troops found expression in the Second World War, when two batallions of Garhwalis joined the Indian National Army. The intrepidity of these soldiers encouraged the Garhwalis at home, and made a landmark in the history of the Freedom movement of India as well.

As regards the political movements in Tehri Garhwal State, whatever occurred in the two districts of Almora and Naini Tal, the echoes were sounded in British Garhwal and then they resonated in Tehri State. Since the third decade of the 20th century, the people in Tehri Garhwal State tried to associate themselves with the mainstream of the national movement. In Tehri, in the initial stages, the uprisings were against feudalism but soon the repercussions of British Garhwal were felt in Tehri Garhwal State and the energies of the people were channelized in the right direction. By 1945, they started demanding liberation not only from feudalism but also from the fetters of the alien yoke.

It is worth mentioning here that from 14th century, the Parmars were ruling the whole of Garhwal, though their progenitor had come to the throne of Chandpur Garhi much earlier. In 1804, as has been mentioned earlier, they were defeated by the Gurkhas and from 1804 to 1815, Garhwal came under the sway of the Gurkhas. After the British occupation of Garhwal in 1815, Garhwal was divided into two parts, British Garhwal and Tehri Garhwal State. Interestingly, the erstwhile Parmar rulers were reinstalled in Tehri Garhwal State.

This turbulent history provides us a definite due. The Parmars were Hindu kings and so were their conquerors, the Gurkhas. The British encouraged the spreading of christianity through missionary works, but characteristically did not tamper with the local traditions and the basic mechanism of Hindu hierarchy. Thus the religious officials continued to enjoy royal blessings and this protection gave them considerable politico-economic status, particularly during the Parmar epoch. All the copper plate inscriptions found hitherto are land grants and these grants were extended mostly to temples or Brahmins. This implies domination of caste Brahmins in rural/agricultural sector and reinforced inequality in land distribution due to rigid social stratification.

Though similar instances of favouritism are witnessed in Kumaon, Garhwal had another rider also. Unlike Kumaon, major pilgrim centres of all India status are situated in Garhwal. Owing to a long known history of perennial pilgrim traffic in the Garhwal, perhaps petty merchants may have flourished, and enormous wealth amassed at the nodes of these religious activities. This again may be regarded as discriminating as low caste persons cannot be logically expected to serve in supportive activities, for example, as cook etc. The whole outfit thus encouraged high priests and caste Brahmins to accumulate wealth.

Some consequence to religious domination can be cited. Elite domination resulted in massive land acquisition by the priests and high caste Brahmins. Kshatriyas, the hard core of the military paraphernalia of the Parmars, came in the second order. During the short Gurkha regime, although Brahmins remained untouched due to Hindu loyalty of the barbaric Gurkhas, military officials paled into insignificance. Menials and craftsmen had no or insignificant holdings. This gave birth to an oppressive oligarchy as the land symbolizes political economic power in an agricultural society. Often this repressive nature of the oligarchy became more rampant via marriage associations. For example in Jaunsar Babar intercaste marriages between Brahmins and Kshatriyas were in vogue.

Whereas religion and its ritualistic aspects can reasonably be held responsible for relegating technological creativity, in Garhwal it led to an unegalitarian economic set up.

Basic martial traditions of Garhwalis continued to find their most vehement manifestation as early as the 14th century. The mighty dynasty of Parmars claimed sovereignty even during the Mughal rule and every now and then challenged the legendary Mughal might. Thus for approximately four hundred years, Kshatriyas remained the hard core of the elite. Only for eleven years of Gurkha regime, Kshatriyas can be said to be less fortunate than their Brahmin counterparts amongst the elite because of the contemptuous administration of the Gurkha top brasses. In fact, after the death of Pradyumna Shah, his minor son, Sudarshan Shah had to emigrate. It implies that military officials too may be expected to have left Garhwal. But Britishers were shrewd enough to identify martial instincts of the Garhwali tradition and raised their regiment even before exploiting the martial element of the Kumaonis. In fact, Garhwali soldiers came into lime light as early as the First World War. However, it may be pointed out that as a subtle variation of their divide and rule policy, Britishers encouraged Kumaonis to join administrative and secretarial services and it was very late that they raised the Kumaon Regiment. It actually served as an auxiliary of various other regiments before receiving a full-fledged and independent status. The recruitment policy had a tinge of discrimination because less administrators and more sepoys eventually peopled Garhwal.

This recruitment policy also generated another internal cultural barrier, in the form of demographic imbalance, both in British Garhwal and Tehri Garhwal State. The armed forces employed male population of a definite age-group, say eighteen to forty-two. This meant absence of male population from their region during the creative years. Consequent upon these factors viz sex and age as well as migration of the population resulted in stagnation in development of agriculture which further perpetuated the hegemony of a local oligarchy.

A cursory survey of Garhwali literature reveals the importance given to war exploits and memoirs by the bards. Rikhola Lodi Pawara, Madho Singh Bhandari Pawara or Jeetu Bagdwal Pawara etc. may be cited as relevant examples. Though the plethora of eulogies, indicative of a high value of a 'need to achieve' can be witnessed in the literature, the value of particularism did not speak of adaptive changes in the society as it did elsewhere, perhaps because they were channelled into integrative institutions such as the family, clan, caste and kinship in Garhwal.

Whilst the agricultural transformation due to intense participation of females becomes an onerous task, Gurkhas and Britishers can be held responsible of eventual extinction of professionals, poets, authors, painters etc. The benevolent despots of the Parmar dynasty extended their patronage to their professionals and consequently we find a rich cultural heritage, such as the Garhwal School of Painting. These professionals not merely gave an ego boost to the kings through their eulogies but provided a base for cultural coherence and enlightenment also. This core of the elite eventually vanished from Garhwal due to the plundering of the Gurkhas. Britishers were never interested in its systematic revival though some efforts were made by the rulers of Tehri Garhwal State to salvage the decayed and almost a lost heritage.

During the Parmar regime and also in Tehri Garhwal State, Garhwalis traded with the outside population. Though in later years the petty merchandise traffic flourished, the volume of trade remained deplorably low for a long span. Internal trade also mostly consisted of barter exchange at the village level. This is thus responsible for a low number of traders and business men in Garhwal.

While historical changes in the armed forces and agriculture occupations are almost very insignificant so much so that these occupations have become an innate part of the culture, it is the extractive and manufacturing industries of household level which received a severe blow from the Gurkha-British occupation. As evidenced from heaps of 'slug' it can be concluded that extractive industries flourished to manufacture tools, weapons and other equipments. Because of the invasion of British products, household industries crumbled away. The craftsmen and people engaged in tasks regarded as menial by the higher strata were forced by their necessities to seek work as agricultural labourers or to cultivate their meagre holdings. Owing to this late start as well as oligarchic resistance, their holdings remained smaller and with the prevalence of Hindu inheritance law, the holdings were fragmented and sub-divided. Though it was true for the whole Hindu society, the lower strata had to face additional hardships.

Bibliography

Little Known Primary Sources on Undivided Garhwal

1. Inscription of Raja Sahaj Pal of the year 1548 A.D. on the stone door of the temple of Kshetra Pal at Deoprayag.
2. Inscription of the year 1561 A.D. of Raja Sahaj Pal on a bell in the temple of Raghunath ji at Deoprayag. The bell is supposed to be dedicated to the temple by Sahaj Pal.
3. Inscription of Raja Man Shah on the door of the temple of Kshetra Pal at Deoprayag dated 1608 A.D.
4. Inscription of Man Shah in the temple of Raghunath ji at Deoprayag of the year 1610 A.D.
5. Copper plate inscription of the year 1640 A.D. issued by Maharani Karnavati on behalf of her son Maharaja Prithvi Pat Shah.
6. Inscription of Maharaja Prithvi Pat Shah in the monastery of Madho Dass in Laxmi Narayan Temple of the year 1642 A.D. at the village Bhaktiana which is adjacent to Srinagar. The inscription is in the outer portion of the main temple wall.
7. Farman of Aurangzeb of the year 1662 A.D. sent to the Raja of Garhwal.
8. Inscription of Maharaja Prithvi Pat Shah on the southern door of the temple of Raghunath ji in Deoprayag dated 1664 A.D.
9. Inscription on the western doorway of the temple of Raghunath ji in Deoprayag of the year 1664 A.D.
10. Farman of Aurangzeb of the year 1665 A.D. sent to the Raja of Garhwal.

11. Copper plate inscription of the year 1667 A.D. of Maharaja Fateh Shah which bears the seal of Maharaja Prithvi Pat Shah.
12. Copper plate inscription of the year 1700 A.D. of Raja Fateh Shah.
13. Copper plate inscription of the year 1706 A.D. of Raja Fateh Shah.
14. Copper plate inscription of the year 1716 A.D. of Raja Fateh Shah.
15. Copper plate inscription of the year 1716 A.D. of Raja Pradip Shah.
16. Two coins of Raja Pradip Shah which are available in the State Museum, Lucknow.
17. Two coins of the reign of Raja Lalit Shah which are available in the State Museum, Lucknow.
18. Copper plate inscription of the year 1788 A.D. of Raja Pradyumna Shah.
19. Inscription on a stone slate affixed to the wall of the temple of Parshuram at Uttarkashi which bears the names of the kings from Pradip Shah to Sudarshan Shah.
20. Inscription in the temple of Vishwanath at Uttarkashi in which the list of the kings from Pradip Shah to Sudarshan Shah has been given.

Original Manuscripts

1. Sanwari Granth of the reign of Raja Ajay Pal. It is a 'tantrik' manuscript.
2. Sanwari Granth of the period of Maharani Karnawati. It is also a 'tantrik' manuscript.
3. Fateh Shah Karna Granth by Jatadhar.
4. Fateh Prakash by Ratan Kavi.
5. Vrit Kaumudi by Mati Ram.
6. Sabha Sar by Raja Sudarhan Shah.
7. Garh Rajya Vansha Kavya by Mola Ram.

National Archives, New Delhi

1. Foreign Department, Political, Box No. 57, Sunud dated December 10, 1824.
2. Foreign Department, File No. 86, Political Proceedings, 16-30, August 1833.

3. Foreign Department, Political Proceedings, 19-27, September 1833, Letter Nos. 7 and 8.
4. Foreign Department, Political 1848, File No. 62, Letter No. 611.
5. Foreign Department, Political 1848, File No. 63, Letter No. 612.
6. Home Department Political, File No. 393/30.
7. Tehri Garhwal State Records, File No. 220/1905.
8. Tehri Garhwal State Records, File No. 42/1907.
9. Tehri Garhwal State Records, File No. 281/1913.
10. Tehri Garhwal State Records (Political Agent for Tehri State) File No. G-30-8/Tehri.
11. Tehri Garhwal State Records, File No. 55/1923.
12. Tehri Garhwal State Records, Extracts from the fortnightly D.O's of Commissioner Kumaon, Letter dated 1st December 1923.
13. Tehri Garhwal State Records, Copy of the Confidential note on Annual Administration for 1922-23, Letter dated 15th July/1923/Tehri.
14. Home Department, 1930, Political, File No. 174.
15. Home Deprtment, 1930, Political, File No. 174, Letter No. 57915/28/G.
16. Tehri Garhwal State Records, File No. 247/1930.
17. Tehri Garhwal State Records (Political agent for Tehri) Letter No. 6/125-IV A.
18. G.B. Pant Papers, File No. 4/2, Letter dated 11th July/1934.
19. G.B. Pant Papers, File No. 4/3, Item No. 22, Letter dated 17th July/1945.

Central Secretariat Library, New Delhi
1. The Annual Administration Report of Tehri Garhwal State for the year 1935-36, Narendra Nagar, 1937.
2. The Annual Administration Report of Tehri Garhwal State for the year 1936-37, Narendra Nagar, 1938.
3. The Annual Administration Report of Tehri Garhwal State for the year 1938-39, Narendra Nagar, 1939.
4. The Annual Administration Report of Tehri Garhwal State for the year 1939-40, Narendra Nagar, 1940.
5. The Annual Administration Report of Tehri Garhwal State for the year 1940-41, Narendra Nagar, 1941.

6. The Annual Administration Report of Tehri Garhwal State for the year 1941-42, Narendra Nagar, 1942.
7. The Annual Administration Report of Tehri Garhwal State for the year 1943-44, Narendra Nagar, 1944.
8. The Annual Administration Report of Tehri Garhwal State for the year 1944-45, Narendra Nagar, 1945.
9. The Annual Administration Report of Tehri Garhwal State for the year 1945-46, Narendra Nagar, 1946.

State Archives U.P., Lucknow

1. Settlement Letters Issued Vol. I, 1837-39, Letter No. 8.
2. Settlement Letters Issued, Vol. II, 1839-42, Letter No. 56.
3. Report on the Administration of N.W. Provinces, for the year 1875-76, Allahabad, 1878.
4. Pauw, E.K.: Report on the Tenth Settlement of the Garhwal District, Allahabad, 1896.
5. Burh, R.: Census of India, 1901, Vol. XVI, Part I, N.W.P. and Oudh, Allahabad, 1902.
6. Report of the Working of the Garhwal Central Scarcity Committee, from April 30, 1918 to February 28, 1920, Dehradun, 1920.
7. Brahmawar, R.N.: Working Plan for the Garhwal Forest Division, 1930-31 to 1939-40, Allahabad, 1932.

Dynastic Collection. Thakur Shoor Beer Singh, Purana Durbar, Tehri (Source: Garhwal's State Records)

1. Annual Administrative Report of Tehri Garhwal State for the year 1907-1908, dated May 26, 1908, Tehri.
2. Annual Administrative Report of Tehri Garhwal State for the Year 1909-10, dated May 26, 1910, Tehri.
3. Sir Kirti Shah ka Sankshipt Jeewan Charit, Dehradun, 1913.
4. Annual Administrative Report of Tehri Garhwal State for the year 1918-19, dated May 26, 1919, Tehri.
5. Narendra Hindu Law, Tehri Garhwal State, 1919.
6. Doval, Ram Prasad: Revenue Settlement Report, Tehri Garhwal State, Babat, 1924.
7. Niyam Prabhu Seva va Coolie Utar, Tehri Garhwal State, 1930.
8. Prant Panchayat Vidhan, Tehri Garhwal State, 1930.

9. Niyam Vasooli Bura, Tehri Garhwal State, 1930.
10. Tehri Garhwal Rajya, Nagar tatha Pur Panchayat Vidhan, Tehri Garhwal State, 1932.
11. The Tehri Garhwal State Naturalization Act No. 1, of Samvat, 1992, State Press, Narendra Nagar.
12. Tehri Garhwal Rajya ka Dund Sanghra, Tehri Garhwal State, 1937.
13. Tehri Garhwal Rajya, Prant Panchayat Manual, Dehradun, 1938.
14. Tehri Garhwal Rajya ka Kusht Vidhan Bill, Samvat 1996. Dehra Times Press, Dehradun.
15. Niyam Babat Marne Machli va Shikar, Tehri Garhwal State, 1940.
16. Tehri Garhwal Rajya Ke Bhumi Sambandhi Adhikar Niyam tatha Vidhan, Dehradun, 1941.
17. Parganna Pratap Nagar, Jila Tehri Garhwal ke Assessment Report, Lucknow, 1965.
18. Letter No. 560/C, dated 23rd May, 1927 and endorsement No. 1839/50/26-27, dated 13th June 1927, from Tehri Garhwal State to Dhar State.
19. Report of the History Officer of Dhar State contained in letter No. 17, dated 22nd July 1927 and D.O. No. 1004, dated 10th December, 1927 from Dhar Durbar to Tehri Garhwal State.

Forest Department Tehri

1. Khosla, Prem Nath: Working Plan for the Tehri Forest Division, 1939-40 to 1969-70, Tehri Garhwal State, 1941.
2. Saklani, Indra Dutt: Tehri Garhwal Rajya Forest Manual, Tehri Garhwal State, 1940.
3. Raturi, Padma Dutt: Working Plan for the Uttarkashi Forest Division, Tehri Garhwal State, 1938.
4. Pant, K.P.: Working Plan for the Tons Forest Division 1945-46 to 1964-65, Tehri Garhwal State, 1948.

Newspapers

1. Garhwali—January 1907; January 1912; January 1913; November 1913.
2. Almora Akhbar—4, August 1913; 11, August 1913; 20, October 1913.

3. Kshatriya Beer—15, July 1925.
4. Karm Bhumi—31, November 1939; Visheshank, 26, January 1966.
5. Shakti Saptahik—16, January 1921; 23, March 1940; 25, May 1957.

Journals

1. Asiatic Researches, Vol. VI, First Published 1809, Reprint, New Delhi, 1979.
2. Asiatic Researches, Vol. XVI, First Published 1828, Reprint, New Delhi 1980.
3. Journal of Asiatic Society of Bengal Vol. XIII, 1842.
4. Tharandter Forstlichen Jahrbuch, 1931, Vol. 82, No. 8.
5. Indian Forester, December 1942, Dehradun.

Gazetteers

1. Atkinson E.T.: The Himalayan Gazetteer (in 3 Volumes) Allahabad, 1866.
2. Walton, H.G.: British Garhwal, A Gazetteer, Allahabad 1921.
3. Srivastava, Madhuri (State Editor): Gazetteer of India. Uttar Pradesh, Tehri Garhwal, Lucknow, 1971.

Books

1. Aitchison, C.U.: A Collection of Treaties, Engagements and Sunuds Relating to India and the Neighbouring Countries, Vol. II, Calcutta, 1963.
2. Awasthi, A.B.L.: Studies in Skanda Purana, Lucknow, 1965.
3. Amar Sandesh tatha Baba Balaknath Ji Ke Jeevani, Mandir Ghot Siddha, Hamirpur 9.
4. Briggs, George W.: Gorakhnath and Kanphata Yogis, Calcutta 1938.
5. Bhattacharya, Pandit Brij Ratna: Skanda Puranantragat Kedar Khand Grunth, Bombay, 1906.
6. Briggs, John (Translation from the original text of Mohamed Kasim Farishta): History of the Rise of the Mahomedan Power in India till the year 1612, Vol. II, and Vol. IV, Calcutta, 1910.
7. Basu, Major B.D.: Sacred Book of the Hindus, Vol. XVI, Calcutta, 1914.

8. Banerjee, Anil Chandra: Guru Nanak to Guru Gobind Singh, Delhi, 1978.
9. Beveridge, Henry (Ed.): The Tuzuk-i-Jahangiri or Memoirs of Jahangir, First Published 1909, New Delhi, 1968.
10. Bernier, Francois: Travels in the Mogul Empire (Translation, Archibald Constable), First Published 1891, Reprint New Delhi, 1972.
11. Berniers Voyage to the East Indies, Reprinted and Published for the Resuscitation of Indian Literature by H.C. Dass, Calcutta 1909.
12. Commaraswamy, Ananda K.: Catalogue of the Indian Collections in the museum of fine arts, Boston (Part V Rajput Painting, Part VI Mughal Painting) First Published Boston, 1926, Reprint Varanasi 1981.
13. Cunningham, A.: Ancient Geography of India, First Published 1870, Reprint, Benares 1979.
14. Chatak, Govind: Garhwali Lok Geet, Dehradun, 1956.
15. C' Wessels: Early Jesuit Travellers in Central Asia, S.I. 1924.
16. Darshan, Bhakt: Garhwal Ki Divangat Vibhutian, Landdowne, 1952.
17. Dayalu, Shiv (Ed.): Itihas Arya Pratinidhi Sabha, Lucknow, 1963.
18. Dewar, Deuglas: A Hand Book to the English Pre Mutiny Records in the Government Records Room of the United Provinces of Agra and Oudh, Allahabad.
19. Dabral, Shiv Prasad: Uttarakhand ka Itihas, Dogadda, 1982.
20. Duff, C. Mabel: The Chronology of India from the Earliest times to the beginning of the 16th century, 2 White Hall Gardens, 1899.
21. Dass, Brij Ratan (Hindi Translation): Mughal Darbar ya Maserul Umra, Benares, 1947.
22. Deshraj, Thakur: Sikh Itihas, Gramothan Vidyapith Sangaria, 1954.
23. Evatt, Captain J.: Hand Book on Garhwalis, Calcutta, 1924.
24. Elliott and Dowson: History of India as told by its own Historians (Muntakhabu-1-Lubab) vol. VIII, Allahabad.
25. Fazal, Abul (Translation by Colonel H.S. Jarrett): Ain-i-Akbari, Vol. II, Calcutta, 1978.
26. Fuhrer, A.: The Monumental Antiquities and Inscriptions in the N.W.P. and Oudh, Allahabad, 1891.

27. Foster, Williams (Ed): Early Travels in India (1583-1619), London, 1921.
28. Gopal, Ram: India China Tibet Triangle, Lucknow 1964.
29. Gill, A.R.: Valley of the Doon, Dehradun, 1952.
30. Husband, Sir Francis Young: Wonders of the Himalayas Indian Reprint, Chandigarh, 1977, First edition, London, 1924.
31. India and the War, Illustrated (1914-18) Compiled and published by the Imperial Publishing Co., Khosla Brothers, Lahore, January 2, 1924.
32. Joshi, Sudha: Kurmachal Kesari, Hyderabad, 1970.
33. Johar, Srinder Singh: Guru Gobind Singh a Biography, Jullundur, 1967.
34. Kumar, Shanta: Himalaya par Lal Chhaya, New Delhi, 1965.
35. Khan, Major General Shah Nawaz: My memoirs of I.N.A. and its Netaji, Delhi, 1946.
36. Munshi, K.M.: The Glory that was Gujar Desh, Part I, Bombay, 1955.
37. Misra, Pd. Brahma Sarkar (ed.): Sukra Niti, Varanasi, 1968.
38. Manucci, Niccolao (Translation by William Irvine): Storia do Mogor or Mogul India, Calcutta 1907.
39. Ram, Mola (ed. by Ajay Singh Rawat): Ganika, Naini Tal, 1975.
40. Moorcraft, William and Trebeck, George: Travels in the Himalayan Provinces of Hindustan and Punjab, First Published, London, 1837. Reprint, New Delhi, 1971.
41. Lal, Mukandi: Garhwal Painting, Delhi, 1968.
42. Maclagan, Sir Edward: The Jesuits and the Great Mogul, London, 1932.
43. Moreland, W.H.: The Revenue Admistration of the N.W. Provinces, Allahabad, 1911.
44. Nautiyal, K.P.: Archaeology of Kumaon, Varanasi, 1969.
45. Nayal, Indra Singh: Swatantrata Sangram Mein Kumaon Ka Yogdan, Delhi, 1973.
46. Pearse, Colonel Hugh: Five Generations of an Anglo Indian Family. London, 1905.
47. Pant aur Tewari: Shikharon ke Swar, Aligarh, 1969.
48. Pande, Badri Dutt: Kumaon Ka Itihas, Almora, 1937.

49. Parmar, Pati Ram: Garhwal Ancient and Modern, Simla, 1916.
50. Powell, B.H. Baden: The Land System of British India, Vol. II, Oxford, 1912.
51. Roy, Pratap Chandra (translated): The Mahabharata of Krishna Dwaparyana Vyas, Vol.II, Calcutta.
52. Rahul, Ram: The Himalayan Borderland, Delhi, 1970.
53. Ramakant: Indo Napalese Relations (1816-1877), Delhi 1978.
54. Raturi, H.K.: Garhwal Varnan, Bombay, 1910.
55. Raturi, H.K.: Garhwal Ka Itihas, Dehradun, 1928.
56. Rawat, Ajay Singh: Uttakand Ka Rajnitik Itihas, Naini Tal, 1982.
57. Rawat, Ajay Singh: Garhwal Himalayas—A Historical Survey, Delhi, 1983.
58. Srivastava, K.P.(Ed.) Mughal Farmans 1540-1706 A.D. Vol. I, Lucknow, 1974.
59. Singh, Shoor Beer (Ed).: Fateh Prakash, Aligarh, 1961.
60. Shastri, Balkrishna Bhatt: Garhwal Jati Prakash, Itawa, 1983.
61. Singh, O.P.(Ed): The Himalaya: Nature, Man and Culture, New Delhi, 1983.
62. Singh, Bhagat Laxman: Guru Gobind Singh, Lahore, 1909.
63. Sirkar, D.C.: Select Inscriptions, Vol. II, Delhi, 1983.
64 Sirkar, D.C.: The Saka Pithas, Delhi, 1973.
65. Stowell, V.A.: A Manual of the Land Tenures of Kumaon Division, Allahabad, 1907.
66. Sah, Shambhu Prasad: Govind Ballabh Pant ek Jeevani, Delhi, 1972.
67. Sankrityayan, Rahul: Garhwal, Allahabad, 1953.
68. Sukhtankar, Vishnu (ed.): The Mahabharata, Vol. III, Bhandarkar Oriented Research Institute, Poona, 1942.
69. Sherring, Charles A: Western Tibet and the British Borderland, London, 1906.
70. Sewak: Fascinating Uttrakhand, Information Department, Luckow, 1963.
71. Tendulkar, D.G: Abdul Gaffar Khan, Gandhi Peace Foundation, New Delhi, 1967.
72. Toye, Hughe: The Springing Tiger, London, 1959.

73. Tod, Lt. Col. James: Annals and Antiquities of Rajasthan, Vol. II, Yorkplace, Portsman Square, March 10, 1899.

74. Woodyatt, Major General Nigel G.: The Regimental History of the 3rd Queen Alexandra's Own Gurkhas Rifles (1815-1927), London, 1929.

75. Watters, Thomas: On Yuan Chwangs Travels in India, New Delhi, 1961.

76. Williams, G.R.C.: Historical and Statistical Memoirs of Dehradun, Roorkee 1874.

77. Yogi, Bhambut Nath: Navnath Katha tatha Goraksha Stavngjali, Haridwar, 8th edition.

Index

Abul Fazal 39
Ajay Pal 18, 19, 26, 35, 37-38, 40, 49
Akbar 38
Amar Singh Thapa 73
Andrade 43, 44, 45, 153
Aurangzeb 39, 40, 48, 55, 89, 92

Balbhadra Shah 39-41
Bal Sabha 157
Bam Shah 73
Baz Bahadur 51
Bhangani 57-59
Bhawani Shah 97-98, 99, 101, 108, 115, 161-62
Bhim Chand 57, 58, 59
Bhushan 61

Chandpur 18, 31, 32, 33, 35, 60
Chandrabadni 163
Chandra Singh Garhwali 158, 173
Coolie Begar 155
Coolie Utar 155

Dapa (Daba) 43, 56
Dara Shikoh 39, 49, 51, 89
Darban Singh 158
Deep Chand 66
Diwan 80
Duftari 79

Fateh Shah 19, 25, 27, 29, 53-64
Father Ceschi 52, 53
Faujdar 79, 80
Ferishta 39, 87
Foster 41

Gabar Singh 158

Gold washing 83
Goldar 80
Govind Ballabh Pant 168
Guru Govind Singh 57, 58, 59
Guru Ram Rai 62
Gyan Chand 60

Harsh Deo Joshi 66, 71, 72, 74
Hasti Dal Chautariya 73
Heske 116
Hiuen Tsang 19, 20

Jagat Chand 60
Jagat Prakash 68, 69
Jahangir 42, 44
Jai Krit Shah 67-70, 73
Jyotik Rai 42

Kalyan Chand 65
Kalyan Shah 26, 38
Kanak Pal 18, 19, 26, 27, 29-30, 32-33, 35
Karnawati 45, 46, 47-48, 49, 55, 65
Khaikar 113, 114
Khan Abdul Gaffar Khan 158
Kirti Shah 73, 97, 98, 100, 102, 103, 127, 128, 135, 136, 140, 146
Kumaon Parishad 156

Lalipat Shah 25, 66
Laxmi Chand 41

Madho Singh Bhandari 29, 45, 46
Mahipat Shah 43-46
Makhowal 59
Man Shah 18, 40-42
Mana 152
Manvendra Shah 103

Mati Ram 61
Maurusidar 113, 114
Medni Prakash 57
Medni Shah 51, 52, 53, 54, 56
Mola Ram 18, 67, 68, 70, 71, 72, 74, 79, 89
Moorcraft 74, 153
Mowdok 159
Mukhtar 79

Narendra Shah 102-103, 112, 127, 128, 135, 140, 169, 173
Negi 80
Niti 152

Padhan 115, 136
Paonta 57, 58
Pilgrim trade 85, 86, 145
Pradip Shah 63-66
Pradyumna Shah 20, 25, 27, 67, 68, 69, 70-74
Praja Mandal 157, 169, 170, 174
Pratap Shah 97, 99-100, 101, 108, 112, 126, 163
Prem Sabha 156
Prithvi Pat Shah 45-46, 49, 50, 51, 52, 53, 54, 55, 56, 65

Rawain 98, 103, 142, 154, 163, 164-167

Sahaj Pal 38, 40, 41
Saklana 113, 168, 171, 172
Shah Jahan 47, 50, 54
Shyam Shah 42-43
Sirtan 113, 114
Srideo Suman 169, 170
Subash Chandra Bose 159
Sudarshan Shah 72, 92, 93, 94, 95, 97, 98, 108, 154, 160, 162
Suleiman Shikoh 48, 49, 50, 51, 52, 54, 56, 62
Swami Satyadeva 156

Thath 81
Thokdar 80, 115
Tibetan trade 84, 85, 144
Trebeck 74
Tsaprang 44, 153

Upendra Shah 64

William Finch 41

Younghushand 152